Eng'd by A. H. Ritchie.

Adelaide L. Newton

A MEMOIR

OF

ADELAIDE LEAPER NEWTON.

BY THE

REV. JOHN BAILLIE,

MINISTER OF THE FREE CHURCH OF SCOTLAND, LONDON;
AUTHOR OF "MEMOIRS OF HEWITSON," ETC.

"He is the happy man whose life e'en now
Shows somewhat of that happier life to come;
Content, indeed, to sojourn while he must
Below the skies, but having there his home."—COWPER.

NEW YORK:
ROBERT CARTER & BROTHERS,
No. 530 BROADWAY.

1858.

"We can make our lives sublime,
And, departing, leave behind us
Footprints on the sands of Time:
Footprints which perhaps another,
Sailing o'er life's solemn main,
A forlorn and shipwrecked brother,
Seeing, shall take heart again."

LONGFELLOW.

STEREOTYPED BY
THOMAS B. SMITH,
82 & 84 Beekman Street.

PRINTED BY
E. O. JENKINS,
24 Frankfort St.

PREFATORY NOTE.

The Authoress of the "Song of Solomon compared with other Parts of Scripture" scarcely needs to be introduced to the Christian public. But many will be interested to trace, in her personal life, a singularly vivid pattern of the heavenly walk there so touchingly portrayed. It is in compliance with a widely expressed desire to have that mind and heart embalmed that the present Memoir appears.

The poet Southey once wrote to James Montgomery:—"I am one who shrinks in like a snail, when I find no sympathy; but, when I do, I open myself like a flower to the morning sun." Such was Adelaide Newton. Not many knew her thoroughly; but there were two or three select hearts to which she "opened herself." To the letters thus called forth this Memorial mainly owes whatever of the life-like it may possess.

A critic lately said of a Memoir now issuing from

the press:—"We wanted a marble bust, with the features delicately chiselled and the features preserved—and we are threatened with a colossus in bronze." It would have been easy, in the present instance, out of the vast mass of letters and papers, to cast a colossus; but the Author has aimed rather at the marble bust.

The writer is sensible how imperfectly he may have caught the delicate lineaments of her inner life. But he is not without the hope that He who made her what she was, will graciously use this "living epistle" to solace some wearied pilgrims and to quicken the steps of some loiterers by the way.

LONDON, December, 1855.

POSTSCRIPT.

After these pages had passed through the press, the Author received from the Rev. Canon Stowell, of Manchester, a communication respecting the subject of this Memoir, in which he writes thus:

"Seldom or never has it been my happiness to see the mighty power of grace so marvellously manifested as in her. She seemed to dwell in the vestibule of heaven—to live on the steps of the throne of grace. The vigour of her understanding, the acuteness of her judgment, the force of her reasoning, the originality of her ideas, and the beauty of her style, astonished me. You could not converse with her without being charmed with the freshness, the vividness, the activity, the refinement of her mind. The spring of all was love to her Saviour, intense desire to glorify His name. This strung up all her energies; this animated all her pursuits. Grace changed the whole tone of her character. From the flexible, tasteful, buoyant girl, she rose into the earnest, elevated, reflective woman; yet all was artless and easy, clothed with humility, and adorned with simplicity.

"The one grand instrument of the work was the Word of God. She lived *on* and *in* the Bible. It savoured every sentiment and toned every thought of her soul. She caught the faintest whisper, and analysed the minutest expressions, of 'the lively oracles.' The Scriptures were wrought into the very texture of her inner life: she fed upon them in her heart. Hence the newness, the unction, the savouriness of her writings. Like the silk-worm, which spins her exquisite thread from her own vitals, fed by the mulberry leaves—so she, from the experience of her own spirit, nourished by the leaves of the Tree of Life, wrought out her lovely tissues of heavenly wisdom. Flesh and blood had not taught her, but the Spirit of her Father in heaven.

"In all she wrote, and said, and did, to glorify Christ was her single aim. This desire was as a fire in her bones. Her zeal was ever burning. Nor was the light of her joy less remarkable. Whilst most humble, she was most assured. Doubt seemed never allowed to overshadow her soul, anxiety to disquiet it. When you entered her chamber, you felt that she was enveloped in an atmosphere of heavenliness and peace. When she mingled with the family-circle, she seemed like the denizen of a higher world come down on some errand of love.

"Assuredly, grace has seldom shone brighter in any vessel of clay. And for the honour of the Saviour and the consolation of His Church, the memorial of what was done in her, for her, and by her, ought not to be lost.

"Manchester, Dec. 4, 1855."

CONTENTS.

CHAPTER I.

CHAPTER II.

CHAPTER III.

CHAPTER IV.

CHAPTER V.

CHAPTER VI.

CHAPTER VII.

CHAPTER VIII.

CHAPTER IX.

CHAPTER X.

CHAPTER XI.

CHAPTER XII.

CHAPTER XIII.

CHAPTER XIV.

CHAPTER XV.

CHAPTER XVI.

CHAPTER XVII.

CHAPTER XVIII.

CHAPTER XIX.

CHAPTER XX.

CHAPTER XXI.

CHAPTER I.

"I LONG so earnestly to be growing in grace hourly—'filled with the Spirit'—burning with love to Christ, and Christians, and sinners—to be a reflection of HIM in the world, and working whilst it is day." So wrote, on one occasion, the beloved disciple whose brief but bright course we are now to sketch. That aspiration was the key-note of her life.

It is fabled by an ancient poet, that, "when Hercules went to unbind Prometheus (a figurative personification of human nature), he sailed the length of the great ocean in an earthen pot, or pitcher." And Lord Bacon, applying the fable to the Christian life, describes the saint as sailing most marvellously in the frail bark of the flesh, through the waves of the world, to that home where he shall be "free indeed."

It was emphatically a frail bark and a stormy ocean which carried Adelaide Newton to her haven. And others who are still on that ocean, "toiling in rowing," may be comforted mightily as they hear the articulate voice of HIM who so often came to her, saying, "It is I; be not afraid."

The town of Derby cannot boast of many holy memories. But He who noted Bethany as "the town of Mary and of her sister Martha," has noted the birthplace of ADELAIDE LEAPER NEWTON. It was on 1st March, 1824, that an infant, who was to leave behind her so precious a fragrance, was ushered into this vale of tears.

"Life," it has been said,

"Beginneth as a little path edged with the violet and primrose,
A little path of lawny grass, and soft to tiny feet."

To Adelaide Newton, life's early years were eminently smooth and pleasant. Of a good family, and surrounded by every earthly luxury, she grew up into girlhood, her sunny morning betokening a cloudless day. "This sweet spot," we find her writing to a friend, on her return home after a short absence, "seems like an earthly paradise." And a singular aptness in acquiring each accomplishment to which she successively devoted herself, threatened, as she rose into womanhood, to entangle her still more firmly in the world's meshes. A surviving sister speaks of "her peculiarly sweet touch in playing, and voice in singing," which "made her music unusually attractive." Her delicate pencil, too, seemed to mark her out for no ordinary success in drawing. And graver attainments were added. "A natural talent for languages" found its development in the acquisition of various of the modern tongues; and, in later years, she added to them Greek, Hebrew, and even a little Arabic. She "particularly delighted also in mathematics." And when, added to all this, was the adornment of a "charming manner," whose graceful modesty was "never for an instant spoiled by the praises which were continually heaped upon her in the social circle," it will be seen that seldom has the world held out a more attractive allurement than to the subject of our Memoir.

"Like yourself," she writes, long afterwards to a school-companion, describing that season of her early joys, "my heart naturally clung very much to the world. Music was my great snare. I took infinite pains to play well, and delighted secretly in the commendation I got whenever I played before any one. Fancy now its being nearly four years since I have touched either piano or organ. And my singing, which I had once even more reason to be satisfied with, is probably for ever silenced. You cannot think how I thank God from my heart that He would not let me gratify the secret pride which was lurking in it, and which was stealing my love from HIM."

Henry Martyn tells, that, in his student-days, when self and self-pleasing was as yet the centre of his soul, he contrived to pronounce himself "a religious man." Adelaide Newton, also, had, for many days, inscribed her name in the same bede-roll.

A child of parents who loved the Lord, scarcely had she known the time when the "things of the kingdom" were strangers to her ear.

"Pleasant as it was," writes her governess, "to teach her in the school-room, it was still more so to be with her at the season for spiritual instruction. She always appeared to enjoy those opportunities:

and on one occasion I remember she said, 'Thank you, I shall now go to sleep on the Rock of Ages.'"

And, as years went on, the "religiousness" had grown more intense. "On one occasion," says her sister, "in 1835, when Mr. Greville was here for a few days, much that he said, both in the family and to herself, deeply impressed her. And I well remember how, about that time, we were constantly reading Doddridge's 'Rise and Progress,' Fletcher's 'Address,' and James' 'Anxious Inquirer.'" And in the following summer the "religiousness" assumed a still deeper hue. The family had removed for a few months to a neighbouring village, to escape the small-pox which had seized virulently a member of the household. In an unfurnished attic of the house, Adelaide, and three others, used to spend—each unknown to the rest—many solitary hours in "devotional reading and in prayer." And the family governess writes: "From the beginning of 1837 to the end of 1839, I had a daily course of private Bible-reading and prayer with dear Adelaide at her own particular request."

But the "religiousness" did not give her rest. "I am the victim," we find her writing, "of the most distressing and painful conflict. Sometimes I feel ready to give myself up almost to despair, while at other times I seem to enjoy religion. When I look back upon the time when I think this conflict first began in me (which I believe is now six or seven years ago), I am tempted to believe that it is quite impossible that one who has trifled so long with such things, sinning against such light and knowledge as I enjoy, shall ever be forgiven." And again: "I am so careless, and so unwilling to pray. Pray earnestly for me, and write faithfully to me. It will not be a small thing to deceive myself on so all-important a subject."

And some years afterwards, referring to this period, she writes: "I can perfectly enter into all your feelings, because I have been in much the same state of mind myself. I was not happy in the world, and could not be, for there is nothing in it which can satisfy an immortal creature. I had no real enjoyment in anything, because I was trying to serve two masters. And this, I now see, cannot be: God will have the whole heart: His promise is, that we shall find Him when we search for Him with all our hearts."

And again, to the same friend: "I have often thought of you since you once wrote me a note saying you could serve God only as a duty. If this is still your feeling, I can assure you from my own experience, that it is only because your heart is not given up entirely to God. You are trying, as I too long did, to serve God *and* Mammon; and therefore you find no true enjoyment either in the world or in religion. I know exactly how you feel, having had precisely the same conflict going on in my heart for a long time."

"Out of about 365 religions in the world," said a highly-educated Jew one day to his beloved child, an accomplished and lovely girl of nineteen, as she was urging upon him the wonderful graciousness of that Divine Saviour whom she had found in the crucified Nazarene, "I don't think your's the easiest; people have to work so hard, and be so distressingly earnest, and so awfully solemn; it makes me ill to think of it." "Ah!" replied the youthful convert, "this religion is a very happy and a very easy one. I have an inward peace and joy which is unspeakable. Jesus is precious; He is Heaven; He blesses me every moment. Oh! his boundless love to me!"

Adelaide Newton had not yet found Him who was Leila Ada's all. "It is the constant life," says she, "of watchfulness and self-denial required of the Christian which fills me with despair." Her conscience not yet sprinkled with "the blood," she was without a leverage to move her to willing service. Her heart, not yet attached to the Lord Jesus, was not, and could not be, detached from a world "lying in the wicked one."

A new expedient was now attempted.

"I did so much wish to see you," she writes, on the 27th April 1839. "You know that I have at times been very anxious about the state of my mind. Many indeed are the convictions God has most graciously granted me; but they have been rejected and slighted. All this winter, however, I have been very much depressed in spirit, and at times quite miserable. When J—— was staying with us, she slept with me. We often talked indirectly on religious subjects; but one night we got nearer and nearer home, till it ended in my opening my whole heart to her. This was no sooner done than I felt a burden taken off my mind, which has been weighing me down foı months. She gave me most precious advice. I had never spoken freely to any one before; and you may imagine what a relief it was. O pray for me! I trust God is bringing me by a way I know not."

And again, to another: "There is something within which keeps me from enjoying perfect peace. If I could once be sure that I am justified, then all would be right. I wish, more and more, every day, to see some clergyman who would tell me what he thought of me. Still, I can hardly think that God would have brought me so far to put me to shame."

But a brighter hope was now to dawn. "If," says Cowper, of the condemned felon, who, "in darkness and heart-chilling fears," hears the warder at his cell-door, about to lead him forth to death,

"If then, just then, all thoughts of mercy lost,
When hope, long lingering, at last yields the ghost,
The sound of pardon pierce his startled ear,
He drops at once his fetters and his fear;
And transport glows in all he looks and speaks,
And the first thankful tears bedew his cheeks."

And the poet adds:

"Joy, far superior joy, which much outweighs
The comfort of a few poor added days,
Invades, possesses, and o'erwhelms the soul
Of him whom hope has, with a touch, made whole.

'Tis heaven, all heaven, descending on the wings
Of the glad legions of the King of kings.
'Tis more—'tis God diffused through every part;
'Tis God Himself triumphant in his heart."

The bard of Olney himself knew little of this joy; but Adelaide Newton was now to realize it as her own.

One morning, at Leylands, at family worship, a visitor* read the third chapter of Colossians. Selecting the first verse—"If ye, then, be risen with Christ," he spoke emphatically of the "If,"—urging the necessity of make sure of this starting point, setting forth Christ and His resurrection-life as the sinner's immediate privilege, and closing with an appeal on the duty of instant decision for Christ. The message went straight to Adelaide's heart. "The words," says her sister, "were used effectually by the Holy Spirit to decide her to be the Lord's."

When Jesus was on earth, the needy "drew near to Him," and found in Him immediate life. Adelaide Newton "drew near" to the same Saviour, and found the same immediate life. Before, she had gone with her burden to the creature; but the creature could not solace. Now she went direct to Jesus Himself, and she was "accepted in the Beloved." "This," we find her writing, "is the only way to life and salvation—'Come, and see Jesus.' This is the way to settle all objections. We may have a thousand diffi-

* The Rev. Dr. H. M'Neile.

culties in our minds; but, by coming to Christ, to see Him for ourselves, they all vanish away."

Brainerd, in his Diary, contrasting his religiousness with his godliness, writes of the former thus: "The more I did in duty, the more hard I thought it would be for God to cast me off. But now I see that my duties laid not the least obligation upon God to bestow His grace upon me. I see evidently that the whole was nothing but self-worship."

And of the latter he writes: "It was the apprehension of a divine glory. God brought me to a hearty disposition to exalt Him, and to set Him upon the throne. I was sweetly composed. I felt myself in a new world. I wondered that all the world did not see and comply with this way of salvation, entirely by the *righteousness of Christ.*"

Adelaide Newton was carried through a like experience. The "annihilation of her religious self" she had found "a bitter work." That work, though in some sense a life-long discipline, was now so far done, that, for the first time, she could say, "Not I, but Christ." And, like Brainerd, she felt an indescribable repose. "It is impossible," she writes, "to describe what a sight of Christ is. One man cannot tell another. Every one must see for himself. It is perfectly irresistible. And there is something transforming in the very act of beholding Jesus. It is the soul's highest joy."

CHAPTER II.

One day Henry Martyn wrote in his Diary: "My soul approves thoroughly the life of God; and my one only desire is, to be entirely devoted to Him. I have resigned, in profession, the riches, the honours, and the comforts of this world; and I think, also, it is a resignation of the heart."

With Adelaide Newton, also, it was "a resignation of the heart." "'Whose am I?'" she writes, alluding to Paul's words that night in the ship: "Why is it that so few, so very few, can at once answer, 'I am thy servant, O Lord?' There is no sin more hateful to Christ than lukewarmness. And yet how many thousands are victims of it in the present day! What numbers are spoken of as 'well-inclined,' or 'well-disposed,' young persons, liking to be thought well of by the Lord's people, and yet shrinking from that 'coming out' from the world and being 'separate,' which alone could enable them conscientiously to affirm, as in the sight of God, 'I am THINE.'"

"Every one living," she proceeds, "must be Satan's slave or God's child. What an alternative! Surely those who continue in this uncertainty have never seriously asked themselves *whose they are*, if they are not Christ's ? or reflected that they can not be standing still in this uncertainty, but that every thought, word, and action, of every moment of their lives, is confirming them in their service of one of these two masters, and is ever giving fresh and still stronger evidence whose they are !"

And she adds: "How intensely important, therefore, the question becomes, 'Whose am I?' There can be no true peace till it is settled. 'Being justified by faith, we have peace with God' (Rom. v. 1); but not till then. And this is the secret why there are so few—so very, very few—happy, rejoicing Christians. It is not that the religion of Christ is a gloomy thing, but it is that so few know the peace it gives under a sense of forgiven sin. How can they be happy, who are bearing about on their consciences the burden of a life of unpardoned guilt?"

From her own conscience that burden was now gone. Like the pilgrim's, it had fallen from her at the foot of the cross. "How did I know," she writes, some time afterwards, in reference to this period, "that my sins were all washed away? Because I was trusting simply to the FINISHED work of Christ, and was not waiting until I had done any thing to evidence it. What we *do*, as Christians, proves whose we are *in the eyes of the world* (Matt. vii. 16—20); but the grand question with us is, whose we are *in the sight of God;* and that depends entirely on our acceptance of the finished work of Christ. Union with Christ makes us Christians; and that should be the test *whose we are.*"

Relieved from her burden, and bearing in her hand "the roll," she now with a light heart ascended the hill Difficulty. "There is blessedness unutterable," she writes, in true fixedness of heart upon God. It enables a soul to 'sing and give praise' (Ps. lvii. 7), even amidst dangers and calamities and reproaches."

In casting in her lot with Christ, she had not omitted to count the cost. "One day, Lady L—— S—— was asking a mutual friend about us," we find her writing some time previous; "and she heard that we were not decided enough to be happy. Her simple reply was, 'Oh, tell them from me not to be half-and-half.' You cannot think how those words haunted me ever afterwards, and how often they have helped me to be out-and-out a Christian in my conduct."

The "soul that loveth," has been compared to the

"Pale geranium, pent within the cottage-window."

"Behold," says the poet,

"How yearningly it stretcheth to the light its leaves!
How straineth upward to the sun, coveting its sweet influences!
How real a living sacrifice to the god of all its worship!"

Such was Adelaide Newton. Fixing her heart on her beloved Lord, she was transformed into "a living sacrifice." "We read," she writes, "of 'many men of Benjamin and Judah,' who came to join themselves to David. And how did they proclaim their true-heartedness? By their entire self-surrender: 'Thine we are, David; and on thy side, thou son of Jesse!'"

Surrounded by not a little to attract the carnal eye, she "chose the better part," and chose it once for all. "What I long for most," she writes, "is an habitual and realizing sense of the presence of God at all times, and the constant recollection that His eye is upon me, and that nothing, however trivial I may think it, can escape His observation. May it be our experience daily more and more, so that we may grow in conformity to the image of Christ and in meetness for our heavenly inheritance!"

Like the "man in the picture," she had not only "the world behind her back," but the "crown of glory hanging over her head." "Every fresh development," she writes, "of the fruits of the Spirit in our hearts is fresh treasure for 'the Lord of the harvest.' Oh! did we but remember this, in what a different light would all the events of time appear to us! In every friendship we form, in every visit we pay, in every letter we write, we are either sowing to the flesh—of the flesh to reap corruption, or sowing to the Spirit—of the Spirit to reap life everlasting! How this ought to quicken us to use our moments in sowing seed for our eternal harvest!"

In an age like the present, when "the form of godliness" is so rife, and its "power" so very rare, it is not wonderful that a sensitive heart like hers should early have been called to solve various problems in the daily life.

One of these problems was "the course to be pursued in regard to worldly society." Writing to a friend who had solicited her judgment, she says:— "I scarcely think it possible to draw the line too strongly between light and darkness. We cannot be real Christians only in private. It is written, 'By their fruits ye shall know them;' and if we are really following God devotedly, it will be evident to all around us. Let me, therefore, entreat you at once to resolve to make up your mind to devote yourself entirely, soul and body, to Him. I know you never can be really happy till you do."

Tersteegen speaks of "love exercising self-denial without tasting its bitterness, and almost without ever thinking of it." One of Adelaide's sisters, who had been absent from home, writes: "I shall never forget the impression she made on me by the intense feeling she put into Gal. vi. 14, which was the first text she quoted as soon as we were alone together; and from that time I saw that the world was crucified to her in a way I had never seen it before." And she herself writes: "The nearer we live to Jesus, and the closer our walk is with Him, the less inclination we have for pursuits and pleasures in which He is not *the* object."

Many Christians seem only half-reconciled, and therefore only half-separated unto God. Dear Adelaide felt at home in her Father's house; and that made her feel a "stranger" in a world which knows not the Father. "Oh! for a heart," some one has said,

"Magnanimous to know
Thy worth, poor world, and let thee go!"

Such a heart Adelaide had gotten at Golgotha, and it cost her scarcely a pang to "let go" whatever had been most dear. "I can not help thinking," she writes to a schoolfellow, "that, if you are much occupied with thoughts of heaven, of holiness, of the meek and lowly Jesus, and how He lived and walked on earth, you will feel a secret shrinking from wordly society, which will make balls, &c., &c., very painful to you. God has left no positive commands upon things of this sort; for He knows that where the heart is given to Him, the life will assuredly be given too. And the motive of Gospel-obedience is, not so much duty, as love. The child that loves its parents devotedly, or its friends, does what will please them at any cost."

It was not in words only that she thus commended Christ. "Her love to Jesus," says one in whose house she resided at Blackheath during her closing years of school, "was her animating principle, and the very joy of her heart. To lead her young companions to HIM was her grand aim. Her winning cheerfulness made the young see how happy Jesus could make them. Every girl loved her, some most devotedly."

In the autumn of 1842 she visited Ireland. "We have indeed," she says, writing to one of that youthful band, "met with the truest Irish and Christian hospitality. We dined one day with Mr. Daly, at Powerscourt. Almost all the Irish clergy, I find believe in the Personal Reign; and it seems to have a very practical influence on their whole life and conversation. We met there Mr. R——. I really think I have seldom seen a more heavenly-minded man. He does (just what I always long to feel myself) in a most habitual manner seem to feel, that Jesus is always present. Oh! to realize this continually is certainly to have some foretaste of heaven."

Wherever she went, she left behind her a savour of Christ. "I never can forget," writes one who met her during that Irish tour, "dearest Adelaide's deeply interesting visit to Glanmore. Though it is thirteen years since, I can well remember how much we were both struck by her deep spirituality, the very enlarged range of her intellectual powers, the chastened tone of her mind, and the exquisite modesty and simplicity of her manners and character. We were not less delighted with the warmth of her zeal for the enlightenment of the poor Irish people."

Scarcely a week passed that some school-companion or other friend was not soliciting her counsel and sympathy in the struggles of the Christian life. Writing to one, she says: "I think 1 Cor. vii. 20–24 plainly shows us, that in whatever position or calling of life we are placed, there it is our duty to abide. A child, for instance, must be in subjection to her parents; and if they would have her do what she dislikes or disapproves, it is generally, I should think, her plain duty to take up the cross and obey them, for God well knows her motive, and by no means judges her of willing conformity to the world in such acts."

And again:—"If you feel obliged to join your family or friends in scenes which give you no pleasure, and if you let them see that you join them from a sense of duty, and not from inclination, I think you will reap the gain of self-denial. But, after all, don't you think that our grand concern is, to aim at close walking with God, leaving Him to order our steps for us, and trusting Him so to order our way as best to enable us to walk closely with Him? Remember that Jesus is each day saying to his Father for you, 'I pray, not that she should be taken out of the world, but that she should be kept from the evil.' May I send you these words to use as your constant plea at the throne of grace whenever you are in difficulty how to act?"

And to another friend: "In one sense, all conformity to the world is forbidden. We could not have stronger language than St. Paul's: 'Come out, and be separate, and *touch not* the unclean thing.' But then he has balanced that extreme by telling us, on the other hand, that, if we kept *no* company with ungodly people, we 'must needs go out of the world.' And so far from this being intended, we are expressly commanded to be "blameless and harmless, the sons of God without rebuke, in the midst of a crooked and perverse nation, among whom ye shine as lights in the world.' Again, we find Jesus, when on earth, accepting an invitation to a wedding-feast (John ii.); and He dined with a Pharisee (Luke vii.), who most certainly was a man of the world. And don't you think He is as much our example in these things as in visiting the poor, and in relieving the sick and needy?"

And yet again: "I think the love of the world may show itself very differently in different persons, and that no one can altogether judge for another, whether they are indulging it in what they do, or not. But I believe conscience tells each child of God in secret. I dare not decidedly judge for you, even in my own mind, how far you may rightly go into the world; but I feel sure that if you honestly seek direction from God, you will certainly get it. My desire for you is, that you may walk as Jesus walked. I don't think we can aim too high. Let your standard be, to be like Him."

"I hope," she adds, "you will not think me severe upon you in anything I have said; for you cannot think how I feel for you. My natural heart was so fond of the same wordliness, though in a different way. I struggled for months—or, I may say, years—between God and the world; but never did I enjoy peace or happiness the whole time. No one knew what I endured. May you be spared the bitter conflict, and choose the better part at once and unreservedly!"

"Dead to the world, we dream no more
Of earthly pleasures now;
Our deep, divine, unfailing spring
Of grace and glory—Thou!"

CHAPTER III.

Lord Bacon, in one of his essays, quotes a proverb of the ancients—"A friend is another himself." "No receipt," he adds, "openeth the heart but a true friend to whom you may impart griefs, joys, fears, hopes, suspicions, counsels, and whatsoever lieth upon the heart to oppress it."

Dear Adelaide had left behind her not a few prized companionships; but others were substituted. "Kindred," some one has said, "is the riches of the heart." That kindred she now possessed. "Oh! what a life," she writes, "the life of a Christian is! I feel so wrapt up in thought this morning, that I really cannot write. How delightful is the feeling that the same High Priest above understands your feelings and mine! It gives a feeling of union which nothing else can. 'One in Christ!'—if we are thus made members of one body, we shall never be really separated."

And to another: "I cannot tell you how thankfully I look back upon the privilege of getting to know you as much as I did at Sandgate. I really believe my chief pleasure in this world consists in having and being with Christian friends; and none but Christians know how real and lasting such friendship is."

The instinct which loves because of natural attractions, and the grace which loves in spite of natural defects, and simply because of what is Christ-like, are very different affections.

"There is a fragrant blossom, that maketh glad the garden of the heart;
Its root lieth deep; it is delicate, yet lasting, as the lilac crocus of autum:
Loneliness and thought are the dews that water it morn and even.
I saw it budding in beauty; I felt the magic of its smile;
The violet rejoiced beneath it, the rose stooped down and kissed it;
And I thought some cherub had planted there a truant flower from Eden,
As a bird bringeth foreign seeds, that they may flourish in a kindly soil."

That "truant flower" is Christian fellowship—the "communion of the saints." And not often has it found a more "kindly soil" than in the heart of Adelaide Newton. "I am thinking so much," she writes, "of you and dearest —— to-night. I can fancy you both looking at that splendid star which I too see again to-night for the first time for ages. How long it may be before we all three look at it together again! Perhaps never! Be it so; may we then only meet to behold together, not a star, but the glorious, unclouded Sun of Righteousness! We could not wish for anything so enrapturing in this world." And again: "I constantly think of you

How wonderfully we are all separated just now! How sweet the thought—

"'Our bodies may far off remove,
We still are one in heart!'"

The saint is not an anchorite, and he never will be. The world has not a friendship which shall survive earth's brief hour; but the saint is linked to his heavenly kindred by an affection which cannot die. His heart can never grow poor. "What a strange and mysterious thing," she says, "our pilgrim-life here is! designed just for a special purpose, and often rendered so sweet by fellow-pilgrims who travel with us a part of the way! but, different work and different paths being assigned to each, we are emphatically taught that our family-gathering cannot be fully realized till those numberless paths and different tracks shall meet in one common centre—the Father's house above. Oh! that our love may indeed grow exceedingly both towards God and towards one another!"

And, writing to one of her sisters, she says: "How I wish, my dearest N——, I thanked God as I ought for all He makes you to me! I love so deeply, that really, when my love is peculiarly called forth, I long to live both to enjoy others' love to me and to love them in return. How intensely difficult to believe that love is to be so increased and perfected in heaven!" And she adds: "As love is that which flows from God, I don't think it is possible to prize it too highly from others, or to love too much ourselves. It is only the sin that defiles our love, which mars it. It is trying to be so near, and not to meet. But our meeting-place is in Christ and in His Word: we need separation to teach us this effectually, I believe."

If she was Christ-like in her love to the saints, she was not less Christ-like in her compassion for perishing sinners. "In 1843," says one who knew her well, "she became a teacher in the Sunday-school—an employment in which she always took the deepest interest. The impression produced on the children's minds was not easily forgotten, some of them even proving their grateful affection by visiting her in her last illness."

And another field of labour was a District in the parish of All-Saints'. Her visits were singularly blessed. The writer, a few months ago, met an aged women who owed to these visits her conversion. As she spoke of "dear Miss Newton," with tears in her eyes, a gleam of heavenly joy lighted up her wrinkled features. "Oh! I was so dark," she said, "when that dear lady came to see me; but she told me of Jesus and His love, and it drew my dead heart to Him. Oh! had she not come to me, I would just have lived on in sin."

Her aim in all her visits was, not to "do a duty," but to "win souls." One of her sisters writes: "Early in the spring of 1844, Adelaide asked me one day to share part of her district, and lend books and tracts at one end of the street. Noticing how long she had waited at the different doors before going in, I asked her, as we were walking home, 'Do you always wait when you knock at a door till they open it?' 'No,' was her reply, 'but I always like to wait a moment, before I knock, to ask for the Holy Spirit to be with my mouth and teach me what to say in each house.' I have often thought of it since," her sister adds, "and have attributed to it her wonderful success among the poor whom she visited."

And what passed within, we may gather from a few sentences occurring in a "private" Diary, marked "Visits to the Poor—1843-6."

"1843. *July* 14.—Saw R. F.: she appeared at the point of death. I never can forget the overwhelming feeling of being asked to speak to a soul on the brink of eternity; perhaps the last words she heard might be mine. I urged her to believe in Christ, who was able and willing to save her. I then prayed with her very shortly, and as simply as I could. I did not improve that opportunity as I might. May God forgive me for it!"

"*July* 19.—Saw M. S., who gets worse in body, but I hope grows in grace. She told me that Mrs. W. began to pray the day before she died, but, finding she could not, she said she found swearing easier; and, returning to her former ways, she died in that awful condition. Oh! that it might be a saving warning to some!"

"1844. *April* 3.—Saw Mrs. L., and read her part of 2 Cor. v., and 1 Cor. xv. She could scarcely speak, but charged me to remember M. She said, 'If Jesus died for sinners, I'm sure he died for me;'

and several times she repeated that she was 'soon going home,' and could now resign everything to God."

"*April* 9.—Heard, from old Betty Fox, of the dying Infidel, Samuel Goode. In speaking of his determination not to have anything to do with a Saviour, she added, 'But *I* hope to trouble Him, for I hope to be with Him for ever."

"*May* 1.—Saw Mrs. H., and read her John iii.; but I fear she depends on supposed innocency of life for acceptance with God. May God open her eyes to see her danger! Oh! that she may yet be brought into the fold of Christ, and be made His for ever!"

"1845. *April* 9.—Went to see E. E.; but her spirit had taken its flight that morning. She knew she was dying, and on the Tuesday desired her mother to give 'her best love to Miss N., for she should never see me again;' and in the evening she asked her to take her a candle, and hold it by her while she read my hymn on 'The Fulness of Jesus.' She also spoke very seriously to her sister S., though the room was full. In the afternoon, while her mother was sitting alone with her, she said, 'Oh! mother, can't you hear it? It is so beautiful!' After listening for some minutes, she said, with her arms stretched out, 'I'm sure Jesus sent those blessed angels to comfort me.' She also said, when asked if she felt afraid to die, 'No, I'm not afraid; the sting of death is quite taken away.' She was sensible to the last, and died peacefully."

"1846. *January* 23.—Spoke to B. of neglecting salvation till we are sick and dying; he was quite affected to tears, and wept some time. He seemed quite cheered when I spoke to him of the precious blood of Jesus."

"*February* 23.—Spoke faithfully to Mrs. D. about her husband, and urged her, instead of trying to talk to him, to talk to God about him."

"*March* 10.—Saw M. W., who had been taken ill on Wednesday. She said she had often wondered if her religion would support her in illness and death; and it did. The world had never been much to her. She was always afraid of having too much, lest it should draw off her affections from God; but now it seemed utterly nothing. She said she felt as if standing on the outside of it. She had perhaps led as upright a life outwardly as was possible, exercising always a conscience void of offence; but if any one should suggest that as a ground of acceptance, she spurned the thought. She would consider everything in that light as 'lighter than a feather to waft her across the ocean.'"

It was thus that dear Adelaide went about, like the Master, from day to day, "the common people hearing her gladly." "I would never," we find her writing, in her diary, at the beginning of 1846, "enter a house without having first asked His blessing—never go to the district without prayer, and prayer especially for a blessing on the books lent." And this other entry: "The time is short; work while it is day; the Lord is at hand: occupy till I come."

Her sickle preserved its fine edge; and that made her so successful a reaper in His fields.

And the sickles of other reapers she sought to sharpen. "'Who hath believed our report?'" she writes, in a pointed appeal, widely circulated in various parts of England, "is the sad inquiry of the minister, the teacher, and every one who labours to win souls to Christ. Let us, therefore, put the promise of our God to the proof, and see if He will not open the windows of heaven, and pour us out a blessing that there shall not be room enough to receive it. True, we need self-denial and resolute effort, to get even time for prayer; and we must endure some conflict with Satan and self, ere we are enabled to continue in prayer. But if one hour each day could be devoted by each praying soul in this parish to intercessory prayer on its behalf, what immense results might be expected! Surely we might be more thoroughly in earnest. Surely we might plead more with God, when infatuated men are deaf. Does not the Lord *wait* to be gracious, until He hears our cry (Isa. xxx. 19)? 'Ye people, pour out your heart before Him.'"

In her visitations, not less than in her own hidden life, the "blessed hope" grew daily more precious. "I have always found it," she writes in her diary, "produce a deeper impression upon the poor than any other subject." And elsewhere she says: "It opens the Scriptures to us in an entirely new light. I find, too, that all who receive this view are agreed that it makes them feel less concern and love for the world than anything we can imagine. It gives one this feeling, 'If Christ is coming so soon, what matters it what men think of us, if only we are safe in Christ? and what is there in the world worth caring for, since we shall so soon have done with it?' I know that we may say the same thing with respect to the shortness and uncertainty of life; but we do not *realize* it in the same way."

The "hope" wonderfully quickened her own steps heavenward. "It should ever be the Christian pilgrim's answer," she writes, "to every allurement to loiter or make a home down here, 'I cannot tarry; I am journeying.' (Num. x. 29.) And whither? Even to that land of promise, 'of which the Lord hath said, I will give it you.' He is 'going home.' It is already his by promise and by gift, and he is going to take possession of it! It is not merely a resolution, it is a matter of fact that even now he is *on his way*. It could be no question with Israel of old; for they were neither in Egypt, living in the land of Goshen, nor in Canaan; but between the two—'journeying.' And they felt it—knew it—to be so.

"'We are on the way to God:'
"'And nightly do we pitch our tents
A day's march nearer home.'

We make progress in a journey: we expect none of the rest, or ease, or comforts of home, but press onwards. And the promise of God leads us on We can trust to it.

4*

"'Though the shore we hope to land on
Only by report is known,
Yet we freely all abandon,
Led by that report alone,
And to Jesus
Through the trackless deep move on.'"

Schiller, in one of his tragedies, has a personage who, in her enthusiasm of attachment exclaims, "He sails on troubled seas—Amelia's love sails with him; he wanders in pathless deserts—Amelia's love makes the burning sand grow green beneath him, and the stunted shrubs to blossom; the south wind scorches his bare head, his feet are pinched by the northern snow, stormy hail beats round his temples—Amelia's love rocks him to sleep in the storm. Seas, and hills, and horizons are between us; but souls escape from their clay-prisons, and meet in the paradise of love." That is but a fond creation of the fancy, without a counterpart in life's realities. But the Christian pilgrim finds, in the hope of his Lord's "appearing," a gladness which is here but faintly shadowed. "Jesus endured the cross," writes our pilgrim, "for the joy that was set before Him; and that we may endure it, He would have the 'fulness of joy in His presence,' and the crowns which He promises to 'those who overcome,' to be ever before us." This annihilates intervening "seas, and hills, and horizons." "Make haste my Beloved!" the soul cries in its struggle, lifting heavenward its faith and hope, "and be thou like a roe or a young hart upon the mountains of Bether."

Her thoughts at times took the form of verse. The lines which follow, though very simple, have a sweet pensiveness about them, betokening the heart of the stranger whose eye is upon the Canaan-rest. They are founded on Col. i. 27, and are dated "May 10, 1846:"

"'THE HOPE OF GLORY.'

"So bright is the hope of the glory before me,
I'm often impatient, in haste to be gone:
I long, blessed Jesus, with saints to adore Thee,
Those glorified spirits surrounding Thy throne.

"So bright is the hope, that *I would not* live alway
For pleasures this poor fading earth can bestow;
They never can satisfy, never can cheer me,
For each one is tainted with sorrow and woe.

"Of this body of sin and of death I'm so weary,
I cling to the bright '*hope of* GLORY' in store
For the souls who have found all on earth to be weary,
And long to attain to the heavenly shore.

"Lord, hasten the time of Thy blessed returning,
To give us the peace and *the rest* that *remain*
For Thy servants who stand with their lamps ready burning,
To enter Thy glory, and *with Thee to reign!*

"This—this is the Hope that is now set before us;
Oh! when shall we enter that glorious rest?
Welcome, pain! welcome, death! if it brings us to Jesus,
And banishes *hope* in our pleasures POSSESSED."

CHAPTER IV.

He who tempers the wind to the shorn lamb, had been solacing His servant with this "strong consolation," before laying upon her His chastening rod.

Her unceasing labours in the "district" began at length seriously to undermine her never very robust frame.

In April, 1844, we find her "going round a new district, containing at least one hundred houses," and "fairly tired out with each day's work." "I have been this evening," she writes, in June of the same year, "to see another poor woman, very much like Mrs. ——, but more anxious. I have had two deeply interesting talks with her. Only think, what a privilege to be allowed to speak to poor sinners of a Saviour's love! May our unworthy efforts be blessed!"

And in March, 1845, she writes: "If you knew how fully every moment has been occupied lately, you would not wonder at my long silence. Suffice it to say, that last week I was out at district-work four days out of the six, from breakfast in the morning till four or five in the afternoon."

Often protracting her visitations until she was obliged to hasten home too late for dinner, she at last sat down one day overheated, and caught a chill. It was in June, 1846.

It speedily became apparent that only a season of entire rest could afford any hope of real amendment. Writing from Malvern, to which she had gone "for change of air," she says, of date June 30: "You ask about my health. I am not well, but not ill. A troublesome cough has got me at last into the doctor's hands. He has ordered me to the sea-side, where I may get my constitution strengthened and have no temptation to work as I was doing at home. He has positively forbidden me to go into crowded rooms, Sunday-schools, &c., or to sit in the open air. I have had appliances to my chest; and I hope, in time, to be either restored to health again, or to go where pain and *sin* are known no more—to that perfect 'rest which remaineth.' My times are in His hands."

Vinet has remarked, that "those who hope and trust in Jesus Christ present us with a strange spectacle—that of weak, frail, mortal men, for whom suffering and death are no longer a necessity endured involuntarily, but in some sort an act of the will, because, by consenting to those chastisements, they transform them into sacrifices." It was so, emphatically, with Adelaide Newton. Not suffering "in spite of herself," but consenting cheerfully beforehand to the Master's will, she was to find in her coming sufferings, only "a bitter dew," which should develope and mature in her soul the germ of faith and of hope.

> "Then shall these powers, which work for grief,
> Enter Thy pay,
> And, day by day,
> Labour Thy praise and my relief:
> With care and courage building me,
> Till I reach heav'n—and, much more, Thee!"

"What an unspeakable mercy it is," she writes to a fellow-sufferer, "that God should give us these trials, and should care so much for us as to watch over them, and over us in them—that, through them, we may be brought nigh unto Him! You are, I am certain, being 'led by the right way;' and if it is a darker way, will not in all probability the result be brighter?"

And to another: "You know that each drop in your bitter cup is measured out to you by the unerring hand of your heavenly Physician, who never makes mistakes, or ceases to watch His patients for one moment. Sometimes I rejoice to think how very soon I may die; for I am sadly tied and bound by the chain of sin, and long to be delivered from this body of corruption: but I oftener think there is too much to be done in me before I am 'made meet' for glory, to allow me to die yet. How calming it is to remember the words of that hymn—

> "'Till He bids, I cannot die;
> When the time He wills is come,
> Nought can keep me from my home.'

And then to think of our meeting in glory, where there is fulness of bliss for evermore! Oh! surely this is a prospect which may well cheer us in our wearisome pilgrimage through the wilderness of life temporal. Life eternal we cannot understand at present; but what we know not now, we shall know hereafter. I will try and pray for you in your present trouble. Let us not double the anxieties of to-day, by adding those of to-morrow: 'Sufficient unto the day is the evil thereof.'"

Cecil observes, that "such is the state of the world, and so much depends on action, that everything seems to say loudly to every man, 'Do something—do it—do it!'" Dear Adelaide had hitherto been an earnest doer: now she was to be a patient endurer. But, though no longer able to "speak" much about "the King," her "tongue" was transformed into "the pen of a ready writer;" and greatly was the Lord to bless her words.

"Is it not wonderful," we find her writing, for example, to one who had not yet decided for Christ, "that you can love such a world so well? It is very hard to give up all and follow Christ; indeed, with men it is impossible. But, blessed be God, when He makes us willing, He gives us the needful strength for every trial. What a wonderful reality there is in these things—so different from the head-knowledge which so many possess, who never will be partakers of heaven or of Christ! It is hard, very hard, to become a true Christian; but think, only for one moment, what is the only alternative! Do not you shudder at the bare idea of dying unprepared? Oh!

my dear F——, can you go on unconcerned, at the brink of everlasting death? If I may speak from my own experience, I would urge you not to leave the spot where you now are, nor to let the present moment pass by, without making up your mind at once to give up the world and devote yourself to HIM. Forgive me, and don't be offended; it is all because I love you so much."

One day, a friend remarked to Gerhard Tersteegen, "God has much trouble in bringing up his children." "Yes," said Tersteegen, "and in bringing them down." The detaching and the attaching usually go hand in hand. "I think," we find Adelaide writing at this period, "God has been teaching us both the same lesson, though by different means—namely, that we must be weaned from a love of earthly objects and find happiness in Him alone. I have by no means learned the lesson yet myself. No sooner is one idol removed than I find myself setting up another immediately. God finds in me, I am sure, a most rebellious, wayward child; but He deals most wisely, most graciously with me. Pray that we both may find our faith growing exceedingly, and our love to each other abounding, whilst the love of so many waxes cold."

Wandering about in search of health, she writes to one of her sisters thus: "I have been getting my Irish-reader collection made up, and, through God's help, sent 16*l.* yesterday. One of my trials now is such a feeling of indolence and inability to arouse myself—the re-action, I suppose, of over-exertion in times past. How you would laugh, could you see me at this moment! sitting all alone in my bed-room, at the open window, with bonnet, shawl, and everything on! I quite enjoy the air and the sun in this way; and I must submit to not seeing my friends, remembering the blessedness of being left alone with Jesus. You taught me that!"

And she adds: "I can't make out what —— means to do; but it is the very best thing for us to have the world embittered to us in all ways. Should we ever have been what we are, if we had had the uncrossed lives so many young people lead? And I believe, the more we know of conformity to the 'Man of sorrows,' as He was 'acquainted with grief,' the more we know of Himself, who is all our happiness, our joy, our peace. May He be glorified in you, dearest N——, where you now are, and ask the same for your fondly attached sister, Adelaide."

"The "Irish-reader collection" was an object very near to her heart. "I am sure," she writes to the Secretary, on the occasion above noted, "when I look upon my first originating this little plan, I cannot but wonder at the marvellous success which God has been pleased to grant—not so much in my own case, as in raising up, through us, three other instruments in the same service." Four missionaries were now in that field, all of them owing the means of cultivating it entirely to her exertions. And the money was the least element contributed. By maintaining a constant correspondence with the agents, and communicating the leading features of their labours to a large circle of friends, she kept alive in many hearts a glow of devotion on behalf of the work, which bore its fruits in the singular blessing with which their words were attended.

In July (1846) she returned home "much worse." "The air of Malvern," she writes, "was too keen and bracing for me. And now I am ordered, as soon as possible, to go to the sea, in some warm, sheltered place. I get quite impatient at times to have done with sin, and with this body of sin which I carry about with me; but I must learn to wait the Lord's time. It is difficult to learn to leave everything in the hands of God; but it is a lesson we must learn, and we must be thankful for *any* means by which we are taught it."

Later in the season we find her at Sandgate. Rejoicing over one who had at length consecrated herself to God, she writes, on Sept. 29: "God has dealt wonderfully with you, in enabling you to separate yourself from others who serve Him by profession only. I cannot help rejoicing with you. It seems as if He were dealing with you as with a choice plant, whom He would shelter from the withering blasts which would have assailed you at home. I am sure of one thing, that it is all love, and that it is just because He loves us that He thinks it worth while to try and to prune us. But I must ask you to pray that the end of His present dealings with me may be fully answered, and that He may still make use of me in His service, though in a different way from that I have been used to."

From Sandgate she went to London. There a gleam of sunshine seemed to break upon her. "Mr. Evans' words to me yesterday," she writes, on Nov. 2, "were—'I think I see in you beginnings of that improvement which, I fully believe, will end in perfect restoration by the time you are leaving Torquay.' So that I must look upon this winter," she adds, "as a precious opportunity, which I may never have again, of growing in the knowledge of God. It may be, that a life of active service is still in store for me; but I delight to think that the future need be no source of anxiety to me, and that our chief object ought to be to live habitually in dependance on that sweet promise, 'As thy day, so shall the strength be.' How sweet it is to lie passive in His hands, and tc know no will but His!"

CHAPTER V.

"OUR drive through the vale," writes a Swiss traveller, "brought us full in the view of the snowy Blumlis Alps at sunset. What a form of majesty and glory! How he flings the flaming mantle of the evening sun down upon us, as if he were himself about to ascend in fire from earth to heaven!" Adelaide Newton now enters on a course of discipline which reminds us, at every step, of that sun-mantled Alp.

Torquay is a spot around which not a few assemble sadly fragrant memories. Dear Adelaide is not the only saint whose evening sun has here shed its cheering rays. But not often has

> "An unimpeded commerce with the sun"

illumined with so bright a glory a pilgrim in her evening-hour.

She reached Torquay in November, 1846. At first it seemed as if she might again be restored to health. "I submitted," she writes, "to a regular visitation from Dr. —— this morning. So far as human foresight can foretell future events, I suppose I may expect ere long to be back again in the world, as I shall call returning to my old pursuits. It is giving up self," she adds, "which is so hard, and which makes us most like Christ."

In her Diary, we find, under January 1, 1847, this earliest entry: "Begin this year at Torquay, having been ordered here by Dr. Latham, and in God's merciful providence, placed under Dr. ——'s care. May I this year realize by faith, and prayer, and meditation on such chapters as John xvii., 1 Cor. ii., Eph. i. and iii., the personal and substantial presence of the Holy Ghost within me, maintaining an absolute oneness with the very body of Christ, and in Christ, with His Godhead—John xvii. 23. His body, the Church, filled with all the fulness of God! This is the hope of my calling, and this the exceeding riches of the glory of my inheritance in the saints!"

From her new home she writes: "When you think of me, pray that I may have grace to make a diligent use of my present opportunities for growing in the knowledge and love of God, whilst laid aside from ordinary home duties and pursuits. Never apologise," she adds, "for filling a letter with thoughts about Christ's Second Coming. What theme so worthy of those whom He has taught to be looking for Him? I only long to have my own thoughts more perpetually turned towards Him."

And a week or two later, alluding to an instance of Divine power attending the words which her correspondent had spoken, she writes: "I hope it will encourage you to visit all you can, sowing the seed of the Word, which God will own. You inquire about myself. Sometimes I am very happy, and sometimes under a cloud; but Jesus is always the same. Let us seek to grow up into Him more and more, till we can say from the heart, 'Christ is ALL.'"

Her symptoms became less favourable. "Yesterday," she writes, January 8, to one of her sisters, "I was saying to Miss E——, I should really be sorry when the time came for me to leave Torquay. 'I'm not sure,' she replied, very kindly, 'that you ever will have to leave it.' I instantly replied, 'Oh! I'm not going always to live here.' And she added, 'Well, from all Dr. —— has lately told me, he has quite given me the impression, that he thinks it will be necessary for you to live in a mild climate.' I am not much given to anticipate; and when I think of the extreme uncertainty of life, it would be vain to be looking forward: but it proves very plainly to my mind, that I have little or no prospect of ever being strong, which at times comes over me with a degree of shrinking; and yet if it is to make me reflect more of the image of a suffering Saviour, I am sure I ought to be the last to complain."

And to the same, on January 15: "You cannot think how I enjoyed the Sacrament; only I got so tired. I don't think I am so well altogether since I came here. Some time ago, I never could have believed that I could be so happy—cut off from all active work for God as I am now. I feel as if it would be quite a blessing to have a constant reminder, in this body of sin, that this is not my rest. It will be a constant proof of the chastening hand of God upon me."

And again: "I am more and more persuaded, that it is wrong so to long for death, as I sometimes do; for nowhere in Scripture is it set before us as a subject for hope, but always the Lord's Second Coming; and, therefore, it is not our own selfish gratification in the release from such a life which is our hope, but the glory of Christ in the perfected condition of the whole body at His coming. At the longest, it is but 'a little while.' Oh! what a comfort! I am enjoying 'Howe on the Righteous' very much; on Ps. xvii. 15, he speaks so very animatingly of likeness to God, and of the glory we shall then enter upon! But what a subject it is for worms like us to think about! Oh! for growing likeness to Him now!"

It is not easy to praise the Lord in the fires. And yet if these fires, not touching a hair of the garment, only loose the bonds, is there not cause for praise? "I am beginning to think," dear Adelaide writes to a fellow-sufferer, at the beginning of February, "that His chastenings are actually the strongest proofs of His intense love to us; and how sweet that makes them, none know but those who learn it, as you and I are learning it now."

As the winter advanced, her illness grew more alarming. A sister, whose "happy privilege it was to be appointed her companion," writes: "At the end of January she became much worse; and she continued very ill indeed through February and part of March; but, towards the close of that month, the hectic fever and the unceasingness of her cough rather abated."

And another trial was added. "I never remember to have endured," Adelaide writes to another of her sisters, on February 22 (1847), "more intense pain than during the last fortnight; and, the last day or two, mental anguish has aggravated bodily suffering, to a degree I never at all understood before. I have no doubt that Satan took advantage of the state of extreme weakness I was reduced to, to make his temptations the more effectual; but stronger is He that is in us, than he that is against us, blessed be God! And I delight to tell you, for your own encouragement, that yesterday in the midst of such mental darkness and bodily pain, I still felt the assurance that God was the same unchanged God as when I was able to feel Him precious to me. I could not help thinking that it might be in answer to a prayer I have often prayed with trembling, 'that I might know Him and the fellowship of His sufferings,' that I was made to taste of the bitterness of that cup which He drank when tempted of the devil; for that, too, was at a season of peculiar bodily weakness."

And she adds: "I like to tell you all this, dearest N——, because I feel it is *real* experience, which is worth many thousand times as much written from head-knowledge of Bible-truths. I am certain now that it is only in the furnace we are purged from sin. And, however trying it may be, I hope you will pray that God may accomplish all His will in me. I want to feel more thankfulness for His chastening love, and not to shrink from suffering."

She began to "get into smoother waters again." "Positively, I am wonderfully better," she writes, April 9; "and what is more, I am thankful to be so. It is God's mercy, and shall be continued at His pleasure. At one time Dr. —— thought very badly of me, and I really hoped my pilgrimage on earth was nearly run; but if God should call me back to the world again, do pray that I may be kept from a worldly spirit. In this 'light affliction' God has been making me feel, by gentle pressure, that He is holding me tightly in His hand. Oh! what a mercy to be so kept!"

Nothing proves so affectingly our lack of likeness to God, as the faintness of our compassion for perishing souls. God loved the world so much that He gave His dear Son for it; we love the world so little, that too often we feel it an effort to tell men that God has given Him. One of the lessons which dear Adelaide was learning in the school of trial, was an intenser sympathy with God in this matter. "I wonder," she writes to one of her sisters, "what you and G—— are doing to-day to make known the riches of God's mercy to fallen men. Oh! the honour of rescuing but one soul from—oh! I wish I thought more what it is from. How much more thankful we should be, if we did!" And, on another occasion, referring to a woman in her district, who was very ill: "Do give Mrs. P. a kind message from me when you see her, and ask her if she remembers a long conversation I had with her last May, urging her not to put off seeking Christ till she came to be ill? I suppose she had a 'Just as I am;' will you ask her to consider that as my message to her, and entreat her not to rest happy one moment till she has come to Christ? I have so often repented of not having sent a special message to poor Mrs. R——, that I am doubly anxious not to lose this opportunity; and I never but once spoke faithfully to Mrs. P——."

If dear Adelaide was unworldly, she was not unhuman. Her warm, genial heart had an ear for nature's symphonies. "The day was lovely," she writes, April 14, "and this place so exquisitely beautiful, that perhaps natural feelings excite me too much. Yet God has given us all these things 'richly to enjoy;' and when we can enjoy them, I believe we ought. Sometimes it is a burden to me even to hear the birds sing, so little do I yet know of the joy God has in all His works!"

One of her greatest trials this winter was her inability to attend public ordinances. In her Diary, she writes: "*Sunday, April* 11.—The thirteenth Sunday spent at home! 'Lord, show me wherefore thou contendest with me.'" And writing to a friend, April 20, she says: "It is now fourteen Sundays since I was in church; and you may imagine what this is to me, who, sooner than stay away, have more than once actually got up out of bed to go.

But God is able to make all grace abound towards me."

A little incident, which had occurred at Leylands the previous summer, illustrates this feature of her character. Living at some distance from town, she was not in the habit of attending evening service. "We were dreadfully starved," writes one of her sisters, "with our afternoon sermons that summer; and she and I were allowed to go in the evening again in consequence, as long as daylight lasted. But each Sunday we feared it would be the last. When it came, I was comforting myself by singing hymns in the garden, whilst the bells were ringing for evening service. Presently she came out, saying, 'How can you sing?' I reminded her of an exposition we had heard and enjoyed at a friend's house, on Ps. cxxxi., and said, 'I was trying to behave and quiet myself like a weaned child.' 'Oh,' she said, 'so was I; but those seem *so* blessed who can *still* be praising God in His house—who can *dwell* there;—I long for it so. To hear the bells is more than I can bear; I shut myself in my room, and buried my head, while I was trying to bear the disappointment.'"

And she "took heed how she heard." The same informant adds: "She never would speak, if she could avoid it, after leaving church, and often begged I would not talk to her as we walked home, even though it should only be about the sermon we had heard."

But, shut out from the sanctuary, dear Adelaide

had other joys. "I enjoy my Bible," she writes, April 23, "when quite alone, so that I have no room for complaining. I can never be sufficiently thankful for having such an opportunity of learning something of God, and of what He becomes to us in Christ—a very present help in trouble." And to her sister, a day or two later, thus: "I sometimes enjoy my lonely Sundays very much, and they go quicker than ever. And no wonder, when they are spent in the study of that blessed Word which is the very life of the soul! God can feed us both with Himself, dear N——, without either ministers or church; and it is well worth being deprived of the comfort of either or both, to be driven to Him, the fountain of living waters.

"'Break all thy schemes of earthly joy,
That thou mayest find thine all in ME!"

Is not that just our experience at this very time?"

And in another direction she was tasting the same flesh-crucifying but soul-profiting experience. "I see plainly," she writes, "that both in you and in me there is a tendency to form an idolatrous kind of attachments; and God in mercy makes us feel that they are not HIMSELF. What a bitter lesson it is to learn, and how much teaching we have taken to learn even what we have learned!"

Herbert, in his "Country Parson," has a chapter on "The Parson in Circuit," in which he describes, after his own quaint fashion, the method of a true shepherd. Describing a visit from a dear servant of

Christ, who had come a considerable distance to see her, Adelaide writes, "April 9 (1847):"

"Mr. Dallas walked up to the window at Holm Cottage with B., about half-past two; and as he came into the room, and took my hand—while we stood, he prayed that the Holy Spirit might be with us, to make our intercourse profitable and to God's glory, for Jesus Christ's sake.

"As B. walked up with him, he had asked if he might speak out plainly to me, or if I could not bear the thought of death, &c.? She said he might; so the moment she left the room, he began to talk to me, asking me if I thought much about going to be with Christ? if I could bear to think about dying, or if I felt afraid of it? When I said I did not, he said it was right to have a sense of the horrid nature of death as part of the curse of sin, and that it should not be regarded as a light thing. But he was 'very thankful' to find that he might talk to me so quietly about it; and he said, what a wonderful thing it was that two redeemed sinners could talk in that way of what the world shrinks from the bare mention of. How it magnified the grace of God, which had wrought such a change in us! He said he hoped I could look on death as a sunken fence, and look over it and beyond it to the glory on the other side. Then he talked a great deal about the Second Coming of Jesus, the first resurrection, and how near he thinks it is.

"He spoke next to me about depressions in illness —the mind being acted on by the body—that at such times, whatever we may feel, the believer is just as safe as when asleep, and that the very sorrow we feel at our inability to pray, &c., is actually communion with God—it is the Spirit working in our hearts. He also talked to me about sleep. He said the best remedy for calming an agitated mind (which, after all, was the cause generally of wakeful nights) was to fix the mind on one thought, such as Christ upon the cross.

"Then he knelt down and prayed for me, that I might enjoy much of His presence—much of the Spirit's teaching—very near and close communion with God—a sense of acceptance through Jesus, that all God's purposes might be fulfilled, and the end of my coming here, &c., be fully realized, and that I might have patience to wait God's appointed time for going to be with Jesus, &c., &c. Then he prayed for B., and for each member of our family, and for all we loved in the Lord, and that such as were not yet, might be speedily gathered into His fold; so that, whether we were among the dead in Christ, or the living who were to be caught up to meet them, we might be 'for ever with the Lord.'"

We give these jottings, both as indicating the method of visitation which meets such an invalid's necessities, and also as opening up a glimpse into dear Adelaide's own heart.

Grace had adorned with a most engaging patience a temperament naturally somewhat quick. "As we moved from lodging to lodging," says her sister, who was with her, "suiting the warmer and lower situations to the colder weeks of winter, she rejoiced in believing that in each she gained something which she could not have had without the move, though that moving was in itself irritating to her natural disposition, and sometimes, when so ill, a real trial."

"In every lodging," her sister adds, "she studied to make friends with our landlady and servants in order to do them good. Though I chiefly waited upon her, some things—such as cleaning her rooms, lighting her bedroom fire, &c.—brought her into immediate contact with the young servant girls, and her patience with each one having to be taught exactly how she wanted things to be done, often struck me. One, a girl named Jemima, especially annoyed her. She was very dull; yet dearest Adelaide begged me to try and teach her about spiritual things—would often ask about her interest in them, and if I observed any—and afterwards she took her in hand herself. Indeed, several of these people have told me how they prized her words, and that they believed they 'had got quite a blessing from her.'"

In May, "it was thought that the journey and the excitement of going home would most probaby aggravate her illness beyond the hope of recovery." "I have had a most precious winter here," she writes, May 14, "during which God has been teaching me for eternity. Oh! how sweet it is to hold communion with our Heavenly Father! It is just a foretaste of what heaven will be; but there we shall be freed from these vile, clogging bodies. To be told you have an incurable disease is nothing alarming to me ; so far from it, that it only makes me hope God will soon accomplish His work in me, if such be His will, and then take me to be—where He is ! What a thought !"

A month later, however, she had so far recovered as to warrant her return to Leylands. "And so ends," she writes in her Diary on June 15, "my happy, privileged sojourn of betwixt seven and eight months at Torquay ! I think it has been with me a training place for heaven, though God has not seen meet to transplant me there. Oh ! for a more thankful heart for the very peculiar tenderness which has marked all His dealings with me, and rendered it so sweet, so endeared a spot to me during my pilgrimage, especially in regard to the sweet communion with Christian friends, much of which will, I trust not pass away as fruitless, but remain for eternity ! I thank God for giving them to me just when He knew I needed the comfort of them. May I trust Him for sufficient grace for every future need !"

And on reaching home, she writes to a friend : "I am here again for a time, though I must spend the few next winters in Torquay, they tell me, if I live. Oh ! what an *if* that is ! God has been preparing me for going to be with Him in His own time, be it sooner or later. I only pray that, if His will is that I should live, my life may be more than ever devoted to His single service."

And, indeed, she "did what she could." Writing at this period to the Secretary of the Irish Missions, she says : "I enclose O'Connor's salary for the next quarter. I am thankful to be well enough to write and read, and work. I think now that it will become my duty to do what needlework I can for the Society, as more active work is impossible. In that and in some such ways I may do something, however little, in the service of that Redeemer who, when He bought me, bought my time and talents, and requires all to be used for His glory."

One of the methods by which she helped forward the work in Ireland was by her pen. We close this chapter with a specimen of some of her earnest appeals to the Irish heart:

"A SECRET:

"'His secret is with the righteous.'

"I've just heard a bit of uncommon good news from Ireland; and in these times, when the plague is already begun among the people, I think it is a shame to keep it to myself.

"Everybody knows how bad the cholera is, and nobody can say that they mayn't be the next to be taken with it; but everybody does not know *how to live through it.*

"I've just heard of *a 'Healer;'* and if you like to know where He is, I'll tell you. The word 'Jesus,' in Irish, means 'Healer;' and Jesus is the most wonderful man for healing disease that ever was heard of. It is true He is out of sight; but then He is in heaven, every bit as true a man as He was when He came down from the mountain and the leper met Him, saying, 'Lord, if thou wilt, thou canst make me clean. And Jesus put forth His hand and touched him, saying, I will, be thou clean.' And His Word had that divine power in it, that 'immediately his leprosy was cleansed.' (Matt. viii. 2, 3.)

"If Jesus was a Healer then, Jesus is a Healer still. But the most wonderful part of the secret is, that *His Word* has got that divine power in it, that, to anybody who asks, He can give *life without end*, and cure them of death altogether. 'The gift of God is eternal life through Jesus Christ our Lord.' (Rom. vi. 23.) He can send a breath of the Spirit of life into us, and make our bodies temples of the Holy Ghost, so that no matter what may happen to the earthly hut of these clay tabernacles which we now inhabit—they may decay and they may die, but the immortal inhabitant lives on and on for ever! The spirit of life which is in them only changes earth for heaven; and, since it came from heaven, it's no grief to it to return to heaven. It only wants to take all it loves along with it.

"Who will come? Who will get this heavenly life, and go to heaven when they die? I verily believe it only wants *asking for*.

"There is one thing more about this secret, and that is, why so few people give any credit to it? My answer is, just because it is 'secret.' If Jesus the 'Healer' was seen walking in the streets, some few might believe their own eyes when they saw Him. But this is what I have to say:

"He *will* be seen soon—for 'every eye shall see Him'—but it will be too late to be healed then.

He is the Healer—NOW. The cures are wrought by faith, not by sight. The life is the Holy Spirit. It is secret now—'Your life is *hid* with Christ in God.' But it will be plain enough by and bye, 'For when Christ who is our life shall *appear*, then shall *ye* also *appear with Him* in glory.' (Col. iii. 3, 4.)

"'A man shall be as an hiding place.'"

CHAPTER VI.

"I AM certain there must be more growth in grace, more study of the Word and character of God, and more time given to it—in fact, it must be more our business (Luke ii. 49)—if we are to be exalted Christians." In these words—written in June, 1847—Adelaide Newton indirectly expressed her own personal life.

"It was indeed a privilege," writes one who knew her well at this period, "to be with her and to enjoy her heaven-born thoughts.

> "'In everything she said or did,
> There was a touch of heaven.'

I was struck, especially, with her complete absorption in the Bible. She was always digging in the precious mine; and this gave to her mind a peculiar tone—that of searching for the mind of God in everything."

In reading the Word, she was never content if God was "silent" to her. "Silence," we find her writing, "betwixt our souls and God is one of the most painful trials we endure; even as we know the bitter trial it is when a much-loved friend will not speak to us. David felt what it was to be silent towards God through his sin. 'When *I* kept silence, my bones waxed old through my roaring all the day long; my moisture is turned into the drought of summer.' It brings such withering deadness over the soul. Oh! why do we not 'acknowledge'—speak out—'our iniquity?' David knew also what it was for God to be silent towards him: hence his prayer—'Be not silent to me; lest, if thou be silent to me, I become like them that go down into the pit.' The word rendered 'silence' denotes a willing or voluntary silence as opposed to being 'dumb' and unable to speak. How often we provoke the Lord to silence! like a father who cannot talk freely to his child, because it has displeased him! Alas! how many hours and days, as well as moments, we lose in silence, which might be spent in happy, holy intercourse with our God! How blessed it is when He is '*not* silent'—when we hear His voice in every word we read in Scripture—when we hear Him speaking 'peace!' 'Speak, Lord!'"

Here lay the secret of her heavenly walk. It was literally a walk with God—a living fellowship—an interchange of thought—God uttering His thoughts to her in the Word, and she uttering her thoughts to God at the throne. On either side she could not brook "silence."

It was this holy and happy fellowship with the Father and with the Son which gave to her words and to her whole life so sweet a fragrance. "I am sure that letter-writing only on ordinary subjects," she says, July 7 (1847), "is a sad waste of precious time, and very unpardonable amongst the Lord's people, who ought, in their writing, as well as in their life and conversation, to be different from the world around them." And she proceeds: "It is very trying for all three of you to be so much out of health; but, dearest M——, you are able to feel that it is all exactly right and for the very best, are you not? We who know something of the utterly unsatisfying nature of this world's worth, through sickness or bereavement or other trials, feel the want of One who can sympathize with us in it all, and is in Himself sufficient to make amends for all. And surely Jesus is! We only need to know Him, to be sure of it; and every fresh view of Him shows but the more entirely how 'altogether lovely' He is."

A friend had asked her if she thought it "a duty to pray for restoration to health." Replying to the inquiry, July 9, she says: "Don't you think it would not be wrong to do so, even though it were God's purpose not to grant it? for we have the example of Christ Himself praying earnestly for what God never intended to grant; only, it was with Him, and ought always to be with us, accompanied by, 'Nevertheless, not what I will, but what thou wilt.' From this, would it not almost seem as if we might pray about anything and everything, so long only as we ask all in submission to the will of God? Don't you think that God will in some way or other hinder us from asking what we ought not, or asking too determinately for any particular thing, as He did St. Paul? He was set upon the removal of the 'thorn in the flesh,' and prayed (he says) thrice about it; and then God stopped him, not telling him he had done wrong, but only assuring him that His grace was sufficient to enable him to bear it. I readily believe He will deal with us in the same way, and that sincere prayer for the teaching of God's Spirit in prayer will save us from praying sinfully."

In her Diary, on July 14, she writes: "Read Canticles. Oh! to come into the chambers—the secret presence—of my Beloved! to have sweet foretastes now of the heavenly communion to be enjoyed with Him in glory! (Ps. lxxiii. 25)." And, another day, she records a visit from a friend who prayed "that, having been separated from others for so long, it might be evident to them now that she had been with Jesus."

Like Andrew going forth that morning in search of Simon, to speak of HIM with whom he had passed the night, dear Adelaide now with a new devotedness everywhere commended Christ. "Oh! what a God we have to do with!" she writes, on July 15: "what tenderness, sympathy, and wise, unerring love, guide His hand in all His dealings with us! If any one ever had reason to boast of the loving-kindness of the Lord, it surely must be myself. Time would fail me to tell of the great tenderness He has shown towards me: but you may take encouragement, from what He has done for me, that you, too, will find Him the same God. He changes not!"

Her state of health since her return home, she notes in the same letter, thus: "I am come home much better, but weak and good for nothing, and quite obliged to be idle. I believe I look very well, and at times I feel very well; but there are hours of weariness which none know but those who know what real illness is. How precious to feel that each is measured out by our loving Father, and is really working out for us a far more exceeding and eternal weight of glory! I have thought of you very often in your peculiarly trying circumstances. To see the hand of God in each, renders them almost welcome; for it is a peculiar honour and privilege to suffer with Christ, and will assuredly end in 'reigning with Him.'"

She was no cynic, but rejoiced, like the Master, to make all around her happy. Delicately tempering congratulations with a seasonable admonition, she writes to a schoolfellow thus: "Well, dear F——, as you have often sympathized with my sufferings, you must now let me sympathize with your joys. Provided —— be (as I cannot but suppose, from your choice, he is) a fellow-member of the one Body likewise with us, and one who will seek to strengthen your hands in the Lord, I offer you my heartfelt congratulations. I am far from looking on marriage and love as trifling or *unsacred* subjects; they are designed of God amongst men, as I feel convinced, to set forth the love and marriage-union of Christ to

His Bride, the Church, and are, or may be, sweet and holy earthly ties. But it has strongly been on my mind lately, that they are ties only for time. In heaven, they neither marry, nor are given in marriage, but are as the angels. And now, they that have wives, are bid to be as though they had none, because the world passeth away! It must be remembered constantly that the sweet enjoyments of such mutual affections must be held in subordination to the lasting, ceaseless, pure, and unrestrained affection which, through time and eternity, must exist between the soul and JESUS! All that comes in subordination to THIS, dearest F——, I wish you; and this itself, the strongest, purest, and most intense enjoyment in personal interchange of love with Jesus, I wish you also!"

"I am very decidedly stronger as to general health," she adds, "and get on very well as long as I don't attempt to get into the carriage or go beyond the garden. But my chest is often painful; and, though slowly, I believe disease still makes some progress there. It is only doing the divinely-appointed work, and in God's own time and way too."

Some Christians take a morbid pleasure in "making little confessions" of their unprofitableness; and they mope over their vileness, until they grow proud of their very humility. For this "sore evil" Adelaide understood the Divine remedy. "I have had such a dear girl with me to-day," she writes, "the niece of those two sisters who were with us at Torquay, and who are both gone home. She used to say to me there—'Oh! if I only knew that I was God's child, how happy I should be!' and I used to tell her that the less she thought of herself in that way the better—for if she tried to think of God as her Father, she would soon find out that indeed she was His child. She has grown in grace wonderfully, and kept telling me over and over again to-day what a HAPPY thing religion is! She tells Jesus *everything*—all her wishes, all her feelings, right and wrong, and all her little hourly troubles. No matter who is by, she tells Him everything, because nobody can hear her; and when she is alone, she reads her Bible, and prays over it and feasts on it. Yet not one of her family now is like-minded. Her two aunts, who loved Christ, are gone to be with Him. It has done me good to see her, her faith is so very simple. Just what she finds in the Bible she believes; and she says that sometimes, when she feels too wicked to dare to pray, she says to herself, 'Oh, but *I* am nothing. *I'm* not seen; *it's only Jesus that is seen;* and *I* don't pray, but the Holy Spirit makes intercession within me.' I can't help just telling you about her, becauss you will see how others feel with regard to those precious truths I have tried to tell you of. They were an unspeakable comfort to a lady in York," she adds, "to whom I wrote frequently till she died this summer, only telling her of Jesus. That prayer in Psalm xxxv. 3, 'Say unto my soul, I am thy salvation,' struck her very much. I told her I thought it said so VERY much in so few words—

God doing everything for us from first to last, so that our salvation is wholly in HIM."

And again she writes: "One thing which has particularly struck me lately is the freeness of God's gift of Christ, especially in those words in the fifth of Romans—'the grace of God,' and 'the gift by grace'—given without one single thing in us to render us deserving of it. "Oh! are we not obliged sometimes to give vent to our grateful astonishment in those words, 'Thanks be unto God for His unspeakable gift?' I think it is the freeness of it which makes it such a stumbling-block to many. We can't give God credit for being as good as He is."

In one of his touching little sonnets, Herbert utters a longing of his heart thus:

"I go to church; help me to wings, that I
Will thither fly:
Or, if I mount unto the sky,
I will do more."

Again, this summer, dear Adelaide was shut out from "church;" but her soul, nevertheless, was ever "mounting to the sky." On August 1 (1847), we find her, whilst alone in her chamber, throwing her thoughts into the following simple lines, founded on Song ii. 3, and on Ps. lxxxix. 15:

"While from Thine earthly courts ascend
Loud Hallelujahs to Thy praise,
Lord, to the 'still small voice' attend,
Thy feeble ones in secret raise.

"While others taste the bread and wine,
The outward signs which Thou hast given,
Oh! feast our souls with love divine—
That 'living bread' sent down from heaven.

"While they are walking in the light,
Which flows from Thee, its living Source,
May we sit down, 'with great delight;'
To the same Fountain have recourse!

"Beneath the 'shadow' of the Rock,
Defended from the burning sun,
Refresh Thy weary, feeble flock:
Thence streams of living water run.

"May those who tarry still at home
'Divide the spoil' with those who go:
Spirit of truth and comfort come,
Make every heart with joy o'erflow!

"Oh! May Thy Church below now 'taste'
The sweetness of redeeming love;
And to the Church triumphant haste,
To share Thy fulness, Lord, above!"

As the autumn approached, she began to contemplate another removal to Torquay. "I honestly confess," she writes, on August 21, "I am not yet reconciled to the idea of leaving home so soon again. As you most truly said, if our wills were conformed to the will of God, we should no longer know what trials mean. I was greatly struck with an observation of Lady Powerscourt yesterday, that where God sends a trial, He sends it where He knows it will be felt."

Then alluding to the "cloud of witnesses," in Heb. xii. 1, she adds: "Some of them have lately been almost more present to me than the earthly witnesses. I do so like the feeling of having them there; it's almost like a resting-place for one's thoughts, though they are kept waiting for us to be perfected. But they have bidden adieu to this changeful, up-and-down world, and are *with the Lord;* and there is certainly something that gives one a feeling of calm repose in that thought, which cannot be got at by any other means. And yet we are in Him as truly as they are; and when faith gets uppermost, and sinks sight and seen things below the surface for a while, one can catch glimpses of their joy. Alas! that they should be so few and far between! But we shall soon be there too. How quickly time is hastening our re-union, is it not?"

And, writing to another friend, on September 9, she says: "Since I have been at home, I have been studying in Canticles with great delight; and I hope I have got to realize the union of Christ with His people in a way I never did before. It is union in the covenant, so that all the changers in one's feelings, affections, &c., &c., &c., alter it not. We are married to Christ; and what God hath joined together, can in no wise be cut asunder. With Him 'is no variableness, neither shadow of turning.' Precious truth! He loved us while we were sinners, and He loves us while we are backsliding (Hos. xi 7, 8, 9); for His is unchangeable, everlasting love. (Jer. xxxi. 3.) I am so thankful that, amidst terrible seasons of coldness and indifference, and want of realizing anything of these eternal truths, He has mercifully enabled me to remember that He changes not towards me!"

A friend had written to her, complaining of being content to seek after "Jesus in a lukewarm, heartless spirit." Adelaide replied: "I got a kind rebuke from a dear Christian friend the other day, which points out the true remedy, I am sure for the evil which you lament, and, in short, for every evil, every sin, which separates betwixt us and God. She says, 'I find a great help, when tempted to be low in mind, to shut out as much as possible thinking of self, in any way, or even of death, but to meditate on Jesus, to remember His presence with me, when I think, or speak, lie or sit. Oh! it is sweet thus to enter into Jesus—to delight in Him—to think of His perfections—His love, His humility, His patience. If we ask God's Spirit to give us these sweet, lively, realizing views of Jesus, will He deny us? Is it not His especial office to 'take of the things of Christ, and show them unto us'? I shall long to hear that you have again found sweet 'access with confidence' into the holiest by the blood of Jesus. So inexpressibly precious is that blood to God the Father, that the soul on which it is sprinkled becomes unspeakably precious to Him also. And the very mention of it in prayer is a plea from which He can never turn away!"

Her health continued in the same infirm state. "I am only able," she writes, September 9, "to go downstairs for prayers and breakfast; and the rest of the day, except when I am out, I hardly ever move off the sofa. Still, through God's mercy, I am able to write, read, and work; and I trust He is making use of me in some humble ways, though not just the ways I should choose."

In her diary, on August 31 (1847), we find this entry: "Mrs. Fitchett came to see me: she told me Betty Fox had charged her with the message that, if we never met again in this world, she believed we should in another; that she owed more to me than she could ever say, and to my going round the district, where it seems as if God had condescended to make some use of me; for Mrs. Fitchett told me she could say the same thing, and she was sure many others could, too. May the Lord keep me from vain-glory, or from taking more comfort from hearing such things than He intends! Ps. cxv. 1 ought to be my heartfelt language; for how much more might I not have done, had I only had a *single eye!* Double motives must have robbed me of much of my reward."

Will not the measure of future glory depend upon the measure of present service? *A* place in the kingdom depends upon the "finished" work of Christ; but does not *the* place depend upon the individual attainments in suffering and in service? "I have been wondering so much this morning," says she, "why, and for what ends, God is dealing thus with me, and what my life is now preparing for me in eternity. I have thought so much about 'sowing seed' lately (Ps. cxxvi. 5, 6), that my reason seems to say, 'I wish to live;' and yet my heart rebels as much as ever. I hope God will bless 'The Shadow of Death.' S—— told me 'she felt as if it were to be the means of delivering her from the bondage she had been in all her life.' Don't be distressed if you find you cannot speak to the people as you wish. Remember, it is not you that speak, but God that speaks through you. My constant comfort just now is, that God's Spirit may breathe through us."

On September 21, she again reached Torquay, her "general health so much better" since she had left it in May, that her physician, on examining her shortly after her arrival, "could only thank God for His blessing."

CHAPTER VII.

"MARTYRDOMS," says Lord Bacon, in one of his Essays, "I reckon amongst miracles, because they exceed the strength of human nature."

Of martyrdoms there are two kinds. "Perhaps," writes Cecil, "it is a greater energy of Divine power which keeps the Christian from day to day, from year to year, praying, hoping, running, believing, against all hindrances—which maintains him a LIVING martyr, than that which bears him up for an hour in sacrificing himself at the stake." Bacon, in his Essay above quoted, has the same thought; for, after "reckoning martyrdoms amongst miracles, because they exceed the strength of human nature," he adds: "I may do the like of superlative and admirable holiness of life."

It is this kind of martyrdom which is before us in the subject of our Memoir. And each successive season seems to encircle it with a brighter halo of Divine glory.

Writing to one of her sisters from her "new tent in the wilderness," she says: "The first note I write is to you, on a day which, I trust, is to both of us but a foretaste and pledge of that eternal Sabbath which 'remaineth' for us. Oh! what a prospect for souls which find no rest for the soles of their feet on the ocean of life! Tossed to and fro, sometimes in their temporal circumstances, sometimes from one home to another, sometimes in their souls—beat about and buffeted by the god of this world, and tormented by the evil workings of their corrupt natures, till really they do literally feel like the dove, out of the ark, hovering over a boundless expanse of ocean! I never felt so more than lately. I have been tried both outwardly and inwardly, and can most heartily sympathise with you in those words you used, 'Not doubting, but hoping against hope.' I feel satisfied that this very experience, dearest ——, is the strongest proof that we are in Christ. We are like vessels tossing about upon the water, yet firmly and securely fixed to the anchor. As long as the confident hope and expectation of the soul is from CHRIST (however little comfort or enjoyment there may be in looking to Him), the soul is exercising true and living faith; and perhaps faith is never so strong as when it clings to Him in the dark—I mean, without sensible enjoyment."

How was she girded for this "living martyrdom?" "Her enjoyment of prayer was frequently expressed," writes her sister, "when we were together in Devon; and she would often get upon the subject by questioning me as to my own stated times for prayer, comfort in ejaculatory prayer, and whether I felt able to continue the habit she knew dear Mr. Dallas had urged me to seek—I mean, praying when I walked. She loved herself to pray at night near the window, gazing up to the stars; and, in every room she occupied, she had one particular chair or spot thus consecrated. 'Do not I fill heaven and earth?' was once quoted as comforting her with the delightful consciousness of being so surrounded with God, that her very prayerful thoughts—I mean prayerfulness not taking so distinct a form as to pass into words—were known, and, as it were, heard by Him. And thus, when occasionally out in a Bath-chair, I have heard her express her felt communion, and her delightful realization of His near and all-pervading presence."

Herself "comforted of God," she knew how to solace fellow-pilgrims. "It seems to me the only comfort," she writes to a bereaved mother, November 22 (1847), "in looking at such of God's dealings with us as are otherwise perfectly inexplicable, that He is doing what He wills with His own; and, since 'He does all things well'—since 'His work is perfect'—since all He does He makes 'to work together for good to them that love Him,' it seems to leave us without ground of complaint, whilst God is trying our faith, to see whether we can trust Him so to order each event of our lives now as best to promote our eternal happiness and His own glory. It is a great exercise of faith; and yet how can we doubt it? I never felt the comfort of that twentieth chapter of Matthew so much before as I do now: to think that your dear, dear baby, who had literally 'continued one hour only,' should be made equal to those who had 'borne the burden and heat of the day,' is a very precious thought to me, and seems to magnify the sovereignty of God's grace. I can only pray that God may enable you to trace His 'bright designs,' 'treasured up,' as Cowper so beautifully says, 'in deep unfathomable mines of never-failing grace.' May the God of love and peace and of all comfort be with you!"

On another occasion, after "a most dreary and desolate day," she writes: "This kind of life makes me feel as if, perhaps, it were God's way of answering my prayer to be conformed to Christ's image. He was perfect through sufferings—sufferings of all kinds; and so, I suppose, must His followers be. A thought," she adds, on Gen. xxix. 20, "has made me feel quite ashamed of being in such a hurry to die; if years of service seemed so little to Jacob for the love he had to Rachel, what ought they seem to us for Chirst?"

For six weeks that her sister was obliged to be absent from Torquay, Adelaide was one of a small circle in a boarding-house. Alluding to her "utter inability to speak to these people," she adds: "But I pray that God may use me to say what He wants saying to them. My mind was very much struck in reading Ps. cxxiii. 1, 2, some days ago, with the idea of looking up to God every morning for direction what to do, just as a servant to a master or mistress. This seems to me the secret of real happiness—to be what God makes us to all around us."

Three years afterwards, a lady who had been of that circle died. On her deathbed she informed the minister who visited her, that to Adelaide Newton she owed, instrumentally, her conversion. And four other inmates of that house looked upon those precious weeks as a season to them of new life.

It was thus that she sowed beside all waters the seed of the kingdom. And the sowing quickened her own heavenliness "In Phil. i. 22, 23," she writes at this period, "Paul evidently considered that 'the fruit of his labour' made it worth while to abide in the flesh, however he might long to depart. I believe this is the lesson I have been learning most of late."

Only one life! one sowing-time! one season of laying up treasure in heaven! Realizing that thought with a new vividness, she writes: "I don't feel as rebellious about life as I did. I have been thinking about it as the sowing-time for eternity. Oh! that we were only sowing continually to the Spirit! What a rich harvest we might expect to reap hereafter! and what a full compensation for all our tears by the way!"

Her illness was again manifesting bad symptoms. "You will be sorry to hear," she writes on January 13 (1848), "that my chest is much worse." And she adds: "Such are our poor frail tenements of clay. Is it not very humbling to look upon all kinds of disease as the fruit of sin and of the curse of God?"

But her soul mounted up on wings as eagles'. "Oh! how I wish," she says, "that I could live up to my privileges, and walk worthy of my high calling! Pray for me, that, as I draw near the close of my earthly pilgrimage (and how the days and hours, weeks and years, do fly!), I may more and more realize my true position as 'accepted in the Beloved.'"

And one feature of her growing heavenliness is singled out thus: "Is there not a selfish feeling in desiring one's own happiness after death, rather than desiring the perfected bliss of the whole body at the glorious appearing of Christ? Nowhere in Scripture is death set forth as an object of hope, but always Christ's Second Coming. I believe you will find meditation on the Second Coming to be of all truths the most quickening. I don't know how you feel; but of late I have been *horrified* to find a secret backwardness to cry with my whole heart, 'Come quickly!' and this, too, whilst I have thought of death as the greatest 'gain.'"

In her diary, on January 1 (1848), we have the following: "Commenced another stage of my journey—another year of my pilgrimage through life, at Torquay. May *every step* be 'ordered *by* the Lord,' and *in* His Word—'leaning on my Beloved!' 'My times are in Thy hand,' O Lord. Living or dying, may I be Thine, and have no will but to do Thy will! Whilst I live may I sow seed for eternity every moment, which shall yield an abundant harvest to 'the Lord of the harvest!' And in close union and communion with Jesus—in the power of resurrection-life, may I be dead to sin, and 'be clothed with *humility*,' whilst soaring to the height of that glory which He gives to His members!"

The "humility" which arises from "soaring to the height of the glory" is not a counterfeit but a real humility. It is in the joyful fellowship of a reconciled Father, not in a "fearful" doubting of His love, that the heart is truly humbled.

"Well said the wisdom of earth—'O mortal! know thyself;'
But better the wisdom of heaven—'O man! learn thou thy God.
Learn God; thou shalt know thyself."

"Don't you think," Adelaide writes, "that it is exactly in proportion as we walk in the light that we become aware of surrounding darkness. I have fancied that this was implied in 1 John i. 7; where, after speaking of our walking in the light it is immediately added, 'And the blood of Jesus Christ His Son cleanseth us from all sin'—as if we could not bear the sight of what the light would expose to our view, without that to fall back upon."

Cecil writes: "The man who is yet carnal, if taken into a closet and forced to meditate on God and eternity, will find it insupportable. But the spiritual man is born, as it were, into a new world; he has a new taste; he savours the thing of the Spirit; he turns to God, as the needle to the pole." With dear Adelaide it was natural to speak of Christ, not forced and artificial. For example, in a very familiar note to one of her sisters, we find her pouring out her heart thus: "Except on the one subject, which never grows old, it's of no use writing anything, in a note which may not reach you for many days; but on that I must scribble a few words. What a theme! A Saviour's unchanging love! I have been thinking very much of the Levitical offerings lately, and especially of this—that the ground of comfort and true satisfaction to the conscience was to see the blood on the mercy-seat, *i.e.*, to see the evidence that God was satisfied with the atonement made. That is the point. It seems to me so comforting to feel, that, if we have equal evidence that Jesus, our atonement, is accepted for us, that's enough; we need have no doubt as to our own acceptance. I have not been able at all lately to think realizingly of God; and it has troubled me a good deal; but, through His mercy, I have not one doubt of His willingness to accept me, even in spite of my wretched guiltiness and unbelief."

"I hope you pray for me," she adds. "I don't mind owning to you, if you will keep it strictly private, that I have not been outwardly so comfortable since I came here. I have a thousand little daily annoyances, and no one to tell them to. But I know, if God saw them not necessary, He would remove them; so they must be right. How sweet to know God reigns and orders all our daily lot! May He abundantly bless all your labours in His service! Sowing in tears now, you shall reap a joyful harvest hereafter, and perhaps be rewarded, for a long and toilsome carrying of the seed-basket, with many sheaves. God grant it to you and to me!"

The seed-basket she was ever carrying. "The text I shall send you," she writes, "is—'He satisfieth the longing soul, and filleth the hungry soul with goodness.' It is so sweet to think, that, as Jesus is satisfied in seeing of the travail of His soul in us, so we shall be satisfied in Him. All fulness dwells in Him—enough to fill us with goodness. Don't you find, more and more, that the things which occupy the minds and hearts of others lose their interest with you? There is a craving of the immortal soul for higher objects; nor can it be satisfied with anything short of God for its portion. How He comes to be more and more the Alpha and Omega—the All and in all! And how communion with Him, when we can realize and enjoy it, seems to bring us into the very holiest—the presence-chamber of Jesus!"

And again, to another: "We are hasting to 'that day.' Oh! what a very comforting thought! Certainly I do more and more realize its nearness. I often feel now quite a wish to see it, and to work whilst there is room for bringing in the many sons whom He died to bring to glory. I can pray for them when I cannot go and talk to them; and I can ask God to make you and others talk effectually; and so I think I may be a sharer of your joy in the day of Christ. I so earnestly covet the honour of turning many to righteousness, in order to shine like a star. It is not, however, for selfish ambition that I seek higher glory, but to reflect more of Christ's glory, which glorifies Him."

And, in another letter: "I have been looking out lately all the texts which connect the sufferings of Christ and His glory. I thought Heb. ii. 9, 10; 1 Pet. i. 11; Heb. xii. 2; and Rev. v. 6—14, peculiarly beautiful. The Lamb, as it had been slain, in the midst of the throne! And no less than seven times in Rev. xxi. and xxii. 1—5, is 'the Lamb' mentioned in the description of the heavenly city—as if we should remember it as much then as now, and should still 'glory in the cross of Jesus Christ,' even in heaven!"

"Love," it has been said, "is the king of words, carved on Jehovah's heart." The same word is carved by the Lord on the heart of each of His children. "I have been greatly struck," writes dear Adelaide, "with the pre-eminenence which is always given to love among the Christian graces. 'Above all things, put on charity.' And, in 1 Cor. xii. 31, it seems as if charity, in the next chapter, were *the* fruit of the Spirit in which, above all others, God is glorified. And the first epistle of John also leads to the same conclusion in my mind: for there it seems to be the very essence of God's nature, and to reflect most of it in us. Love and light, hatred and darkness, stand in such strong contrast; and, evidently, where they are spoken of in reference to fellow-creatures, it is only to show how much it must be so betwixt us and God. The communion and fellowship in that epistle are so sweet to think of because it is through this fellowship that the likeness to Him is realized. The more we see of Him now in communion by faith, the more we reflect His image; just as, when we see Him face to face, we shall be like Him perfectly then—now, only in part."

And writing, Jan. 29 (1848), to a schoolfellow, on her marriage, she says: "May you but be united in the bonds of Christian love, and I have no fear of excess or of danger of diminution. For, in its very nature, it is everlasting; and, as one of the fruits of the Spirit, it will grow and increase continually. Poor M——, on her becoming Mrs.——, once wrote to me so very strongly about the blessing of having at least one earthly friend to whom she could confide everything; and when I reminded her of the possibility of losing that one earthly friend, and the blank which would then be felt—poor girl! she could not bear it. How different it is to have our Maker for our Husband! But I trust you have. Then, if you marry 'in the Lord,' you do well."

The trials of each new day quickened her steps heavenward. After mentioning that a friend had been "praying with her most beautifully about our bearing the image of the heavenly as we had borne that of the earthly," she says: "Oh! if we could but realize what that will really be! and to think that it is nigh, even at the door! Oh! that all knew the preciousness of being safe 'in the ark,' ere the floods of Divine wrath are poured out and the windows of heaven are opened! What a weighty figure that is of the Lord's awakening, as if from a dream, to take vengeance on the ungodly! (Ps. lxxii.) And how very precious the contrast is, that if all this time He is sleeping, as it were towards the wicked, 'His eyes are open to the righteous'—He 'never slumbers nor sleeps' towards us! Oh! how little those whose eyes the Lord has not yet opened know of these wondrous and life-giving truths! and how we may praise Him for so teaching us—adoring His free, sovereign love!"

Her thoughts were occupied at this time with a subject which often afterwards engaged them. "Have you ever thought much," she writes, on January 24, "about self-examination? Systematic arrangement of questions, or diligent looking into one's own heart, is what I can see no Scripture-warrant for—I mean examining as to our growth in grace. 2 Cor. xiii. 5 and 1 Cor. xi. 28 are the only two direct passages I can find in the New Testament; and in both it is an examination as to being a Christian or not, and not as to growth in grace. There are many indirect passages, such as 2 Cor. vii. 11; 2 John, 8; Gal, vi. 4; Rev. ii. 5; and Heb. xii. 15, which imply a kind of self-examination; but I believe these refer rather to cases of backsliders (so in Lam. iii. 40) than to careful search as to how far one is growing in grace. Out of all this arises the query, whether self-examination, as generally enforced, does not rather lead to a looking into one's self which is not enforced in Scripture?"

Another object than her own dark heart attracted

towards it her steady gaze. "'Behold ME,'" we find her writing, "'Behold ME.' Of all occupations, none can be so blessed, so transforming, so strengthening, so enrapturing as that of *beholding Jesus.* O! to be ever hearing and ever yielding to the sweet whispers of His Spirit, speaking through the Word, and saying, 'Behold Me! Behold Me!' Here, indeed, is the object of faith—a living, personal, ever-present ME. This is not truth merely, it is Christ—His own Self."

"God the Father," she continues, "summons us to this act of beholding Jesus—'Behold my Servant, whom I uphold; mine Elect, in whom my soul delighteth.' And Jesus calls us to linger over the wondrous scene of Gethsemane, of Calvary—'Tarry ye here and watch.' Hear even Pilate say to you, 'Behold the Man!' And hear the voice of His messenger, who, 'seeing Jesus' for himself, said to those around, 'Behold the Lamb of God, which taketh away the sin of the world.'"

And she adds: "Grow not weary of this act; look to-day, and be found looking to-morrow. 'Again, the next day after John stood; and looking upon Jesus as He walked, he saith, 'Behold the Lamb of God!' Does not this tell us that it should be a daily act? and that, while we look upon Jesus, we should say to others (as if re-echoing His own emphatic words), 'Behold Him, Behold Him?' Behold Him when you are in trouble; 'so shall ye be delivered.' 'Mine eyes are ever toward the Lord; for He shall pluck my feet out of the net.' Behold Him when you are beset with fear: 'They looked unto Him, and were lightened' (*lit.*, their countenances were made bright). On 'that day,' 'thine eyes shall see the King in His beauty:' 'when He shall appear, we shall be like Him; for we shall *see* Him as He is.' These eyes shall see Him on that day—the God that died for me."

With the returning spring her feeble frame gathered new strength. "I am altogether now very much better," she writes on March 9. "For your sakes, and for some friends' sakes, and for my own (perhaps), I could wish it. May my wishes only be in accordance with His will concerning me! I have gone through a great deal of spiritual conflict; but, on the whole, I never knew so well what it was to be stayed upon the Rock of ages. I should like to send you an expression I was exceedingly struck with lately in the Prayer-book version of the 73d Psalm —'It is good for me to hold me fast by God.' I am certain that the further we get on, the more we are made to feel that HE must be EVERYTHING to us. Have you ever felt the comfort of the words, 'Thou art my hiding-place?' I can give you no idea what they have been to me—to hide in Jesus, and let God's eye rest only on Him!"

And again: "It seems so long since I heard of you; but time rolls so very, very rapidly down the stream, that much intercourse by the way seems impracticable. O for ceaseless communion in heaven! I hope you are getting on. I have had such very real and solemn thoughts at night—the sense of every thought of my heart being as truly laid bare before God as if I were standing before Him in the judgment! And then to know that Jesus *is* in heaven to answer for me, and that only this veil of flesh hides Him from my eyes! O how wonderful it is!" And a few days later: "We ought indeed to be thankful—full of praise; for He is crowning us with the richest of all blessings, 'the light of His countenance.' May we be led to praise Him more and more, and to go on our way rejoicing! not always expecting happy feelings in ourselves, but always remembering that Jesus is the same, yesterday, and to-day, and for ever."

Other lessons she was learning, as she sat at the Master's feet. "It struck me," she writes, "when I read your note about coming here, and giving up your work at home, how often we are made to feel that it is just the fruit-bearing branches which He purges and prunes. As soon as the fruit appears, He uses His pruning-knife—perhaps to cut off the opportunities we have enjoyed, and when we are beginning to see that it has not been in vain—lest we should begin to work by sense and sight, and not simply by faith. I have thought so much of this lately—what a mystery the life of *faith* is. That passage, Heb. xii. 2, 'The Author and Finisher of faith'—not of 'our faith,' because it has reference mainly to His own life on earth, as a perfect life of faith from first to last, and applies only in its secondary meaning to us—it has been a great comfort to me, as it may be to you."

And, on March 30: "I should exceedingly like

to know all about you and dear M——; above all how you are getting on in the Sion-ward way; for how little, comparatively, everything else signifies! I cannot tell you how often I thank God for placing me in circumstances where I may, and almost must, spend my time in such pursuits—learning to know Him better. For months before I left home (two years ago nearly, now), this had been my constant prayer; but how little I thought how God would answer it! But unerring wisdom brought it to pass in the way in which He knew He would be most glorified. I believe it is one of our most difficult lessons, to live by faith and not by sight, trusting to His ordering of things, when they seem so against us, still to be the best. The life Jesus led upon earth teaches this best of all, I believe, if we only understood it; but how little we know of such separation from the world! You will like to praise Him for and with me," she adds, "in one instance that has just come to my knowledge of a young lady, to whom a lady here gave one of my 'Thoughts for Sleepless Hours,' and to whom it was made the instrument of conversion. She has since entered on that day that knows no night."

A fortnight later, writing to one of her sisters, of whom she "had seen very, very little lately," she says: "I suppose it is to make us both remember that we are not to be seeking our enjoyment here, but only to try to live for God, and to use whatever intercourse He allows us for helping each other on to glory. How soon we shall know that *nothing else matters!* that whatever is earthly in our love, or in our duties, or services, or our friendships, or in anything will take away from, instead of adding to our eternal happiness! O! N——, what earthly creatures we are! I actually feel as if I regretted that there can be nothing earthly in heaven. May God forgive me, and give me holier thoughts and feelings! How horrid of me to be writing all this to you—dwelling on self and its vileness, when we might have our eyes all engrossed with the loveliness of Jesus! but we shall only think of that in heaven. All the tears which now fill our eyes, in thinking of these things, shall then be for ever wiped away. So we will comfort one another with these words."

In the beginning of May (1848), she once more left Torquay, "the progress of her disease decidedly retarded," though without "any very material alteration in her state." "It is indeed," she writes, "a sweet and privileged spot, and endeared to me beyond any other *on earth*. God seems to have brought me to lie down here in such green pastures as I hardly thought could be known on earth; for I think bodily suffering, however severe, is scarcely to be compared to mental suffering—and yet I ought not to shrink from either. How comforting it is to remember that, 'in a little while,' we shall see Him! I am sure I ought to own, to God's glory, that I have not felt half so rebellious about things I don't like, as I used to do. Sometimes I can wish to be 'ready to do *whatsoever* my Lord the King shall appoint' (2 Sam. xv. 15); and yet I have been learning, too, how very hard it is to 'kick against the pricks,' when it pleases God, according to His promise in Hos. ii. 6, to 'hedge up my way with thorns.' As for dear ——, I sometimes think her letters betray a ripening process so rapid as to make me wonder if she is to be early called to her eternal home; but it may be only to prepare her for more active service here. I think God has more to do in me yet, and may, perhaps, allow me more sowing-time, so that I may reap a richer harvest hereafter. How sweet it is to trust Him to do the best, whichever it is! I certainly am stronger, and only want a more thankful spirit. Positively it seems as if I had nothing but Satan's snares and sinful self to mar my happiness. And you have not much more; only the world —but what an 'only!'"

And, writing to another friend before leaving, she says, in allusion to her physician's opinion, that, "by God's blessing, her bodily suffering might be greatly alleviated and her life prolonged:"—"I feel as if to go Home, and to be for ever freed from sin, would be such an unspeakable mercy. But I know that nothing can prolong life beyond God's appointed time, and that He will not suffer me to die until He has made me meet for glory. And now it seems as if, more than ever, I were bound to devote whatever is left of my life, be it weeks, or months, or years, to His service only. I am so anxious to ask you to pray that I may be taught how I may best employ my time here, both for my own growth in grace and for the good of my fellow-creatures. I have felt very much for you in losing ——; but one thought has so struck me, which may perhaps occupy your thoughts, too, in a happy way. It is the delight which Jesus, in His humanity, must feel, as He gets back one and another to be with Him. Should we not sympathize in this His joy, while He sympathizes in our sorrow?"

CHAPTER VIII.

In her Diary, she writes: "*May* 6 (1848).—Left Torquay, and reached Bath at three P.M. *May* 9.—Dr. M'Neile talked to me at breakfast on Cant. vi. 12, and on the holy, rapturous delight we ought to enjoy. He expounded 2 Thess. i., and Ps. vii., especially with regard to calumny. *May* 15.—Left Clifton at one, and reached Leylands at half-past eight; truly 'upheld;' crowned with lovingkindness and tender mercies."

Elsewhere, in the Diary, she says: "'The Lord is in His holy temple.' '*Ye* are the temple of the living God.' Lord, dwell in me, and 'rest in thy love' towards me! Hear the voice of the breathing—the cry of thy hidden ones. (Rom. viii. 26, 27.)" And again: "Dear —— called, but only had time to allude to the communion which is to be perfected in heaven, and of which the foretastes here had made some of the happiest days on earth." And another day: "At half-past five, M—— B—— was sent for, to be conveyed in the chariots of angels to the heavenly banqueting-house, to go no more out." And on April 3: "This day I finished Canticles; how often I have wondered whether I should live to do so."

And on the day following: "This morning I awoke betwixt three and four, with such a sense of extreme difficulty in breathing, that I really thought I was dying. I believe I never felt this in my life before. I was obliged to get up, but found relief in a fit of coughing. I did not wish to die at that moment, but even prayed to be spared yet a little longer! That very near feeling of death was very painful to flesh and blood. The Lord give me the victory over it when He calls me to pass through the shadow of it!"

And on July 9: "My precious and beloved Harriet B—— ruptured a blood-vessel at nine P.M., and her spirit fled to Jesus! Blessed sovereignty of our unchanging God, who does what He wills with His own! The last time we ever met on an earthly Sabbath in God's earthly courts was on Easter Sunday, when we both went to meet at His table to commemorate the resurrection of Christ the Head! When we next meet, will it not be in our eternal Sabbath, in our heavenly Father's house above, to join in the marriage-supper of the Lamb, at the resurrection of the members? Thrice blessed fellowship in Jesus!"

The summer of 1848 was spent at Leylands.

Herbert counsels him who would bear worthily God's message, to "dip and season all his words and sentences in his heart before they come into his mouth, truly affecting and cordially expressing all that he says, so that the auditors may plainly perceive that every word is heart-deep." For some time back, dear Adelaide had been engaged in a study which very peculiarly needed such a method. "In 1847," writes her sister, "she had begun her notes on the Song of Solomon, looking into the Bible for illustrative and parallel texts, whenever her suffering in the head would allow her; and thus had commenced a MS. which afterwards expanded into 'The Song of Solomon, compared with other parts of Scripture.'" And, on May 25 (1848), she herself writes: "I am now re-writing my texts on Canticles, and fresh beauties open to me in every verse. And yet how intensely little the most deeply experienced Christian knows of the fulness of the Word of God—the living Word in the written Word?"

And on July 4, she writes: "I am now in chap. vi. Ask for quickening grace, for 'the wind to blow upon my soul, that its spices may flow out,' and for more of the mind of Jesus. I was thinking yesterday how little we know of sympathy with Him—how ltttle we are sharers of His joy, His peace, His sorrows, His expectations—'from henceforth expecting.'"

And to another, on July 10: "His 'Notes on Judges' open up exactly the same truth which I have been dwelling upon in Canticles—that repeated declensions cause greater and more lengthened seasons of distance from the Lord, and He does not so immediately give the renewed sense of His presence. Many, many times lately, when I have been tempted to the recommission of the very same sin, with the full conviction that I should have to go and ask forgiveness as soon as I had committed it, I have painfully felt—exactly what Mr. B. says, that it *is* a very serious thing to be drawing on God's forgive ness."

It was thus she was dipping day by day the Word "heart-deep." "Whilst any book," says her sister, "particularly if it were original and deep in thought, which threw light upon the one Book, she would listen to or eagerly read for herself, her precious Bible grew in preciousness—type, prophecy, history, parable, alike fed her, and, in feeding, 'satisfied' her. Often when I came in from a walk, she would, with the brightest look and smile, say how she had been 'revelling' in such a passage, or in such a sentence!"

"O Book!" her whole remaining pilgrimage seemed to say—

"O Book! infinite sweetness! let my heart
Suck ev'ry letter, and a honey gain,
Precious for any grief in any part,
To clear the breast, to mollify all pain.

"Thou art all health; health thriving till it make
A full eternity. Thou art a mass
Of strange delights, where we may wish and take.

"Heav'n lies flat in thee,
Subject to every mounter's bended knee.

"Oh, that I knew how all thy lights combine,
And the configurations of their glory!
Seeing not only how each verse doth shine,
But all the constellations of the story!

"Such are thy secrets; which my life makes good,
And comments on thee.

"Stars are poor books, and oftentimes do miss:
This book of stars lights to eternal bliss."

In July an arrest was laid upon her pen. "One rather unfavorable symptom," she says, "has appeared lately, which makes the doctor urge all rest from mental effort that I can make." And to another: "I never felt so completely compelled to bow before the sovereign will of God as at this moment, I think. You would hardly believe how fierce the conflict sometimes is, between longing to be spared for active work in the vineyard, and thirsting for that nearer, closer, and more uninterrupted communion with Him we love, which heaven only can afford!"

And, writing to one of her sisters, she says: "I have often been thinking of you all, and wishing you much of that presence of the Lord which makes the hearts of His disciples 'burn within them while they talk together by the way.' And how truly are we on the way, 'journeying to the land of which the Lord hath said that He will give it to us,' pitching our tents nearer and still nearer the heavenly city! I am so fond of that contrast: 'tents' now! but 'a city which hath foundations' then—'eternal in the heavens!' These are the thoughts with which we must 'comfort one another;' and our 'hope maketh not ashamed.'"

And to another, a few days later: "Precious—

very, very precious—is the sovereignty of our God! Don't you think it is a truth one learns to prize more and more each step of the way? It used to strike me so much, when I first went to Torquay, in Mr. Fayle's sermons—how very much he dwelt upon it; and now I see why I was to hear it just then. But it is a pity," she adds, "to speak of one's-self to any who love better to hear of JESUS. Writing of Him is like talking of Him to others; it quickens our own souls, as we learn from the Bride in Cant. v. And though we may have Him in own our hearts, and speak of Him there, still it is a pity to drink from a muddy stream when the Fountain is nigh. Have you seen much of Him in the Word lately? I know it is God's wisdom which so places me, that I should have to go direct to HIM. And how able and willing He is to give me all I ask! 'Open thy mouth wide and *I* will fill it.' I should like your letter, when you write, full of your late 'gleanings' from the fields of our 'Boaz.'"

Love to the brethren was, with dear Adelaide, not a dogma of creed, but an instinct—a passion. "It would, indeed," she writes, "have been a delightful refreshment to have some communion on earth with one who seems to live so near to his God and our God; but the Lord saw it not good at that time." And to another: "I often wonder at God's goodness to me, in letting me have so many of HIS friends as my friends on earth—some who seem to live so near to Him that I think they must be peculiarly dear to Him, if that is possible. And there does seem to be such a difference betwixt those who are 'scarcely saved' and those to whom 'an abundant entrance' is given—those who have lived for many years in fellowship with Jesus here, and those who have but given themselves to Him at the eleventh hour."

God in everything—in the little things of life, not less than in the great! and *my* God! *my* Father! what a secret of calm rest!

> "Teach me, my God and King,
> In all things Thee to see;
> And what I do in anything,
> To do it as for Thee.
>
> "This is the famous stone
> That turneth all to gold;
> For that which God doth touch and own
> Cannot for less be told."

Dear Adelaide was daily learning more of this heavenly alchemy. "May it go forth and prosper," is her counsel to a friend, regarding a Work with which her correspondent was occupied, "and God's blessing go before you in it! 'All *Thy* works praise Thee.' May He give you to see HIS hand in every single fibre and leaf you arrange and classify! and then you will be learning heavenly lessons in earthly things. If I might venture to say so to you, I should very strongly advise you not to take one step in the publishing of that work without prayer. Pray for God's blessing to go with every letter you write about it, and, in short, with all that concerns it and you and your friends. 'Whatsoever ye do—whether ye eat or drink (or arrange seaweeds, might it not be said?)—do all to the glory of God.' Do, if you can, make that a higher aim and object even than your own benefit. Forgive me for saying so; it is because I have found such precious enjoyment in turning my ordinary employments to spiritual good in that way, that I mention it to you. It is *not* irreverent to pray to God about such things: there is not an act of our lives He does not see, nay, that He did not foresee from eternity; and He would have us like children, speaking of everything which interests them to their father."

And she adds: "Whilst writing these thoughts, B. came to the window with some lovely 'forget-me-nots,' saying, 'They may forget, yet will I not forget thee.' Was not that exactly carrying out what I was saying? Oh! dearest M——, let us earnestly seek closer *hourly* communion with God in Christ. It carries one calmly through bodily and mental suffering; and this glorifies God."

And to another: "I am indeed delighted that you are so fond of tracing His hand in the little daily events of life. I find it makes the most disagreeable things, and *people*, a cross to be borne after Jesus, and so—a privilege."

To "wait" and to "work," are equally "living sacrifices," when offered up in faith and in hope. "I cannot say how very unsatisfactory my life seems at times," she writes, "nor how difficult it is to believe that I am just in the very best position; but I suppose we shall understand it all very soon. Talking is such a trouble to me; but it is foolish to write about it. How very little it matters! I am often obliged to say to myself,

"'Tarry thou the Lord's leisure,'

whilst at the same time I dread sinking into lukewarmness. Oh! how difficult it is to let our 'moderation' be known! I never satisfy myself about anything until I can desire to lie like clay in the hands of the potter, that HE may make me what He pleases, both in bodily and in spiritual things."

Reverting to the subject of self-examination, she writes, on August 7 (1848): "I am learning one lesson at least just now—to see more of my own vileness. It is a lesson I would shrink from learning through examination of my own heart to know its secret evil: but I have asked that I might be taught what God saw it needful for me to know, and I desire to leave it to His way of teaching. I often fear I may lose by not searching it out for myself; and yet I believe that watchfulness at the time, and not retrospective self-examination, is the scriptural thing. Do you catch my meaning? Did you ever get upon that subject with any of your deeply-taught friends? It is as interesting and important to my mind as ever; and so is 'crucifying the flesh.'"

Her health, with the exception already named, continued, this summer and autumn, much the same. "I am a regular invalid still," she writes to an old schoolfellow, on Aug. 31, "always lying on the sofa—better in the summer, worse in the winter, and obliged to spend half the year at Torquay. Still I am able now to employ myself quietly in my own room, without any of the intense suffering I have had. Dear E——, don't you feel more and more every day how very little temporal, temporary things have to do with our real, lasting, eternal happiness? I hope you are very happy, not only in the full enjoyment of earthly blessings, but in the possession of that calm, sure, and abiding peace, which the world giveth not, for Jesus calls it '*my* peace.' Most truly can I affirm, that nothing short of it could ever have carried me through the long illness I have had, and the intense suffering of the two last winters. I believe you never knew dearest H—— B——: she, too, spent the two last winters at Torquay; but she is gone Home, and has left me behind."

And to the same friend, on Sept. 11: "I have not heard from A—— for many months: perhaps I wrote more faithfully than she quite liked about her marriage; for I could not help trembling for her at the prospect of uniting herself to one whom she could *only* say she hoped was 'well-disposed!' and I loved her too well not to tell her the truth. I know it is impossible for those who have never felt it, to enter into the feelings of those who have looked upon life from the borders of the grave; it gives a reality and a comparative value to each, which must be learned experimentally to be understood. *How* differently we shall feel when we look back, from another state of existence, upon a life frittered away in vanity, instead of being spent in sowing seed for eternity, I cannot form any idea—the thought is so perfectly overwhelming to me."

And to another, on Sept. 28: "I have had a beautiful letter from L—— this morning. She seems to be growing very fast in likeness to Jesus, quite making that her first business in life. Oh! is it not strange that the things which literally 'perish in the using,' should occupy us more than durable, eternal realities? I will send to both of you Prov. viii. 18, as beautifully expressing what you come into when you go out of the world and are separate from it, and are received by the Father. There, in Jesus, you are heirs to unsearchable riches. May you both find the weight of this scale increasing, as you more and more lighten the other! You will not regret to see the world's side continually rising, if you have the deep, deep comforts which spring from the filling up of the other till it sinks you into eternity, 'filled with all the fulness of God.' Remember me at a throne of grace: you don't know how much grace I need to live with, ere I need dying grace. But it only wants asking for."

"She rejoiced," says a friend who knew Adelaide well, "in every opportunity of studying the holy Scriptures, as one who had found great spoil. Her face literally seemed to shine with serene delight as she elicited, step by step, the unsearchable riches of Christ." "I am longing," she herself writes, on

Sept. 29 (1848), "to hear from you again if you have any rich Bible-thoughts for me. Precious, precious treasure!

> "'My never-failing treasury, filled
> With boundless stores of grace!'

I really do think my Bible is enough for me, where-ever or whatever I am: and the wilderness loses its loneliness, while we lean on the arm of our Beloved. We can forget what a rough, thorny road we are walking on, while our thoughts were engrossed in converse with One so all-engrossing as Jesus!—Him in whom dwelleth all the fulness of the Godhead bodily! Oh! what very amazing thoughts for frail humanity to pen! And yet we are ourselves the very members of that Body in whom this fulness dwells! Oh! to think and write such things with the deep, deep reverence which becomes the beggar raised from the dunghill!"

And, in the same letter, she adds: "I am very much interested in prophetical thoughts just now. If the Lord will, we may, perhaps, go into these depths of divinely revealed truth this winter. I do so covet to know all that I can know by faith, while yet in this earthly tabernacle. No wonder Time should fail, if Eternity cannot exhaust its treasures. 'This is life eternal, to know THEE!'"

Tenderly watching over one very dear to her, she writes: "As a birth-day text, I cannot choose a more comprehensive and glorious assurance for you than Phil. iv. 19—'My God shall supply all your need according to His riches in glory by Christ Jesus. Not according even to my best wishes for you, for these are unworthy of Him, but 'according to His riches in glory!' Nothing seems to me to make the Christian so perfectly happy and contended—come what will—as the certain knowledge that God does it out of His riches of grace, and glory, and wisdom —yea, 'the depth of the riches both of His wisdom and knowledge.' He has no need to act sparingly; He cannot act ignorantly; He delights to act freely, out of the riches of His glory. Oh! dearest M——, are not such thoughts enough to silence all the misgivings of our timid, anxious hearts? Two very favourite birth-day texts of mine are—'*Our* DAYS on the earth are as a shadow,' 'but thy YEARS are to all generations.' I am fond of contrasting the littleness of our existence here with the eternity of the existence of our God. It makes us feel what it is to be safely anchored to the 'Rock of ages.'"

In other letters of this period, she writes: "I have been so greatly enjoying those verses in Ps. lxv. which speak of His showers as 'dissolving' the earth (*marg.*) —such a sweet emblem of the work of the Holy Spirit softening and dissolving our stony, parched, and barren souls." And again: "You have perhaps heard that the Lord has taken my beloved friend —— to Himself. 'Another lily gathered!' As my treasure accumulates in heaven, so may my heart and affections be more drawn thither!" And still again: "I suppose I said, I believe glory to be *consequent* upon suffering. I meant by this, merely the necessary connexion betwixt the two, which I had in my mind. And both come from our *oneness with Christ.* That is one of the most precious of all truths, is it not? indeed, the foundation of everything that concerns Christians: 'no longer twain, but one flesh;' 'members of His body, and of His flesh, and of His bones?'"

As the autumn advanced, we find her at work again. "I am in hopes," she writes, "of getting a Ragged school established in Derby. Will you try to pray about it for me? It is a suitable male teacher we want, and faith to act on Mark xi. 24." Her efforts for this school only ended with her life; and a remarkable blessing followed them.

And other labours she resumed with new earnestness. "I must plead guilty to your charge of very long silence," she says, writing to a friend, on Oct. 8 (1848), "I was forbidden in July to write more than I could help; but for some weeks lately I have been perfectly well able to write, only I have had a Torquay friend staying with me, whose life seems so uncertain that I tried to devote my whole time and strength to her. Till fourteen, she had never seen a Bible, and had known but little of it comparatively since till last winter; and it has been my precious privilege to lead her to see and taste more of the depths and heights of the boundless, fathomless love of that Saviour so richly unfolded to us there. Ah, dear F——, never, never shall we know it all. Eternity itself shall be ever employed in opening up the stores of grace treasured up for us in Him."

In the same letter she gives us a little cabinet-picture of her daily outward life. "I almost feel reluctant," she says, "to waste my moments in writing, and yours in reading, about myself, when there are such themes before us; but, as dear Dr. —— used to tell me, even my body is precious to Christ, for He has purchased it and made it His. So you shall hear what He has done for the 'earthly house of this tabernacle.' I am wonderfully better; much stronger, and suffer but little pain. Still I am not strong enough to bear the carriage, or much exertion of any kind. I live very quietly, chiefly upstairs, and get out a little in the garden whenever the weather will let me. I am not sure yet whether I shall go back to Torquay. I am doubtful whether it will be necessary. How sweet it is to leave ourselves in the loving hands of Jesus, who will do what is *best* for us, even to the ordering of all the little daily crosses and hourly disappointments of life. To see each thing as HIS doing, makes it all sweet, in spite of the trial which it may be in itself. May He make your cup to run over, dearest F——, with the 'wine and milk' which He offers so freely for our use, filling you 'with all the fulness of God.'"

Towards the end of October, it was decided to winter once more at Torquay. "The cold of the last few days and nights," she writes, on Oct. 18, "makes me thankful that I have not had my own way, which would have been to try and stay here.

The more, however, *I devised* that scheme, the more plainly God seemed to open the way for our going; and I feel a great secret pleasure in having my will crossed, and so in being led blindly by a way I know not."

In the interval, she writes: "I believe those who are most purified will reflect the Refiner's image the most brightly. The finer and most exquisite features of the Christian character are brought out only in protracted purification by fire—don't you think so? The soul is safe for eternity, if there have been but the believing look to Jesus; but then the development of the graces of the Spirit have not had time for exercise. There must be trial, ere we can exercise 'patience,' and irritating circumstances to call forth 'long-suffering.'"

And, reverting to a subject before noticed, she says: "Self-examination I have studied with no ordinary care for months. I think Christians are in great bondage concerning it. I hope you will forgive me for saying so. I am so sure that much of the gloomy doubtfulness of the Lord's people, as to whether they are His or not, arises from seeking evidences in themselves, instead of only looking to HIM, which is itself the most convincing of all evidences, that I dread looking much to self for any cause. 'Walking in the light will surely best show us our darkness!"

And, on the eve of setting out, she writes, on Oct. 30 (1848), to one of her sisters, thus: "What I wish for you, above everything else, dearest H——, is, that you may have your heart so full of thoughts of Jesus as to be able to say:

"'I journey through a desert, drear and wild,
Yet is my heart with such sweet thoughts beguiled,
Of Him on whom I lean, my Strength and Stay,
I can forget the sorrows of the way!'

Why should we not? There is no blank, no void which Jesus cannot fill. Does He not create those blanks in order to fill them? We can only learn 'the fulness of Jesus' by being emptied of self. May He make this a fresh means of filling you with all the fulness of God! a fresh creature-stream dried up, that 'the fulness of Him who filleth all in all,' may flow in! Let us see God's designs in trying us:

"'The clouds we so much dread
Are big with mercy, and shall break
In blessings on your head!'

'The balancings of the clouds are His! They come charged with rain, to refresh the dry and thirsty ground. Let us thank God and take courage, and go on our way rejoicing!"

CHAPTER IX.

Her last winter at Torquay opened brightly. "We are very happy altogether," she writes, on Nov. 13 (1848). "May our joy be only 'in the Lord,' and not in our circumstances! As to the future, I am now heartily desirous not to choose or wish for myself, either to live or die. To be content under all circumstances is the highest attainment of the Christian life, and is certainly the summit of happiness. It is a lesson which it seems to take a life to learn; but Paul says he *had* learned it."

Under the same roof with her, this winter, there resided a visitor who found in dear Adelaide "her first spiritual friend." "I think," says her sister, "she was only thirteen, though quite womanly in appearance and manner. She was charmed with Adelaide at first sight; and the affection was mutual, for Adelaide warmly returned it, and had her with her as much as possible—the result being beyond the attachments of earth, for J—— learned to know and love the Saviour. Whenever I was out, J—— sat on a little stool by her sofa, drinking in words of eternal life. She went back to school in February, 1849, loving Jesus as her Lord, and loving her new friend as the means of first opening her mind to see His beauty and to feel His preciousness. She now resides in India, and has since walked most consistently as a follower of Christ."

Her health having on the whole improved, "Adelaide was able," says her sister, "to see more of her friends and neighbours." And alluding to this, she herself writes, on Nov. 22: "I am quite in the world again (to me) here now; and I find it very trying and soul-hardening: but God is able to make all grace abound toward us, and I feel as if we should specially glorify Him by trusting Him to carry on His own work in us as mightily and effectually in the midst of every sort of hindrance as in the quiet of solitude. Are not you too much inclined to put yourself out of the world in order to be wholly given to God, while Christ's prayer for us is—'I pray not that thou shouldest take them out of the world, but that thou shouldest keep them from the evil?' That is the nature of His intercession for us both, as much now as then, and especially so (don't you think?) when He sympathizingly feels how much we both need it."

The Word became increasingly precious to her. "I have been so enjoying Ps. cxix. lately," she writes, on the same date: "it fully says all that I am sure you and I feel of delighting in God's Word so far above everything else. A dreadful conversation with poor R. W. on Monday evening made me go to bed, saying, 'Horror hath taken hold on me;' for he actually owned to me that he dared not, and could not, promise to read the Bible! I believe he has really been to Oscott and joined the Papists! Though he does not quite own it, he can't deny it."

And she adds: "I had a very nice visit last week to Miss ——, a girl just my age, and ill in exactly the same way. She is full to overflowing of Christ—can think and talk of nothing else; and her countenance literally reflects His bright rays. She seems to have felt all I have about life and death, and now at last has learnt to be quite thankful to live, though joyfully waiting to be gone. She told me she had been thinking so much of her need of knowing Christ personally, in order to be able in Him to meet and contend with the personality or the personal agency of the Devil. You will feel it too, I think."

Terstegen once wrote: "Do not think so much upon denying yourselves, upon being faithful, or upon living holily and strictly; but only seek to love—hunger after love—exercise yourselves in love. The love of Christ constrains the believer into suffering and through suffering." Alluding to a trial which had come upon her, Adelaide writes, on Dec. 7 (1848): "I find a blessing to myself in this breaking down of my natural will. It is a daily cross, and a burden; but to take it and bear it *after Jesus*, not doing my own will, but my heavenly Father's, is sweet to me still. Don't you feel more and more, every day, that to be dying to everything here, and living to God, with a full sense of the bearing of each passing moment on eternity, is the grand end of life? To crucify our flesh with its affections and lusts—not, as the Romanists and others do, to feel that they have done a good deed, but because we find it opposed to the life of the Spirit of Christ in us, so opposite as it is to the patience, gentleness, love, meekness, which ought to be reflected in the followers of the meek and lowly Jesus; this is the aim of all our discipline."

"It is most beautiful," she adds, "to see this in some of the tried sufferers here—their cheerful endurance of the most intense pain from day to day without a passing murmur, and their bright hope of glory—'an eternal weight of glory,' which (as one of them said to me the other day) *makes* the afflictions seem light. It is most encouraging to me to see how others are borne up above the billows by that sure anchor of the soul, which entereth within the vail, sustaining them; and I won't shut myself out, for I am sure it sustains me too, through every suffering of mind as well as body."

A closer intimacy with God was her heart's daily longing. "A friend said to me the other day," she writes, "that my chief object ought to be to seek to know God more and more; and I hope I am learning something more of Him. My Bible seems to do me good when nothing else does; and it is so sweet to seek the teaching of God's Spirit, and then to get to understand a little of the meaning of one verse after another. I find the Bible so exceedingly full of comfort and beauty, as I get to *think* more about its meaning."

Vinet speaks of that "eccentric philanthropy"

which "passes over the parent to give itself to country, and passes over country to attach itself to humanity; but the Gospel," he adds, "far from despising the private affections, recommends them." Dear Adelaide loved her kindred, and anxiously laboured to help them forward in the way. With two of her sisters at home, she maintained, this winter, a peculiarly touching fellowship; and as it was her last season of absence, we select a few memorials of it.

To one of her sisters she writes:

"SUNDAY MORNING, TORQUAY,
Nov. 19, 1848.

"MY PRECIOUS N——,

"It shall be one of my sweet employments on this hallowed day to minister, as God shall enable me, to your necessities. 'Iron sharpeneth iron,' as I have been thinking very often lately; and so God shall use us as fellow-helpers and quickeners to each other, as we bend our steps, on each successive Sabbath, not indeed to the same 'worldly sanctuary,' but to the same heavenly temple not made with hands—to present ourselves as living sacrifices on the altar of that temple, even Jesus, in whose whole burnt-offering of Himself we, as the members of His body, are offered likewise to the Father.

"Dead and risen in Him! for the same Spirit which baptizes us into His death, makes us equally, of necessity, partakers of His resurrection also. This is the grand marvel to me, that we are now as truly risen as we are dead in Jesus, and our life is, as truly as His own, hid within the vail. And this makes it so essentially of necessity, that the Christian must live holily—*i.e.*, in exact proportion as he realizes his resurrection-life. His conversation or citizenship is in heaven; and his conflict and his warfare are consequently said to be 'in high or heavenly places.' (Eph. vi. 12.)

"I heartily thank God for giving you more of Himself, directly from Himself, in place of its coming through an 'earthen vessel,' which both limits the abounding flow of His fulness, and also gives an earthy taste to the living water. The smallest and most muddy stream of that water quenches more of the thirst of the soul than the greatest abundance of earthly good; but it is a pity we are content with impure and limited draughts of what we might drink 'freely' (Rev. xxii. 17) and 'abundantly' (Cant. v. 1) from 'the wells of salvation,' 'the fountain of living waters;' and I really account it a great mercy to be driven to this.

"Go on from strength to strength, testifying of Jesus while He gives you time and strength to speak for Him; and, in telling others about Him, you shall yourself find Him to be your Beloved and your Friend, as in Cant. v. I praise Him heartily for M. W. Ask Him to make all you say to be the breathing of His Spirit through you, and it shall be life-giving and quickening. He blesses you wonderfully; above all, in the circulation of His own Word, which never returns void to Him who sends it. What an amazing thought! The Lord bless you abundantly in your own soul and in your work of faith and labour of love to others, till He takes you that He may be glorified in you for ever and ever! So prays your sister in Him,

"ADELAIDE L. NEWTON.

"I have a very good hope of poor M. W. 'Be not faithless, but believing.' 'He willeth not the death of a sinner.'"

And to another of them, she writes:

"SHRUBLANDS, Dec. 2, 1848.

"MY DEAREST G——,

"I was so thankful to get your note the other day: I have been longing to write again. If anything connected with myself could have been more truly refreshing to a sometimes weary, faint-hearted pilgrim than another, it was the tidings of God's having owned and accepted one of my tiny tracts. May I have grace to render Him the glory due unto His name, remembering that I am but the earthen vessel which contains what He puts in and sends forth through me of His own life-giving Spirit!

"I cannot tell you how thankful I am, too, for you. You may not be enjoying the happiest frames of mind, but you are indeed a vessel hung upon the nail in a sure place. You cling to Him even the more because you find rest nowhere else—not even in His work in you. You are like the Bride in Canticles, crying out, 'None but Christ—none but Christ.' The very threshold of His house is a delight to your panting soul, and you love to tread His courts. Ah! dearest G——, these are sure, very sure pledges; they are actual earnests and foretastes of a delight as far exceeding what you now feel as the heavenly sanctuary, the house not made with hands, shall exceed the glory of His earthly courts.

"This longing after Him sometimes seems to me even more blessed in reality (though less enjoyable at the time) than the enjoyment of Him. What do you think? I have felt it so exceedingly strong at night lately, having had a long succession of very sleepless nights, an intense longing to know God, which nothing seems to satisfy. Believing 'that He is' does not seem half enough; I want more, and yet I don't know what. I dare say it is longing after what I must die to know. And I don't feel as if this were wrong, though I more and more believe that wishing to die is wrong. It is a child fancying it knows better what would promote its happiness and welfare than its parent! But we must learn our lessons in God's way of them. We cannot teach one another, though He often uses us as the instruments of His teaching.

"But I see every day that telling other people what I have learnt is useless, unless God is telling them what He means them to hear through me: so that, after all, secretly asking His blessing is the secret of everything.

"I greatly enjoyed some hours at M—— last Saturday. —— seemed fuller of heaven than ever. We both talked and seemed to feel we were here as pilgrims, and enjoying a little intercourse by the way; whilst it did really feel like way-side talk, and nothing more. God is teaching me to do without ——, even here; and I feel that it is to make me rest on 'unseen' things and not seen.

"I am glad you got occasional talks with ——. Her very disagreeableness to me by nature made our love to Jesus more manifestly the only tie that bound us together: it gave a reality to the friendship, which I liked. How mysterious the simplicity of faith is! and how immense the privileges it opens to us! Literally everything that Christ is and has, because we are literally made to belong to Him—to be part of Him! Dear G——, what more can I say? The thoughts are too vast, too immense, to be grasped by my poor finite mind. May the Spirit, in teaching the deep things of God, reveal them to us as we are able to bear it from day to day. So prays your fond

"Addy."

And again, on Dec. 28: "What a word that is in Luke xii. 12, 'It is not you that speak, but the Holy Ghost!' This is very sweet, indeed, in connexion with John iii. 34, '*For* God giveth not the Spirit by measure.' So that everything depends on the indwelling, and on the measure of this indwelling, of the Holy Spirit in us. 'Be filled with the Spirit:'—is not that a nice New-year's-day text? And with it, for our comfort in every feeling of coldness and deadness and lukewarmness—'It is the Spirit that quickeneth.' He quickeneth us, and quickeneth others through us. May God abundantly bless all your seed sown, dearest N——, and give you a harvest of many sheaves!"

And to the other sister, of same date: "I am sorely tried: you don't know what it costs me sometimes. I am positively amazed at that power of God which carries me through it all. It calms me to that degree that I *cannot* be agitated, if I may use such an expression. Oh! it is wonderful! it is so real—so divine! Let me send you Phil. iii. 7—14; it is what we feel, especially as we begin to come under the near influence of a ray of light from the heavenly city. Then, indeed, may all things else be counted as loss and as dung, as the beautiful lines of a hymn say—

"'All things, beside, which charm the sight,
Are shadows tipt with glow-worm light.'

B. sends those four words in Ex. iii. 7, 'I know their sorrows.' I will add Phil. iv. 19, 'Even His riches in glory by Christ Jesus.'"

A snare to which her peculiar habit of mind exposed her, was a tendency to occupy her thoughts unduly with the mysterious side of God's procedure. Her searching intellect was ever sounding depths which it is not given to man to fathom; and the pain of failure was at times almost overwhelming. "To own the truth to you," she writes on Jan. 19 (1849), "I have been trying lately rather to lay aside all difficult subjects in Scripture-study, from the conviction that I was studying them intellectually rather than spiritually. Perhaps, it is a danger few are so much exposed to; but, having so much time to spend mentally, I am in great danger, I am sure, of falling into this snare. And though I feel that this may be given to me as a time for laying up knowledge which may hereafter be called into practical use, I still think and feel that 'knowledge puffeth up,' while 'charity' alone 'edifieth.' God has been very good to me in calling forth my energies in many practical ways lately, which, though less pleasant to my nature, I am sure has been necessary for me."

"If a man is to find life," says Vinet again, "he must find it elsewhere than in a deceitful and sterile view of himself. A look, a simple look (I mean not an argument, a study, a toil)—a simple look converts." And the same look daily renewed, renews the heart's brave purpose. "If you will allow me for once to say what I think," she writes on Feb. 2 (1849), to one who was "distressing herself about her hardness of heart," "you will find the greatest possible help in studying the character of CHRIST, not your own. Read the Gospels, to trace out—in every miracle, and word, and act, and touch, and in every step of the path He trod—what was His character, and how it developed itself; and I think, with the Spirit's help, you will forget your walk in thinking of His, and your emptiness in His fulness; and thus, by beholding as in a glass the glory of the Lord, you will be changed into the same image, from glory to glory, even as by the Lord the Spirit. I do think that Satan hinders Christians more by discouraging them with showing them their perpetual shortcomings and failures, and their sad want of conformity to Jesus, with all its sad results, than in any other way; and I cannot help feeling strongly that, in urging self-examination in the way so many good clergymen do, they really aid the mischief. I like what M'Cheyne said, 'For every look at yourself, take ten looks at Christ;' only I would double and treble it, and almost say, Never look at self at all."

And the intense "looker" is the earnest worker. "Looking," says Vinet, "alone can give to action, not that feverish vivacity which our passions will always give in abundance, but that beauty which passion can never give." And Adelaide writes: "I believe that it is when we are most occupied with Christ that we are most useful to others, however unconscious we may be of it, and however conscious we may then be (as, of course, we shall be more than ever) of our unlikeness to Him. Did you ever notice this in Canticles? It was when the Bride was pining after Christ and not realizing the happy sense of His presence (chap. v. 9), that, in telling what she was in search of, she regained her own happiness, and excited in others the desire to seek Him too. (Chap. v. 10–16; and vi. 1.) This is most encouraging to me."

And she adds: "Oh! I love to see how God is using you, dear L——, and how your 'faith is working by love.' How unspeakably good He is to us, to give us hearts willing to 'occupy' for Him while He is away! Will it not be delightful, when He comes again to have so traded with our 'talents,' that we can point to one and another who heard of Him through us, and cast our crowns (richly set with many jewels) before His feet, to whom we shall glory in yielding up all the glory we have gained?"

As the spring came on, her health again was shaken. "Yesterday," she writes, on February 2, (1849), "I really could do nothing, having been awake almost the whole night through, hearing every hour strike, except from two till four, and being quite done up. I am quite surprised my cough could have got so bad so soon. But enough of 'things seen and temporal,' 'passing away!' Oh! for a mind to dwell only on eternal realities! I so often think of that line,

"'The strong He'll strongly try.'

What a comfort, that He who tries us is He who knows our strength! I was so pleased with a thought of ——'s the other day, that God sends His children many a storm to dash them on the Rock, that they may find out its firmness, security, and elevation."

We may be occupied about God, and not be occupied with God. Watching against this peril, Adelaide writes, on February 21: "I am doing texts for ——, on the love of God; but I am in such danger of doing it all *intellectually*, that I often feel afraid to go on. Do you ever feel it? It seems so easy to like to be occupied with religious things, and to follow out a train of thought on these wonderful subjects, and yet not to get nearer Jesus by it. 'A broken and a contrite heart, O God, thou wilt not despise,' has been my text lately; and my uppermost desire has been, to be able to feel like a child coming to its father, as in Gal. iv. 6, 7. Is it not amazing to have 'the Spirit of His Son' in our hearts? Oh, how holy we ought to be, and how Christ-like in all things—the life which acts in us being God's own Spirit moving about these earthen vessels to do His work!"

Payson once wrote to a friend thus: "A MAN now fills the throne of heaven. And who is this man? Mark it well—it is a man who is not ashamed to call you 'brother.' You may not now know what He is doing with you; but you shall know hereafter—you shall see the reason of all the trials and temptations, the dark and comfortless hours, the long and tedious conflicts—and you will be convinced that not a sigh, not a tear, not a single uneasy thought, was allotted to you without a wise and gracious design." Payson had learned this lesson, not out of books or from the lips of men, but through the things which he himself had suffered. And Adelaide Newton was learning the same lesson by the same personal discipline. "However my wishes and feelings," she says, "may vary with the fluctuations of bodily disease, my chief and highest desire is, that He should have His own way with me—prolonging life, or snapping it asunder, or doing what shall most promote HIS glory, in whatever way He pleases, in His soverign wisdom and *love.* 'Oh, for a deeper entrance,' dear M——, 'into His heart of love!' as a very, very dear young friend, at this moment dangerously ill upstairs, said to me lately. God has been doing it all; and, trying as I own I have felt it, I would not have one link in the chain broken."

"It has been such a strong feeling with me lately," she continues, "when thinking very much of the sorrows of others and wishing sometimes the removal of their trials, that we little think what we are doing when we begin to wish to have anything changed in any degree from what it is. How we should mar the perfect work and plans of God if we hindered one thing from happening at the precise time and in the particular way in which God hath purposed it! and how, as partakers of the mind of Christ through the indwelling of the Spirit, we should shrink from the very idea of a flaw in God's works! Yet don't you think our rebellious feelings, when He crosses our inclinations, all tend to this in reality?"

And she adds: "These few hints of what is passing in my mind will tell you how to pray for me; and that is what I care for above everything else. Desires of the heart, and inward groanings of the spirit, and weariness of sin, and pantings after holiness—are all open to the eye of Him who dwells in His upper sanctuary, but hears 'the groanings of the prisoner.' How full of comfort to know that muttered desires and groans are heard! Plead my cause at the very highest of all courts, because you are one who has 'access to the holiest by the blood of Jesus.' Oh, may you have sweet communings with Him, when you take up my cause for Him to plead with His Father! I hope you enjoy sweet fellowship with Him. We shall uninterruptedly hereafter."

The "very dear young friend upstairs," alluded to above, was soon afterwards taken. "The death of dear B—— C—— last night," she writes, on March 1 (1849), "has so pre-occupied my mind, that I scarcely feel able to turn it back to other thoughts again. A more perfectly peaceful 'falling asleep in Jesus' could hardly be; and all the circumstances attending it have been *so* full of love, that even poor ——'s first words were, 'Bless the Lord, O my soul; and all that is within me, bless His holy name!' Dr. ——'s kindness, too, has been so great; and his way of directing one's mind to look entirely beyond all that which is painful to the realities of unseen things, has seemed altogether to make it (I might almost say) only a fresh instance of displaying to us what God is."

And to another, two days later: "Instead of grieving over dear B——'s death, I feel most deeply thankful to have witnessed it, and to have had such a proof of the reality of my religion. Oh, it is such a real thing to be trusting in Christ, and to feel that we are alive *in Him*, not in our own bodies, which are mortal! Dear ——, too, is so supported by the same reality; it is falling back upon God, the living God—is it not? But my thoughts are too large to express on paper, or even in words. I seem quite lost in such immensity."

Henry Martyn, in a season of sore trial, wrote in his diary this entry: "My dear Redeemer is a fountain of life to my soul. With resignation and peace can I look forward to a life of labour and entire seclusion from earthly comforts, while Jesus thus stands near me, changing me into His own image." Adelaide Newton was realizing, amidst her increasing trials, the joy of the same fellowship. "It is so strange," she writes to a friend, on March 8, "to contrast the scenes of gaiety and of sorrow this world is so full of: if you had all been at the concert, we were in the midst of death! And yet,

"'Although the world may think it strange,'

most truly could we have affirmed,

"'We would not with the world exchange.'

I have so exceedingly enjoyed of late Gal. iv. 5–7. The thought of our having the Spirit of Jesus, as the Spirit of Life which actuates us, seems so wonderful! I like so very much to think of the Spirit as the breath of Christ's body—that very body of which He is the Head and we are the members! Tell —— how very thankful I am that he should be at work in the Lord's vineyard. He won't understand Solomon's Song, viii. 8, or I would add, 'Those that keep the fruit must have two hundred.' You can take it, though, for yourself; and so can ——. How God is making you both 'grow up into Christ!

And we can bless Him for the clouds which break in showers to water our thirsty souls."

It is recorded of the martyr Ridley, that on earth he lived so near heaven, that, when he died, he had not far to go. Dear Adelaide seemed in spirit to be drawing nearer and nearer her home. "Happy girl, to be gone before!" she writes, on March 12 (1849), alluding to the death of B——, "younger than myself by some months, and younger, I should think, too, in spiritual life, and yet more matured and more ripe for glory! But I can use the language of the Great Forerunner, and say, 'Yet a little while,' and we shall see each other, because I, too, 'go to the Father.' Anything so intense as the longings I have felt lately to see Him and be 'satisfied with His likeness,' I have scarcely believed could be anything but the desire put into my heart for what God was intending to give."

Christ's PERSON was more and more realized by her as the centre of all her hopes and joys. "The object of Christianity," says Vinet, "is not an abstract truth. It is a fact, a person, Jesus Christ, Jesus Christ crucified. We believe not in Christianity, but in Jesus Christ. Every Christian act done in the world, is done, not by Christianity (which is itself only an effect), but by Jesus Christ. The relations which we bear as Christians are not intellectual relations—relations between our mind and a truth, but relations between person and person—relations between us men and Jesus Christ, both man and God. The object of our faith is invisible, but not impersonal. He is not seen with the eye of flesh, but nevertheless He is seen. We do not converse with Him as with an idea—that is to say, in substance with ourselves, but as with a Being who is with us even to the end of the world." Dear Adelaide found this reality to be daily growing more real. "I don't know whether others feel it," she writes, "but it seems to me that we so little realize the *Person* of the Saviour. We think and talk of *doctrines*, but they are not CHRIST. Oh, what a wonderful depth there is in those three words—'Thou IN ME'—the Father embodied in the Son! And then, to add to this, the taking of *us* into union—into oneness—with both! Oh! is it not amazing?"

And, writing, on March 15, to one who, like herself, was sorely tried, she says: "How marvellous the dealings of God are! How He brings us at times into the depths, that we may know by experience that He is the high and lofty One! 'The rock that is higher than I.' G—— said your thoughts were too high and too large for others to understand. It is quite remarkable how exactly I have been feeling the same thing lately; but I have thought it has perhaps been in answer to the cry which has been so uppermost with me, ever since Christmas, for 'a broken and a contrite spirit.' I cannot tell you how low I seem to have been brought; but last night I was exceedingly comforted by Ps. lxxiii. 21–23. The 'nevertheless' there seemed so very, very precious, in spite of all our ignorance; and I was so pleased to find the pricking at the heart so exactly expressed. How well God knew every thought and feeling which could ever oppress us, when He caused that precious Book of Inspiration to be written for our comfort! Does not Ps. cxxxix. 6 also express what you feel?—and don't you like Matt. xi. 25, 'Revealed unto babes?' I am writing quite at random, not knowing whether such thoughts may at all fall in with yours; but, at all events, we must have one meeting-place, and that is, the Person of our adorable Redeemer! Oh, to be able to have our eye fixed on Him!"

A month later, she writes to one of her sisters thus:

"TORQUAY, APRIL 19, 1849.

"MY DEAREST N——,

"I am so glad to-day to be able to send you a line. I hope you have not thought me unkind, for I really have not felt able to write. I have been passing through very real trial lately, and very painful—learning so keenly the bitterness of creature-disappointment; and yet, if I will lean on idols, what else can I expect? Rather, let me tell you what I really do feel to be ground for thankfulness: that God has made me feel quite thankful to learn my folly and to be disappointed in the midst of what must, without His teaching and His restraining grace, have filled me with bitter complaing. I will tell you more about it (D.V.) when we meet.

"These wilderness-lessons are sweet, amidst all their bitterness, when they show us that we are thereby made to come up out of the wilderness, leaning more and more exclusively on our Beloved. To our shame be it spoken, that we should slight His all-sufficiency by leaning at any time on any other arm. O! how we do dishonour Jesus!

"I like 'Tekel' very much, and bought two copies. How sweetly it shows us how 'bold we may stand in the great day' with Jesus on our side!

"I hope you have not been much bored with ——. I think it is so difficult to be unselfish in religion, and to be willing to speak and act for God in the way and with the people He chooses, and not ourselves. O! may we be guided rightly in all we think, say, or do!

"Make yourself quite happy about old ——; it is our privilege to pray for him (Matt. x. 42). I am sure I ought to feel this; for —— says, in a letter I had lately from him, that he thanks me for sending such cups of water to his thirsty soul, in the tiny notes I have written him: so God, indeed, chooses weak and base things, that the excellency may all be His! I think the time is very short. O! to be kept blameless till we see Him come!

"Yours in Him, A. L. N."

And again, on having been at the Lord's table: "Only think of my having been down, this morning, to Trinity, for the early Sacrament (of course, without leave)! I have really felt lately so 'barren and withered' a branch of the Vine, that I resolved, if God threw no obstacles in my way to show me I was wrong, I would for once rush into His courts and get at least a glimpse of Jesus through the lattice-work of the ordinances; and I hope I did, in spite of all the bodily feelings which sadly hindered the upward flight of the Spirit after a risen Jesus, which I ardently longed for. O! when shall we rise too?

"Both the last times I have shared this sacred feast, it was chiefly the connecting the outward signs of the bread and wine with the absolute reality of the things signified being now in glory, which occupied and comforted me: Jesus clothed in that very body and blood still. It leads one's thoughts to Him. My Good-Friday text struck me very much in the same way—'Who His own self bare our sins in His own body.' How strong the words are—are they not? And then to think that we are the members which form that body (in another sense), adds another wonderful thought too."

Another thought, suggested by the same occasion, she gives elsewhere: "This do in remembrance of me.' There is a volume of thought suggested by the extreme simplicity of these words—'Remember me.' 'Behold my hands and my feet, that it is I myself; handle me and see,' were the words of Jesus while still on earth. Now, he says, 'Do this' (*i.e.*, eat the bread and drink the wine, which are the outward signs of the body and blood of Christ) 'in remembrance of me.' Don't forget my Body; remember it still, all the while I am away, till I come again! Where, then, is the body of Jesus now? Thither let the eye of faith be turned, whilst feeding on these outward remembrancers of it. Think not only how Jesus has once died, but, 'rather,' how He now lives! It is Jesus 'as He is,' that He bids us remember, to our great and endless comfort."

Her sojourn in Torquay was now drawing to a close. "I am glad," we find her writing, in reference to her intended departure, "to solve every difficulty and bury every anxiety in the certain assurance that I am best wherever God sends me. I mean to waste no more time over the body, further than simply to tell you that Dr. —— expressed thankfulness and surprise that my illness had made so little progress. I am often very thankful that it is such slow work in my case; for I am certain I shall be, with God's blessing, an eternal gainer. I begin to feel it sweet to have even life to offer and devote to Him, though I hope I shall never be unwilling to lay down a body of sin. To depart and be *with Christ* must always be 'far better.' Thank you, a thousand times, for the paper on John xx. and xxi.; it was peculiarly a word in season. Truly, a risen Jesus would not have us selfishly seeking the enjoyment even of His own society, so much as to be proving the reality of our love in real devotedness to Him. What a test it was to Peter, when 'Lovest thou me?' was followed up by 'Feed my sheep'—not by 'Come and lay down your life, that you may be with me.' I think this is very, very strong, when we remember how shortly before Peter was wishing to die that He might follow Jesus."

And she adds: "I meant to indulge in sending you some of the thoughts I have been greatly enjoying to-day on the Transfiguration, but I must not send more than one. Did it ever strike you? Peter desired prolonged intercourse with Moses and Elias; but 'a cloud overshadowed them' (put them into the shade), and a voice out of it said, 'Hear Him,' to make Jesus the prominent One; and they then found themselves left alone with Jesus!"

Looking back upon the way by which she had been led that season, she writes, April 19 (1849): "I have been thinking so much lately of those words 'Count it all joy when ye fall into *divers* trials,' &c. Mine have been very varied this winter; and sometimes the variety and the prolongation of them seem to induce a spirit of 'heaviness.' (1 Pet. i. 6, 7.) But we are going onward through the wilderness; and it is a grand and wonderful thing so to be brought through it as to be willing to be, more and more, bereft of every stay, that at length we may come up out of it, leaning on our Beloved alone! We shall be very anxious for further tidings of your dear brothers. Don't you think God often stirs up the prayers of His people for any one particular object of His mercy, by some trouble which attracts all eyes to centre on that one person for a time? I believe this is often the secret of the showers of blessing which follow such afflictive dispensations. May it be so abundantly in this instance! and, if it be His holy will, may both brothers be given back to you, even in this life, as Lazarus was to his sisters, though, after all, it can be but for a season! I am sure we get to feel, more and more, that we cannot wish or ask for any such things unconditionally; but, in holy submission, it is our privilege to breathe out every wish into our Father's ear, and He delights to answer, and even to do for us far more exceeding abundantly than ever we ask."

She left Torquay finally in May (1849). "A delightsome land it had proved to be," writes her sister, who was with her; "not only because a measure of health had been one result from our sojourn in it, but, most especially, on account of Dr. ——'s spiritual watchfulness over his beloved patient. His communings with her were what she valued above everything else." But she rejoiced to follow the Lord's leading. "'He fed them,'" she herself writes, indicating to a friend where her feet stood so firmly, "'according to the integrity of His heart, and guided them by the skilfulness of His hand.' *His* heart, His hands, His integrity, His skilfulness! it is according to this measure we are fed and guided. 'Fed' implies the whole pastoral care of a shepherd; and all this care God takes of us, according to the integrity or *perfectness* of His heart! What surer provision could be made for us?"

"The Lord's my Shepherd, I'll not want;
He makes me down to lie
In pastures green; He leadeth me
The quiet waters by.

"My soul He doth restore again,
And me to walk doth make
Within the paths of righteousness,
Ev'n for His own name's sake."

CHAPTER X.

Adelaide reached home once more in May (1849), not again to leave it until she should reach her home in the heavens.

In her Diary she writes: "*May* 12. 'Therefore, with joy shall ye draw water out of the wells of salvation.' How precious the sources of our joy are! Not summer or winter streams, but WELLS! May we not say of Jesus—'*The* well is deep?'" "*May* 15. Greatly enjoyed Deut. vii. 20, as an answer to the prayer, 'Cleanse thou me from secret faults.'" "*May* 16. Thought very much of the comfort of knowing that God accounts our litttle span of life 'long-suffering,' and that He should so appreciate our difficulty as to taking it joyfully, as to apportion *such* strength for the need. (Col. i. 11.)" "*May* 19. 'Tarry ye here and watch.' Lord, grant that I may act thus, whilst thou art interceding for me in yonder heavens within the veil!" "*June* 3. *Trinity Sunday.* 'Your life is hid with Christ in God;' a very sweet Trinity text, connecting the thought of the quickening Spirit with our 'life.'"

Elsewhere, in the Diary, she writes: "Received the Lord's Supper, to offer and present myself, body soul, and spirit, to be a reasonable, holy, and lively sacrifice to Him who died for me!" And again: "Bodily exhaustion seemed to hinder spiritual perception all day; but I could 'cling to Christ.'" And, another day: "Spent the whole Sabbath at home, but fed upon the WORD." And another: "Enjoyed Rom. viii. 34, with v. 10; the emphasis laid on the resurrection of Him who is our life." And another: "'I have prayed for thee, that thy faith fail not.' There is something very precious in knowing that Christ *has* prayed for us, even before *we* know our danger."

Her letter-writing, like all her other engagements, continued to be consecrated to God. "I always feel the interchange of Bible thoughts," she says, on May 26 (1849), indicating her method of serving the Lord in this employment, "a kind of letter-writing, which cannot be classed as waste of time or as a frivolous pursuit. May I look to you now and then, for a word in this way, to help me on 'in the knowledge of our Lord and Saviour?' I have been thinking very much of the real test it is of love to Jesus, when the enjoyment of Christian friends, meeting together to talk of the things they love best, is broken up that each may be sent forth as a messenger to others, to tell sinners of the living 'WAY.' Jesus, after His resurrection, tarried not to indulge the fond affections of His people, but, rather, just showed Himself to them, and then sent them forth to do His bidding: For example, Mary—'Touch me not, but go to my brethren, and tell them,' &c.; or, the disciples—'As my Father hath sent me, even so send I you;' or, Peter—'Feed my sheep.' In no case did Jesus stay to converse with them for mutual enjoyment, but would have them engaged in telling

"'To sinners round,
What a dear Saviour they had found.'

And, hard as it may sometimes be to tarry here willingly, even for such a purpose, we certainly may well be content, if Jesus gives to us first, and then tells us to distribute to the multitude."

With a rare *naïveté*, we find her indicating, in allusion to a friend's intended marriage, a characteristic feature of her own heart, thus (June 8, 1849): "I hope they may help each other to give themselves first unto the Lord: but I own I often look on and wonder and adore, when I think of the way by which *I* have been led; for, had I had a husband to please, I believe I should just have plunged into love in that 'out and out' way which would have made the words, 'She that is married careth how she may please her husband,' apply, with more than ordinary force to me. I know that my heart knits so closely to those I dearly love, that it is not without reason that I have been hindered from setting my affections on an earthly object, but allowed One, in human form, on whom I may legitimately indulge in centering them all, and that, too, without fear of disappointment!"

And, with a chastened delicacy, she adds: This natural feature in my character betrays itself in my peculiar love for, and enjoyment in Canticles; for there is, perhaps, no character in which I so love to think of Jesus, as He who has given Himself to His Bride, loving her even more than she can love Him, and allowing her that closest of all kinds of intercourse which else could not have been known. Is it not a sad, sad proof of our fallen state, that the very ordinance which God appointed to shadow forth this is so often the one which, more than any other, draws off our hearts from Him?"

Vinet writes: "How difficult, while enjoying external peace, to keep awake! What exertion is necessary to move forward on a sea whose waters have been rendered heavy as lead by a fatal calm!" Tasting this reality, Adelaide writes, June 14 (1849): "How thankful it made me to find that you had got the peace inwardly, amidst your sufferings, which I got so exactly in the same way! I never was so happy before, as when I was so ill, I have found even my partially restored health bring with it many new and painful trials and conflicts, and could sometimes almost prefer the bodily pain. But, oh! if we can but choose nothing for ourselves, and calmly accept the needed discipline in the form and under the circumstances God chooses for us, happy are we!"

And to another, on June 23: "I hope you will write to me soon—though, if you have very little time to spare for me, I would sooner ask you to use it in *prayer*. I do so want quickening! I can get plenty of ideas, and am strong enough to study and think just now; but is it not worse than nothing, if one finds pleasure in these intellectual enjoyments, short of Christ? Are you able to get into real, close communion with Him at present? If so, do take me with you into the Holiest. I really am afraid to indulge my pleasure in 'knowing,' lest it interfere with simple 'feeding.' Still, I do believe God is leading me onwards and upwards in His own way; and it is well to be humbled."

In the same letter, she adds: "I am a good deal stronger; but I fancy my chest retrogrades, from a few bad symptoms. But they may be only temporary. *I* don't know. May I only ripen for glory!"

And, on June 26 (1849), she addresses another friend thus: "I hope you are enjoying the 'strong meat' of the Word: this is one of the precious privileges belonging to those who, through a longer sojourn in Mesech, 'have had their senses exercised.' Is not that a strong word? I am so fond of it in Heb. xii. 11, the fruit of righteousness being one of the gains to be reaped from being exercised by chastenings! 'Exercised thereby.' Oh! it speaks volumes; it tells of days, and weeks, and months, and years, it may be, of inward conflict and outward trials, exercising us; and not in vain, for the peaceable fruit of righteousness shall be reaped in due time. So let us comfort one another with these precious words, dear M——, counting it still all joy when we fall into divers trials, for the trying of our faith worketh patience; and when patience has had her perfect work, we shall be 'vessels unto honour,' to display throughout eternity the exceeding riches of the grace and glory of Him who wrought it all in us!

Milner, in his "Church History," writes: "To believe, to suffer, and to love, was the primitive taste." Henry Martyn, in his Diary, says, that "no uninspired sentence ever affected him so much." Dear Adelaide was growing more and more in this "taste." "I can, in my little measure, sympathize and weep with you," she writes, June 27. "I have been so struck with Ps. xliii. 4, that I must tell you about it. The expression which we render 'God, my exceeding joy,' is in the Hebrew, 'God, the joy (or gladness) of my joy' (as in the margin); and the two Hebrew words have each their own specific meaning—one signifying, properly, the throbbing, or quick beating, or palpitating of the heart in joy; and the other being a word of gesture (from the root, *to roll*), and hence meaning a 'joy which expresses itself in the gestures of the body, as in leaping or jumping up and down for joy.' So that the two together seem to imply the being pervaded through and through with joyousness, from the indwelling of that God who is Himself 'our exceeding joy.' One can hardly find words to put such thoughts into. I think Ps. xvi. 11 beautifully expresses it, 'In Thy presence is fulness of joy.' And did it ever strike you as rather remarkable, that David should have used that expression about God, at the very moment that he was complaining of being 'cast down?' It seems to me so comforting; for it shows what our real portion is in Him, even when we feel desolate, and cast down, and disquieted, does it not?"

Her trials were giving her that tender sympathy with fellow-pilgrims, which mere knowledge cannot give. "It seems to knit my heart closer than ever to you," she writes, "that we are both being made to feel the gentle pressure of the hand in which we are held. There are trials peculiar to illness, especially to protracted illness, which none can know but fellow-sufferers under them." And to another: "I do, indeed, feel for your poor sister. Do send her this text, 'Strengthened with all might, according to His glorious power, unto all patience and longsuffering with joyfulness.' How blessed to think of the end to which we are strengthened with such amazing might! Not to do some great deed, or accomplish some mighty act, but 'unto all patience.' And not only to the mere endurance of evils which we cannot escape, but 'to all longsuffering with *joyfulness.*'"

Her health this summer rather revived. "I daresay G—— told you," she writes, July 15, "how well I am just now. I am thankful, because it enables me to write and speak for Jesus; and one word in a letter may be a word in season. To be vessels of mercy filled with the Spirit, so as to speak only as He breathes through us, is indeed an honour. May we both richly enjoy it during whatever time we have still to sojourn here—be it years, months, or days! And then to be vessels of glory! Oh! may we not well rejoice with joy unspeakable, in prospect of the glory which shall be revealed in us? Rom. viii. 18, with Eph. i. 17, 18."

The Christian self-reproach is oftentimes misunderstood.

Henry Martyn, for example, writes: "The pride which I see dwelling in my heart, producing there the most obstinate hardness, I can truly say my soul abhors. I see it to be unreasonable, I feel it to be tormenting." But, almost with the same breath, he adds: "I wish for no service but the service of God, in labouring for souls on earth, and to do His will in heaven." Dwelling more "in the light," and realizing more vividly his heavenly calling, he is, even whilst progressing in holiness, weighed down with a growing sense of the unworthiness of his walk."

"I do feel so strongly," Adelaide writes, Aug. 13 (1849), "what you say of the need of 'being stirred up to do what we can.' It is marvellous we can be such triflers on affairs of such moment! Do you not find an increasing sense of calm confidence, that all the horrible coldness, deafness, lifelessness, which so characterize our walk with God—while they hinder our enjoyment—still cannot affect our safety? I fancy it is a thing only to be learnt by experience—and for this good reason, that, if we felt it before our sense of sin had become deep and distressing to us, we might be careless about sin; but, in the after-experience of the child of God, when he has learned (or, rather, is learning) by habitual watchfulness to detect the little, hourly, secret sins which cause him such an aching heart, he learns, at the same time, that, while the waves of corruption may dash him back when he ought only to be flowing towards the shore, they still cannot make him lose his hold of the Rock to which he is anchored. I seem to rest very much on such thoughts as these, of late."

Another lesson experience was teaching her. "Though I have the character of being very well," she writes, Aug. 14, "it is not without many days and hours which weariness of mind and of body renders almost useless, except, indeed, so far as they are part of that chastening whereby I am 'exercised.' I have thought very much lately of the gain it will be to have lived a certain time after one's conversion, in order to learn out the lessons one can never learn in heaven. I believe we shall all 'meet the Lord' with such varieties of feeling;—the young Christian with the ardour and warmth of 'first love,' but the matured believer with a depth and richness of attachment which would characterize, in its measure, the meeting of old and long-tried friends after prolonged separation, and which others can never know. Don't you think this is quite consistent with each having the full share of happiness each is capable of? or do you think it is taking earthliness of feeling too much into heaven? I do think our light afflictions work out a *far more* exceeding weight of glory."

Paul speaks of the "law in his members" warring against the "law of his mind." A poet has written:

> Compulsion, from its destined course
> The magnet may awhile detain;
> But, when no more withheld by force,
> It trembles to its north again:

Thus, though the idle world may hold
My fettered thoughts a while from Thee,
To Thee they spring, when uncontroll'd,
In all the warmth of liberty."

"I cannot tell you," Adelaide writes, "how I dread worldliness of spirit returning on me. Oh! how bitterly one has to learn the folly of wandering from the side of Jesus, or rather, I would say, of grieving His Holy Spirit; for that is what I believe Christians lose by, strictly speaking. I think that is the source of all our misery and unhappiness." And, referring to various acts of service which she had been doing on behalf of Ireland, and also of the Jews, she adds: "One only longs for willing hearts to devote ourselves and our substance, our time and strength and talents, to Him whose own purchased property they are. I do long, as you say, just to live each moment as if the opportunity might soon be gone."

A craving for an intenser fellowship of hearts than earth affords, took a faster hold upon her day by day. "Your visits," she writes, Sept. 17 (1849), "quite refreshed our old friendship, though they were so brief. There is something so essentially binding and lasting in Christian love, that, wherever it exists, friends are and must be friends, however seldom or often they may meet, till they meet for eternity. No words can tell the delight I feel in every such friendship—begun in the bud in time, to ripen and bear fruit for ever. Oh! for better communion! We shall have it, when we have 'patiently endured.'"

A friend was taken away, and she writes: "I am

left: pray that I may not be a cumberer, but a good steward of time, health, and talents, still lent to me to trade with. It is quite remarkable how many whom I loved are gone, and have left me behind, more and more bereft of all but Jesus; but HIS fulness often fills my little earthen vessel to overflowing, and—but for sin within and without and all around me—I should be happy indeed."

And to another: "I am truly sorry for you, in one sense, for the loss of your dear baby; but surely I must rejoice with you, too, if it is a treasure laid up for you in heaven, and drawing your affections thither also! Accept this tiny little book—will you?—as saying what I like to say on that subject. I wrote it just after dearest H—— B—— died. I have since lost my most intimate friend; but I love to think of her as a treasure there, and I feel how good it is for me to be weaned from earthly objects of affection. Oh, that we may all be found enthroned with Jesus in glory—serving Him here, praising him there!"

Another bereavement drew forth her sympathies thus: "I cannot think of your brother as buried in the ocean of this world's sea, without much more thinking of him as buried in the fathomless oceanfulness of the love of God throughout eternity. While the earthly house of the tabernacle of clay was sinking in the waters of time, the spirit of life which inhabited that earthern vessel soared on high, and winged its flight to those unmeasured heights of the love of Christ which pass all knowledge, and into which he has passed to all eternity. Oh, dear E——, may God in Jesus, by the abiding indwelling of the Comforter, enable you to bury all your sorrows in the depths of His sovereign love! Very many of those I loved most are gone before me; and I find it such a blessing to have my treasures laid up there instead of here."

And she adds: "But I could not try to comfort you under an affliction such as this, in any other way than by speaking of Christ, who is Himself the embodiment of all the members, and in whom we shall so soon all meet, to be for ever with Him. To think of ourselves only as members of His body (so as to forget ourselves as separate individuals, and think of ourselves only as parts of a whole), or to think of our trials and circumstances less in reference to ourselves, than as parts of God's perfect plan, are the two great objects I try to aim after, and which I think you will find most calming. It seems to put man in his place, and God in His. But I am so afraid of wounding where I would only wish to pour 'the oil of joy,' that I shall not try to say more. May He who is anointed to do it, give you all that 'oil of joy!'"

As the winter approached, her health appeared to suffer less than usual. "I have not known what it is to be as well for years," she writes, October 16 (1849). "Even this severe cold does not hurt me; but how long it may last, I know not. The character of God is my grand subject this year. I have got it in fifty-two points, with six texts on each; and it is such a rock to rest upon! To see what God is, and that He IS—an eternal present! Oh, it is wonderful, and so precious, as contrasted with all the tossings to and fro of frail man, even though he be a vessel of mercy! The water in the bottle may be spent, but not the water in the well." (Gen. xxi. 15—19.)

With that delicacy of touch which only one dwelling in "the light" can attain, we find her handling a feature of the hidden life thus: "In regard to *meditation*, forgive me if I say I think you are in bondage about it. My idea of it is this, that it is a thing one cannot set one's-self to as a prescribed duty; nor do I think it is enjoined upon us as such in Scripture. It is not within the reach of the newly-converted soul, but belongs to those who, in studying the precious Word of life, begin to see such beauties, and such heights, and depths, and lengths, and breadths in Divine wonders, that, as they read, they are constrained to pause, to wonder, to adore, to get breathing time in which to admire the intensity of the mysteries of Divine revelation. Thus St. Paul seemed to give vent to his meditations in Rom. xi. 33, or in Rom. vii. 24, 25, on a quite different subject. Don't you agree to this? Old writers dwell upon it till they put it almost in the place of a Saviour, just as more modern ones write of other parts of Christian experience. Cant. v. 10—16 is the sublimest meditation I know of, and it came out of the overflowings of a full heart, and not out of one set about to meditate because meditation was 'sweet' and profitable. I think the way to arrive at meditation, is, to read the words and revealed thoughts of

God, till you can't help it. Your own thoughts become so full of it, that you meditate almost unconsciously.

"Would that I knew more of this most blessed occupation!" she adds. "God grant that your letter may stir me up to fresh enjoyment of it by leading me more into those green pastures where (to use a homely illustration) one may eat the grass, and then chew the cud. I have kept up very well this summer in my invalidish way, living almost entirely up-stairs, and never once stirring beyond the garden. But I have suffered very little to what I used to do, and only long for grace to consecrate every energy of mind and body to our Jesus. Humanly speaking, I may live a great while longer in this sort of way. God bless you, while you live and when you die, 'and make you a blessing.'"

And again, on Oct. 19: "What depths of grace and of sin Christians have to learn out! The lower I sink, the higher grace rises. Ps. xcviii. 1, with 1 Cor. xv. 57, have been an immense comfort to me, God getting the victory *by* Himself and *for* Himself, and then in free grace giving it to us, so that we don't even conquer, but He does it all."

And to another, on Oct. 29: "Your gourd is withered before your eyes; but 'rejoice in the Lord, and joy in the God of your salvation.' You will find it an immense help to you in your spiritual advance to have made the sacrifice to God, no matter in what light the act may appear when viewed in reference to other things. I have long felt, that in our fear of denying ourselves, or doing good works *meritoriously*, we run into the opposite extreme of self-indulgence, and of amusing ourselves with innocent worldly pleasures and doing nothing for God. How we need to be kept in all these things, by the guidance of the Spirit of truth, lest in one way or other we fall into error!"

And she adds; "Oh! if one may but win one soul to Jesus, it is worth the sacrifice of one's whole life to do it; but *I* think we ought to *expect* to do a great deal, seeing that all the power is God's and He only wants to use us as a manufacturer sets his machine in motion. The wheels and pins don't do the work, and yet it is done by them. Is not that a strong expression, 'They limited the Holy One of Israel?' I will send you a splendid text—Luke v. 5, 6. It tells volumes of man's impotence (hours of fruitless toil), and God's omnipotence (working wonders in one moment by one word)! Faith, too, is the instrument—'At thy word I will let down the net.' Why don't we launch into the depths of God's love, and enclose such blessings as would well-nigh break our feeble 'earthen vessels?' There are multitudes of fishes in His ocean-fulness, which faith might catch! 'Lord increase our faith!'"

Her life grew more and more intensely earnest, as she hastened towards the mark. Writing to a bereaved friend, Nov. 16 (1849), she says: "Our correspondence has sadly broken down; but I never can keep one up only on one side—I never seem to know what exactly to write about: and to write about *anything* appears more like the unprofitable topics of conversation which too much occupy the world, than like the earnest intercourse of fellow-pilgrims to a better country;—above all, when, as is the case with us, we are both warned so emphatically by illness not to stop and play with flowers by the way. But I have been really anxious to assure you of my true sympathizing love under your late deep trials. With all the fulness of sympathy which is treasured up for us in Him on the way, and with the bright prospect before us of a happy and joyful re-union for ever in glory at the end, have not we enough to change 'the spirit of heaviness' into 'a garment of praise'?"

And a glimpse into her special experience at this period follows: "I do get to feel so much more every day, that nothing but the absolute, naked reality of having God in Christ for my portion and my everything, can satisfy me. I have been stripped bare this summer of those happy feelings which I used to enjoy so much, in order to be made to trust God without them, and, even when walking in darkness, to be stayed upon my God. (Isaiah l. 10.)* It has not made me unhappy, but it has emptied me of any joy which belonged to myself, and has shown me that the only true and abiding joy is in the Lord.

* Alluding to this subject in another letter, she says: "I know I owe this very mainly to dear Mr. Gell's sermons years ago, which the Holy Spirit was pleased to make use of in laying a foundation which no subsequent trials or storms could shake."

"Habakkuk," she adds, "was set to learn this lesson by being stripped of his outward comforts and reduced to poverty and distress—no meat from the flock, no herd in the stall—nevertheless he could say, 'Yet I will rejoice in the Lord, I will joy in the God of my salvation.' And David was set to learn it by bitter disappointment in his friends—'My soul, wait thou *only* upon God, for my expectation is from Him' (Ps. lxii.)—the whole Psalm showing how from rich and poor nothing could be expected in this world. Oh! it is hard—very, very hard—to learn this for one's-self, is it not? It has cost me many a bitter hour; but in one way or another I suppose we must each of us learn it. And I can't help thinking that you and I are being taught it—you more in the way that Habakkuk was, and I more in David's way; though every one has peculiarities belonging to their own peculiar characters and circumstances, and giving a varied colouring to their specific trials."

For a time it was intended that she should again winter in Torquay. "Though in most respects better," she writes on Nov. 17, "I feel conscious of the existence of the underground workings of disease, which others do not see. I have been quite in a swoon whilst writing this letter; but I am better again now, and wish to forget all these little things as soon as they are past. They are but the circumstances of the way, and are unworthy of a thought compared with the coming glory. Oh! that our hearts may be more engrossed with that! How near it may be to each of us! Come, Lord Jesus, come quickly!"

And, on Dec. 5, she writes: "The cold has attacked me at last, and I have gradually been tumbling down each day this week. I am just waiting for the pillar of cloud and fire to move first, and make it plain whether I am to go or stay." And a fortnight later: "I am well enough to have great expectations of staying at home altogether this winter, but God has given me to feel very willing to stay or go as He points out for me. Things seem so much more and more to me every day to be as though they were not: 1 Cor. vii. 29—31 is perpetually on my mind. I seem more to live upon God, less upon feelings and experience."

Another affecting glimpse into her inner life occurs in the same letter: "I long to own to you, dearest ——, though I have said it to no one else, that I have the feeling of having learned so much of such wonders of grace that I don't know what to say. I'm sure I need keeping down; and I don't think I can be thankful enough that the hungering, and thirsting, and fainting state is mine, rather than the fulness of happy joy which I once felt. That I may be emptied and Christ exalted, self crushed, and Jesus set up—these are the things I seem most to want. Only I cannot express it, even to you. Oh! the comfort—the intense comfort—of knowing that God reads the secret thoughts of our hearts which we cannot express! Still one wants to tell of His goodness, and to make our boast in Him. But it is hard to boast in Him, is it not?

"'I cannot make thy mercies known
But self-applause comes in!'"

When Henry Martyn left England and all its pleasant attractions, he "left it wholly for Christ's sake," says his biographer, "and he left it for ever." As he was on his voyage out, he wrote one day in his Diary this entry: "Sept. 23. We are just to the south of all Europe, and I bid adieu to it for ever, without a wish of ever re-visiting it, and still less with any desire of taking up my rest in the strange land to which I am going." It is this spirit of self-sacrifice which alone gives to the Church its power. With it she is like Samson in his Nazarite strength: without it she is Samson shorn of his locks and grinding in prison. "We are too prone by far," writes Adelaide, Dec. 19 (1849), indicating her impression of the Church's real condition, "to cry out for 'money—money,' and to be lamenting that we can give so little, whilst the secret truth is, that what God asks and expects is—OURSELVES. 'My son,' says God, 'give me thine heart;' and well did He know when he said that, that everything else would follow. At the present day few offer themselves to work for God without being well paid for it; and I begin to think we shall have to find that, if missionary work is to be done, it must be done by the sacrifice of ourselves. 'Here am I, send ME.'"

At the close of the year she decided to remain at

home. "God has made His way plain before me," she writes "I never felt so willing to have it all ordered for me before. I have strong indications now and then that the 'love-token' (as dear —— calls it) is not taken away; but my duty is 'patient waiting.' Oh! do ask for quickening grace for me. I hope you have enjoyed this Christmas in thoughts of the great mystery of godliness."

Her own "Christmas thoughts" she records in her Diary thus: "Most holy, holy, holy—*holy* God! we thank Thee that unto us a Son *is* born—unto us a Child is given; that the government shall be upon His shoulders, and that of the increase of His government there shall be no end, upon the throne of David and upon His kingdom, to order it and to establish it with judgment and with justice for ever; that a 'day' is coming in which He shall be revealed as 'King of kings, and Lord of lords,' when His name shall be on His vesture and on His thigh. May we know Him as the Saviour by whom our sins are all forgiven, and not only forgiven, but dethroned more and more every day! May Thy grace be mighty to subdue them all, that, not only in our spirits, but in our bodies, we may glorify God, till at length we come to realize more of the holy anticipations which are set before us in the brighter scenes and nobler society which we hope soon to join, in that countless throng among whom we, too, would cast our crowns before the throne, and before the Lamb who sitteth upon the throne for ever and ever!"

CHAPTER XI.

THIS winter and spring (1850) were occupied with her work on the SONG. "The demand for books at the present day," she writes, on March 16, to a friend who was publishing, "seems to me to make a wonderful opening for saying a word for Christ. And I am always glad when any one writes on the Bible; I think other books are only valuable in proportion as they lead to it. You will be surprised when I tell you that Nisbet has got an arrangement of texts of mine on Canticles. It was my happy employment, the two first years I was at Torquay, to find them out; and I have since written them out, just connecting them together with a few words. The way has been made so clear in regard to it, that I hope God intends for me to be a silent messenger for Him in that manner. It is a sweet subject; it is so full of Christ, and lets one into so much of the feelings of His heart towards His Church."

Henry Martyn once wrote in his Diary: "Read Isaiah the rest of the evening; sometimes happy, and at other times tired, and desiring to take up some other religious book; but I saw it an important duty to check this slighting of the Word of God." Dear

Adelaide found in the Word the very living manna from heaven. "I believe I may say with truth," she writes, "that some of the texts I sent you last have been the language of my heart both night and day. 'My soul thirsteth for God, for the living God; when shall I come and appear before God?' May you find the Lord's words an ever-deepening source of truest enjoyment, opening fresh beauties to your astonished gaze with every fresh discovery of the fading nature of all that Solomon calls 'vanity!' And may you ever have One present, as a Companion to whom you can talk without weariness or *ennui* in your most lonely hours!"

Growing in meekness, she grew in calm repose of spirit. "I do love all God's dealings with me," she writes, "and would have none of them altered, if I could. My burden is only what every Christian groans under—sin; and I know I shall never be rid of it till this body of sin is entirely destroyed, and we are altogether planted in the likeness of Christ's resurrection. Oh! will it not be wonderful to be a body of glory, emitting light in every direction, and dwelling in pure, essential light, 'raised in power,' all our present weakness and dishonour having passed away, so that even Jesus shall be admired and glorified in us? And I have liked so much lately to think how this bright ray of glory, instead of casting a shadow upon everything here, rather sheds a beam of light to gild our pathway heavenwards."

A birthday wish for a beloved sister she breathes forth thus: "*January* 29, 1850. As a tree of righteousness planted in the garden of the Lord by His own right hand, and as a branch of the true vine, grafted into Jesus, may you be daily more and more 'filled with the fruits of righteousness, which are by Jesus Christ to the glory and praise of God!' and further still, may the precious promise be fulfilled in you, 'And her leaf shall be green!' (Jer. xvii. 7, 8.) Even the smallest things about us should be full of the sap of the Holy Spirit."

The "great cloud of witnesses" "declared plainly that they sought a country." Not less plainly did dear Adelaide "declare" to all around her where she was going. "The words, 'household of God,'" she writes, "have often struck me lately as beautifully expressing the full realization of what is now only 'the household of faith.' And when one strongly feels the unsatisfactoriness of seeing 'through a glass darkly,' it is impossible not to long to launch into the full blaze of light—in God, when all the members of the now scattered family shall for ever meet in the 'Father's House.' I don't think I ever knew so well before what it is to be sensibly nearing the port by every passing hour as I have done lately. It is a real and precious truth, whether the time be comparatively long or short; and it seems to help me on wonderfully, though I have no idea whereabouts I am. It is sad and really painful to *be* a child, and have so little of a child's feeling towards such a Father. But if I am only humbled under it, I believe it will magnify the exceeding riches of the freeness of grace."

What joy and what strength we often lose by being overcome of little trials! "In the midst of plenty to try me," she writes, Jan. 11 (1850), "I have been so quiet, that I can only say it shows what 'the peace of God' can do. It is not great troubles, but constant, wearing annoyances, that I refer to—little daily trials; but I don't feel them at all as I used to do. 'They shall not be ashamed that wait for me.'"

The delicate organism of the "new creature" she realized with a growing sensitiveness. "How very precious His thoughts are," she writes, "when we can at all enjoy 'fellowship with the Father and with His Son Jesus Christ!' and yet how easily—oh! I can scarcely believe, and cannot tell you, how easily—I let sin interrupt and hinder me from coming near before Him! But, if it surprises me, it is no matter of surprise to Him who knew from the beginning what a transgressor I should be. Don't you think this thought is one which gives us most confidence in God? If anything could happen which He had not foreseen, it might change His mind towards us; but all His thoughts being to give us 'an expected end,' does seem so intensely to assure our hearts before Him, does it not?"

In spite of an oppressive langour, incident to her complaint at some of its stages, and, this spring, peculiarly trying, she laboured on at her work. "I have lately been transcribing," she writes, Feb. 6 (1850), "the whole of the texts on Solomon's Song. It seems to be the way God has marked out for me to serve

Him; and I desire from the heart, to say, 'Thy will be done.' Precious, indeed, is the privilege of serving such a Master in the humblest ways—whether in passive waiting or in active serving. I often have days on which I am all but good for nothing; but, after all, these bodily fluctuations are but a small thing. How we ought to long for powers to serve God *perfectly!* and yet, let patience have her perfect work first."

Vinet, speaking of "the look directed towards Jesus," and contrasting it with "meditations and discussions on free will, or assurance, or the connexion between faith and works, and even on the properties of faith"—all which, he says, "tend to occupy us too much with ourselves, and give too strong a hold to that vivacious self-interest which catches at and clings to everything," remarks: "In proportion as it is prolonged, it inspires our soul with a holy enthusiasm, a holy love. It makes those dispositions habitual and dominant in our heart. It becomes at once the light and the heat of our life. It facilitates, simplifies, illumines all. It does better than refute doubts, it absorbs them. In its brightness, all their equivocal or false glimmerings are quenched." Adelaide Newton, each new day, entered more deeply into this momentous truth. "The watchword I chose for the new year," she writes, on Feb. 6 (1850), "was—'Heirs of God.' I think we are too much taken up, as Christians, with our Christian character and duties, and meditate far too little on our possessions and privileges. God, and nothing less, is our inheritance; for we are 'joint-heirs with Christ.' 'Tis true that it involves 'if so be that we suffer with Him' now for a few days on the earth; but then it is in fellowship with a risen Jesus, and it leads to everlasting glory with Him hereafter. I send it you to think of, and *make your boast of:* we *may* glory in the Lord, you know!"

It was this peculiar characteristic of her Christian life which gave such fragrance to her words. She was ever herself dwelling in the light; and her aim, in every letter and in every conversation, was to bring others up with her into the same light. "Don't you think," she writes to a friend, on Feb. 7 (1850), "there is something very sweet in being comforted and refreshed together by our 'mutual faith?' I have another most precious word from the mouth of our God to send you—at least one that has been a great comfort to me in giving me fresh courage about dearest ——, when I had begun to be very desponding—'There is no restraint to the Lord:' whether the outward circumstances be encouraging or not, whether 'with many or with few,' it is equally easy to Him to save. And there is one thought which I have enjoyed resting upon, in connexion with these circumstances, very much lately, viz., that what Omniscient love has proposed, Omnipotent love will bring to pass. What a Rock that is to fall back upon, when the waves of affliction toss one to and fro!"

"I enclose," she continues, "some very sweet texts for you. Two, particularly, have struck me very much. One was, when Jesus was praying in the garden for the removal (three times over) of His bitter cup (not composed of one thorn, like St. Paul's, but of a crown of thorns, &c.), instead of His request being granted, He only seemed to get the same answer St. Paul got—"My grace is sufficient for thee.' 'There appeared an angel from heaven strengthening Him.' I thought it was very strengthening to us, in similar circumstances of prolonged trial, to be brought into such evident fellowship with Jesus in His sufferings.

"'I of this cup am drinking,
To be conformed to thee.'

The other text was in the 12th of St. John; the remarkable contrast between those two little prayers of Christ's—'Father, save Me from this hour;' and, 'Father, glorify Thy name.' The first prayer for His own deliverance from trial He Himself seemed to negative—'but for this cause came I unto this hour; whilst the second prayer, for God's glory, was immediately answered by the voice from heaven. Does it not teach us a very sweet lesson about prayer, at the same time affording the precious evidence that prayer for deliverance from the hour of trial is 'Christ-like'—only it is swallowed up in the yet dearer object to a Christian's heart, his Father's glory? It is so blessed to know that we are praying as Christ prayed."

"Oh! I cannot tell you," she adds, "how I feel for all the aggravating circumstances of trial which press on you just now; but 'everlasting arms' are upholding you, and I know it is love appoints it all. What a depth of unutterably precious meaning is enfolded in that one word—'God is love!' I was thinking of the words, 'I will be to you a God,' this afternoon, in the sense of a God of love—'I will be to you Love.' Don't you think it throws a glowing tint, as it were, over all His dealings with us? The words you once gave me—'Thy righteousness is like the great mountains, and Thy judgments are a great deep'—have been helping me to think of the heights and depths of the love of Christ lately; for everything God does, seems to be swallowed up in love.

On another occasion, taking up those words, "Our days on the earth are as a shadow, and there is none abiding," she says:—"It struck me as full of meaning, when our years are counted by days, as they are in Scripture—'The days of our years are threescore years and ten.' It really seems more consistent with the pilgrim character to reckon by days, does it not? (James iv. 13, 14, 15.) 'Here have we no continuing city, but we seek one to come'—'a better country' (or, as some render it, a home, or fatherland)—'Strangers and pilgrims on the earth.' And is it not a gracious contrast?—'days on the earth,' but eternity in heaven! Days of sufferings, but pleasures for evermore! 'Our days on the earth are as a shadow,'

"'But the bright world to which we go
Hath joys substantial and sincere.'"

She was no "lingerer" at the gates of Sodom.

"Oh! why," we find her inquiring, "are we not more transformed into the very image of Jesus? I think it is because we so little seek the indwelling of His Spirit. It is so vain to reform our lives, words, and acts, unless the transformation springs, from first to last, from the *root*, and source, and author of life within us—is it not? I will send you, 'Her leaf shall be *green*' (Jer. xvii. 8), with 'I shall be anointed with *fresh oil*' (Ps. xcii. 10)—the sap or the oil of the Spirit. Dear —— is reading me 'M'Cheyne's Life' again: how sweet it is! He did so realize his full acceptance and completeness in Jesus. And why should not we? I was greatly struck by a remark from a dear friend in D——, the other day: 'I only see two men in the word—Adam and Jesus; and I think God only sees two. All are seen as either in Jesus or in fallen Adam. Christians are lost sight of, and Jesus is seen; and God treats Christians as part of Christ.' Don't you think we should try more and more to forget ourselves as individuals, and to see ourselves as parts of a whole—members of a Body, burying *self*, our *religious* self, quite as much as our natural self.

Her happy thoughts of God both lightened her own trials and "gave her the tongue of the learned to speak a word in season to the weary." "I will not take up your time," she says, after mentioning some details about her illness, "by writing about these seen things, which are but for a moment. How soon they will be forgotten for ever, except as the goodness and tender mercy of our Father in heaven is developed and exhibited in them!" And, writing to another, on February 16, she says: "I really can only think of you and —— as in the midst of the burning fiery furnace heated seven times: but I always see a fourth, like unto the Son of God, with you; and your furnace is heated by love, and not by 'the wrath of the king.' It is 'the furnace of affliction' in which you were 'chosen.' How wonderful to be 'purified seven times!'"

And on February 28: "I shall be entering to-morrow on the twenty-sixth year of my sojourning on earth. Ask for me, that whether for time or for eternity I may henceforward walk in the light of God's countenance. Do you remember talking to me once about 'Jesus lifting up His eyes to heaven?' (John xvii. 1.) How His eye would always meet the downward glance of His Father's eye! It has given me such sweet, happy thoughts about our heavenly Father's countenance. For, in Jesus, the same must always be true of us. And don't you think the Father's face is always irradiated with looks of love, the natural dictates of His heart of love, and that His countenance always beams with lovingkindness? Oh, will it not be wonderful to look up full into our Father's face, and really to be able to enjoy the blaze of that light as it beams from His countenance in glory? I think those words in Jude give us such a wonderful idea of our perfectness in Christ, that He is able to present us faultless before the presence of His glory. In that excess of brightness, that light where there is 'no darkness,' to be 'faultless!' And, dear ——, is it not as true now of you and me in Jesus, as it is of dear B—— C——, who really was presented there this day last year? So that God is lifting up the light of His countenance upon us even now. It does seem so wonderful that we can desire to come into contact with such light—the very thing which by nature we so shrink from: 'Men loved darkness rather than light.'"

And to another: "I have no idea whatever now of seeing you or Torquay. Perhaps never! But it is enough to know, that He who sees, leads His blind ones safely and rightly. Oh, it is sweeter than I can express, to leave it there! How good God has been to me, to make me feel it so! I wish I knew how to be thankful; but I shall not have to wait a bit too long for powers to praise, when Jesus will be Himself the leader of the praises of His people 'in the great congregation.'"

And to a deeply-tried friend, a week later, thus: "The verse I should like to send you is Ps. xlii. 7: 'All *thy* waves and billows are gone over me'—*tides of love*, 'waves and billows' springing out of the ocean of God's love, so that they cannot overwhelm, but only plunge us into its unfathomable depths. I have thought of it many times for you in connexion with Phil. ii. 27—'God had mercy on him, and not on him only, but on me also, lest I should have sorrow upon sorrow.' And it is followed so beautifully in the next verse, by God commanding His lovingkindness in the day-time, and enabling the soul even in the dark night to sing 'His song.'"

Not the Spirit's work in her, but Christ's work for her, was still the object of her daily thought. "I often feel," she writes, "that we go tossing about on the tides of Christian experience, which are for ever fluctuating, instead of lying peacefully at anchor on the Rock of Ages." And in another letter, of March 6: "I cannot find a single instance in which, either in the Gospels or in the Epistles, Christians are taught by example or by precept to make a study of their own hearts. I cannot help thinking that Christian experience has far too much taken the place of the study of Christ and of the character of God, and that this accounts in great measure for the low and desponding state of so very many Christians. Do you not think that the constant study of His character would far more effectually teach us our depravity than poring into our own?"

And on March 30: "This morning, under some peculiarly trying circumstances, those words, 'Be careful for *nothing*,' came home to me with such fresh power! I believe that, in the very act of making everything known to God, His peace fills our souls. Have you ever noticed that joy and peace are the two things Jesus came into the world to bring—'on earth peace,' 'glad tidings of great joy?' And they are the two things which, during His last conversations with His disciples, He seemed most specially to have on His mind—'These things have I spoken unto you, that in me ye might have peace;' 'These things have I spoken unto you, that my joy in you might remain, and that your joy in me might be full.' (This last verse is literally rendered from the original.) So these are the two things I would especially desire for you as your purchased right and privilege to enjoy in Jesus."

Adelaide was, by birth and education, and also by enlightened attachment, a member of the Church of England. But "Christ first, the Church next," was her guiding maxim; and the more she frequented "the light," the more did the two objects assume their due proportions. "As to our own Church," she writes, on April 2 (1850), "in what a fearful state it is in Devonshire! What should we do but for the assurance, 'The government shall be upon *His* shoulders?' I think the Chnrch is merging her character of Christ's bride into that of an ecclesiastical body; and I see no remedy but for each member individually to seek to belong to it rather in the former sense than in the latter—a bride in communion with her Beloved—a believer panting after secret intercourse with Jesus. May each of us enter closer into Him, and hide us deeper in Him! So we shall be safe, come what will."

Her forthcoming book she refers to, on April 15, thus: "Will you take the burden of this work and cast it on the Lord for me? Tell Him the book is His—written with His time, His teaching, His talents, by one whose purchased property it all is. Certainly there is a vast mixture of sinful infirmity to mar and defile it; but then He chooses base things. So, you see, I draw comfort from my baseness! Do implore His blessing on it for me." If works done in His service were oftener gone about in this way, we should seldomer hear of blunt sickles and sheafless reapers.

And, in the same letter, she says: "I have heard from dear ——. She sent me two half-sheets full—very kind, and to me very hopeful. Not a word of actual religion; but then, you know, she is not one to profess even what she feels. And throughout it there is to me an evident consciousness that her whole way of living is wrong and unsatisfying, and that she does not enjoy it, and can't. She declares she likes me to write to her, and says she would write to me if she could say anything worth saying. Indeed, I do think God is at work with her, embittering the world by degrees. She is giving up balls, and wishes for quieter amusements: when she tries these she won't find them the least more satisfying: and may we not well hope that in due season she will give up seeking it anywhere but where it is to be found? He who alone is able to save her yearns over her far more fondly than you or I. What a sweet assurance!"

Notwithstanding the Derbyshire climate, her health this spring rather improved. "I suppose," she says, "I must say a word about the earthly hut! It has weathered the severe winter, under the shelter of 'the shadow of the Almighty,' most bravely; and here I am at home, better rather than worse. I look on and wonder. God is having His way, His 'higher' way than mine; and I am waiting on Him, I hope, to know and do His bidding."

And her soul flourished like the palm tree. "I get calmer rest at times in His love than ever before," she writes. "But I constantly feel that conflict lies before me, and I want very much to be prepared for it. Have you thought much about the Evil One and his associates? (Eph. vi. 12—margin.) What part of the Word is occupying you most? Is it not sweet to be sitting under his shadow? While all other shadows are so essentially 'fleeting,' with Him there is 'no variableness neither shadow of turning.' He is at once the Sun, the Rock, and the Shadow. Precious Saviour!"

The bane of the religious world is religious dissipation. There is not a little gathering of the manna; but there is not much of it eaten. The consequence is, a cry everywhere heard, "My leanness, my leanness!" Dear Adelaide escaped this snare. "I reckon it one of the greatest privileges I ever enjoyed," she writes, April 15 (1850), "to have been taken out of even the busy *religious* world, and led to look into the deep things of God, which He has so wonderfully revealed in His word." It was this earnest, personal, daily communing with God through the Word, which gave to her life so healthful a tone. It is the absence of this intense individual meditation which, like a canker-worm, is eating out the Church's life.

The sympathy of Jesus was ever yielding her

fresh consolation. "I should like to send you," she writes on April 19, "a verse which has been comforting me very much this week; for I felt unusually weary for a few days at the beginning of it. It is Matt. ix. 36 (*marg.*), 'When He saw the multitudes He had compassion on them, because they were *tired* and *lay down*.' If He has still the same feelings which He had when He was on earth, how sweet it is to know that His eye is upon each feeble and weary child, and that His compassion can be moved by the sight of even our bodily tiredness! Oh! if we could but see His look! how feeling a look it is! 'His eyes are as doves' eyes. Just fancy Him, for example, looking down from the cross upon His mother—what a look it must have been!"

"No, I don't find it solitary," said a Tuscan confessor lately to one who was condoling with him on his imprisonment in a cell; "I have with me here Faith, Hope, and Charity." One of these heavenly visitors Adelaide especially prized. "I have been searching out texts on 'Hope,'" she writes on April 30; "they are so beautiful, and it seems to me a grace so very litle cultivated and sought after! Yet surely it is one for the advancing believer to be abounding in, just in proportion as he is 'filled with joy and peace in believing.' There is such certainty in the Scripture-meaning of 'hope;' and I think the real meaning of Rom. viii. 24 is so precious, though our translation dims it—'We are *upheld* by hope?"

With a singular precision we find her defining the Bible-teaching upon another subject, thus: "Did I ask you if you had ever thought of the 'sealing' and 'witnessing' of the Spirit? A Scotch friend asked me about it, thinking they were the same; but I see manifold differences, one especially, that the 'sealing' is a past and finished work in its main sense, whilst the 'witnessing' is the Spirit's present testimony to the truth of all that God has testified about Jesus—a daily taking of the things of Christ and showing them to us."

Her heart was thus drawn away from itself entirely, and was fixed exclusively upon the Word, "My text for you," she writes on April 30, "is, 'I hope in thy Word.' I do so like the naked promise or bare Word of God to be made the stay of the soul. How very, very little we think what it is to rely on that Word with such excessive caution, as if we must be careful how far we trust it! It is surely making God a liar to doubt it. I sometimes think we look upon a certain kind of unbelief as humility, whereas to doubt the truth of the words, 'He that hath the Son, *hath life*,' is as great unbelief as to doubt that 'him that cometh unto me, I will in nowise cast out.' Oh! how little we seem to have learned of the truth as it is in Jesus, when He has been years in teaching us! there is so little 'reaching forth unto things before!'"

Tersteegen has finely said, that "the first poison which steals into faithful souls is, that they imperceptibly place their righteousness and their confidence in their fidelity, in self-denial, in their virtues and graces, in their devotional exercises, and not entirely in God alone. The Saviour then opens our eyes, as with our own clay; and thus His wonder-working hand has alone the glory, and we the shame." "I do really believe," Adelaide writes on May 1, "that it is God's grand aim to humble and empty us; and to be emptied of fancied religiousness is the most painful lesson, I think, one can learn. Since we cannot keep our hearts low, God keeps us in a low condition; and perhaps we are never so truly living on Him as when we feel to lie lowest."

And she adds: "I have been thinking very much lately about Christ being 'made to us sanctification.' Don't you think we are very apt to look to His death on the cross as if our whole salvation lay wrapt up in it alone—forgetting that His death only put away our sin, and that, if we want holiness, it is to the thirty-three years of his life that we must turn? I can give you no idea of the comfort it has been to me, when feeling I could neither pray, nor love, nor believe, nor do anything, to plead all these things as perfectly performed by Christ for me." And elsewhere she adds: "Seriously I do think that many Christians take Christ only as half a Saviour; they so little realize that it is His faith, His obedience, His everything through life, which is to be pleaded as ours, as well as His death and resurrection."

Alluding to a deeply-tried saint at Torquay, she writes, on May 3: "How wonderfully some people are detained in their clay prisons! And yet only that God may get Himself more glory at the appearing of Jesus Christ! Perhaps none will join as cordially in the praises of 'the great congregation' in glory as those who have had most here to be delivered from. Oh! the depth of the riches of God's wisdom, and knowledge, and love! Oh, dear ——, we shall never get to the bottom of that depth—never, never! It is a marvel to be on the brink of being swallowed up in it!"

And, in another letter, speaking of Jesus as "the leader of His people's praises in glory," she says: "Surely His praises in 'the great congregation,' so often referred to in the Psalms, must ultimately mean 'the Church perfected.' And how sweet it is to feel that He will then be able to take the lead in every song of praise which any of us can sing, as *having personally known* every trouble from which we can praise God for being delivered!"

A schoolfellow, after seeking rest in intense worldliness, had begun to seek it in Ritualism. "Don't let it distress you," she writes to a mutual friend concerning her: "she will perhaps try formal religion as she has the world. The latter has already disgusted her, I hope; and 'in due season' I hope the former will, still more. How many try everything but the right thing, till, when everything else has failed, they are just driven to *it* of absolute necessity! Go on taking her to Christ to be healed; and so surely as He never sent away one sickly, miserable body unhealed on earth, so surely do I believe He will send away no sick soul unhealed in heaven, but still He keeps saying, 'If thou canst believe, all things are possible.'"

And to another schoolfellow, on her marriage: "Though you are not to read this to-morrow, it will show you, by its outside merely, that 'the day' is not forgotten. I send you some texts as a very tiny and humble remembrance of it. I know you value God's Word above gold and fine gold, and the adorning which is of such great price in His sight, far more than any little thing I could have sent you to adorn a poor perishing body of clay. When our days on the earth have passed away like a dream, and our outward adorning has decayed and waxed old, *we* shall still be living witnesses, I trust, of the great realities and joys of eternity! clothed with immortality! covered with the robe of righteousness! arrayed in pure white linen robes! beautified with salvation, and crowned with life and glory! Our road to all that lies through much tribulation; but Christ's presence by the way tinges every dark cloud with brightness, and throws a sacred light on every step we take. So, now, dearest A——, I sum up my best wishes for you in the heartfelt desire that His presence may shine on you all through your journey, and crown your journey's end."

Hewitson remarked one day—"I am better acquainted with Jesus than with any friend I have on earth." Dear Adelaide's Christian life gradually assumed more and more of this hue. "Try to cultivate," she writes on May 15 (1850), "the thought of Jesus as a *personal Friend*—a real, true, living Person;—just as truly so in heaven at this moment as I am in this room. You don't see either of us; but you know I am here, and you can think of me; so you know He is there, and you can think of Him. Only with this vast and unspeakably precious difference, that you can only hold intercourse with me at intervals, and by letters or messages through other people, but you can always hold intercourse with Him, at any moment, and without any medium for it to pass through.

"Oh! the mystery," she continues, "is to my mind so intensely wonderful and so sweet, of God's Spirit dwelling at once in Christ and in us, so that we have literally actual personal communion both with the Father and with His Son, through the one Spirit which dwells in us all. It would be frightful to dare to think or speak of it, if it were not so plainly revealed; but now, I think, it is our privilege to know it—and our own fault if we don't, because God says he is willing to give the Holy Spirit to all that ask for it; and 1 Cor. ii. 9—16 teaches us what amazing things we may know if the Holy Spirit is our Teacher."

And she adds: "This is a secret work, just such as you want. No one need know of it but yourself and your Father which seeth in secret. I am convinced that the more you make Jesus your most intimate Friend, breathing out all your secret thoughts into His ear by the Spirit (or the breath of life), the more you will find that gloomy forebodings vanish—you will forget them, not by trying to do so, but by being pre-occupied with weightier matters. And you will never regret going to ——, to be much alone perhaps with the unseen God—if it be, as I hope it will be, a time for leading you to your Bible, in which your spirit may meet God's Spirit, and your solitude be exchanged for the sweetest conversations that can be enjoyed on earth—those, viz., between God and your own soul."

Her "Cómmentary on the Song" appeared at the end of May, and was very favourably received. "I feel thankful to God," she writes on June 17, "for making my book of the least use. It was a bold step, certainly—such a writer, on such a subject! But God chooses weak things and base things, hiding His counsels from the wise and prudent, and revealing them unto babes. And if He choose to make me one of those babes, He had a right to do so, and will get Himself glory in the act."

The "babe" appeared in other ways also. "I used to write with great enjoyment to myself," she says; "but I'm afraid a secret self-satisfaction in so doing had crept over me, for lately I have been peculiarly humbled in this particular way. Even the enjoyment of His own Word God has shown me to be a thing I cannot have just when and as *I* will, but purely by the gift of free, sovereign grace, to be bestowed when and as God sees best for me. It has been just the same with prayer, and in short with everything. I seem to be beginning to find out the bitter and painfully humbling reality that I am literally reduced to the condition of a beggar. Oh! will you ask especially for me more of that love which vaunteth not itself and is not puffed up?"

CHAPTER XII.

It has been said that the Church's life is a perpetual resurrection—an incessant coming forth from the tomb. Daily dying, she daily lives.

"Have you ever thought particularly," Adelaide writes, May 22 (1850), "of 2 Cor. i. 6? It has struck me so much to-day, our salvation being 'wrought' (*marg.*) 'in the enduring of the same sufferings' which the apostles suffered. I do think people make 'suffering' to mean too much and too often bodily sufferings. We don't read of the sufferings of the apostles in illness, but in bearing or doing the Lord's work: and the more I think of it, the more I feel, what I used to feel when I was so ill, that the bodily part was not the prominent part in God's eye even then. It was the struggle betwixt my will and His will; and it is the same still. Indeed, I feel we make too much of these bodies at all times—pampering them with sensual indulgences when well, and, when ill, taking fresh occasion therefrom to serve the flesh! But it seems to me that the mental conflicts, whether in trial or in prosperity, are the sufferings which work so much for our salvation. I am very much tried in some ways mentally—I feel so stagnant! but I am able to rejoice in what God is; and I hope all this is to humble me, and to lay me and keep me low."

The Lord continued to use her as a labourer in His fields. "I have just had a most encouraging letter," she writes, "from an invalid cousin, who has long been in search of holiness, but looked for it in herself rather than in Christ for her. I hope I have been the hand to hold the pen to say what God had to be said to her. Oh! how intensely one is made to feel that we are no more than the instrument through which God the Spirit speaks! We may talk endlessly, and in vain; but HE speaks, and it is done."

Fresh thoughts on the Word rose day by day. "I send you Ps. xxxv. 1–3," she writes to one of her sisters, June 20. "Fancy asking God to take hold of shield and buckler, and stand up for us! as if our armour must be in His hands, not in ours! This so comforted me. And those words in v. 3—'Say unto my soul, I am thy salvation!' It seems to me one of the most comprehensive prayers in the Bible; and so beautifully unlike the gaoler's 'What must *I do* to be saved?' So self-renouncing, and so Christ-exalting! Oh! for more of this spirit! Never do we feel so safe, I am sure. 'Behold, God is my salvation; I will trust,' &c. Then we are happy, let what will fail besides."

Like the heliotrope, occupying itself hourly with the sun, Adelaide occupied herself hourly with Christ. "I have been greatly enjoying the beginning of the first epistle of John," she writes. "One is struck with the all-absorbing theme in the apostle's mind—no truth nor doctrine, but JESUS. And the way in which he introduces Him—'That which was from the beginning!' It seems a natural and favourite train of thought, for he began his Gospel in the same way. Intimate as he had been with Jesus as the Son of man, he loved to go further back and think of Him as the eternal Son of the Father. It would seem as if Jesus loved to go back in thought to the same point—see Prov. viii. 22–31, where He declares that, in the beginning, He was rejoicing always before God. So that it is just a proof how John had caught his Master's spirit."

"And then," she proceeds, "'which we have seen with our eyes.' Jesus said that His disciples were to be His 'witnesses' (John xv. 27); and John could declare that it was no delusive imagination, but actual reality, what he had seen (i. 14.) He had seen the sufferings of Gethsemane, the scenes in the palace of Caiaphas, the death on the cross, the empty sepulchre (xx. 8), and his risen Saviour (xx. 20, 25, 29). Therefore, he could speak with all the holy confidence of a man knowing that he has the truth on his side (xix. 35). But his tender spirit was not content to bear so cold and heartless a testimony; so he added—'Which we have looked upon,' as though his heart had moved him to gaze, to watch, to look with eager eye! As, for instance, when he heard Jesus say from the cross, 'Behold thy mother!' could he ever forget how he had looked up to Jesus, while Jesus looked down upon him? He seemed, too, to notice the very minutest actions of Jesus, twice recording of Him that in prayer He 'lifted up His eyes' (xi. 41 and xviii. 1). It reminds one of our eyes waiting on the Lord, as David says, in Ps. cxxiii. 2.

"Then it follows," she continues, "'And our hands have *handled*.' Is not this very precious experience? as if the 'beloved' disciples of Jesus could never be content with anything short of direct personal contact with Him. He might have been heard and seen, and even looked upon, at a little distance, just as when Zaccheus was in the sycamore-tree he could hear Him, see Him, and even look down upon Him, with ardent delight; but it was as nothing to the joy of receiving Him into His own house! This is something nearer and dearer, involving the intimacy of personal intercourse. Mary might have tasted it, when she 'sat at His feet;' and the poor sinner, in the Pharisee's house, when she washed His feet with her tears and wiped them with the hair of her head; and Simeon, when he took up 'the child Jesus in his arms;' and the poor trembling, woman who came behind Him and touched the border of His garment and was cured. But John, more emphatically than any other, enjoyed the precious privilege, 'leaning on His bosom.' None so 'handled' Him besides, or had that place on His heart."

And she adds: "There are wonderful thoughts connected also with the expression, 'the Word of life.' Life being so clothed in human form as to be rendered visible and capable of being 'handled.' Jesus, too, being the expression of God—'the Word of God.' (Rev. xix. 13; John i. 1, &c.) It has seemed to me as if John felt that he had been uttering thoughts so deep, that they almost needed a word of explanation (in the second verse of the epistle, which he adds in a parenthesis). Do you think it is so? I like to think of his nameless way of speaking about Jesus—'That which was from the beginning;' and, 'That which we have seen and heard:' it is all Jesus; and it is not so much His words, or His actions, as Himself—'My meditation of Him shall be sweet.' And truly our fellowship is with the Father and with His Son Jesus Christ.' I don't think I know any text in the Bible to link with this one, except the 'communion of the Holy Ghost.' It does seem to me such a climax of wonder. Only John xvii. equals it, I think—'As thou, Father, art in me, and I in thee, that they also may be one in us.' Is it not too much for language to give utterance to?"

And to another, on July 2 (1850): "How glad I was to hear you say you felt happier by looking more to Jesus! A nice young woman came to see me the other evening; and, as she was alluding to her lonely position, without father, mother, brother, or sister—and often finding herself misunderstood (she is so very shy) and thought distant when she meant to be kind—she suddenly stopped, and said, 'But I tell HIM all about it, and that always takes the weight off me.' I thought it was so very simple,

Oh! that we did but know more of the simplicity which is in Christ Jesus! It often strikes me so peculiarly about *faith.* People puzzling themselves so, to know whether they are acting faith or not; whilst, if they were looking at Jesus, they would be believing, probably without knowing it, and every look at Him would be strengthening their faith. I think we often lose immensely by studying doctrines and principles instead of a living Christ. He is the image of the invisible God, and the very essence of heaven's happiness. Have you ever traced Him in the Gospels (Luke especially), as betraying in everything He said or did such extreme loveliness of character? It seems to me to draw out our feelings of love and adoration towards Him in return—often, perhaps, insensibly at the time, but very really."

And again, on July 16: "Do you know a sweet little hymn, beginning,

"'Nearer, my God, to Thee; nearer to Thee'?

I am so very fond of it. All day long, my heart seems to be panting after nearness to Jesus. Oh! what will heaven be—to be with the Lord!' But do you not think that we might know a great deal of heaven upon earth, if we only walked more closely with God? if our eyes were spiritually open to see His beauty all the day long, and our ears spiritually open to hear all He has to say to us in His Word?"

And she adds: "It is very much on my mind just now, that we do not think enough of the blood of Christ. Under the Old Testament dispensation, it was the *one* thing they had to think of every day; and in heaven we know we shall be ever singing, 'Worthy is the Lamb that was slain:' and our conduct here as Christians does not seem to agree with all this—do you think it does?"

The day before he died, Samuel Rutherford gave to some brethren who visited him, this charge: "My Lord and Master is the chief of ten thousand of thousands; none is comparable to Him in heaven or on earth. Dear brethren, do all for HIM; pray for Christ, preach for Christ, feed the flock committed to your charge for Christ, do all for Christ!" Dear Adelaide, rejoicing in this self-consecration, writes (July 18): "Oh! it is indeed sweet, dear L——, to lay ourselves out in the service of our covenant-God in Christ. I am certain none can ever regret the time, or health, or life so spent. Each one, in our different spheres, must spend it differently; but if laid out honestly 'to the Lord,' it shall assuredly be abundantly repaid us, in time as well as hereafter. I, for instance, can no longer visit the poor and read to them as I once did; God demands a different service from me now. But still He finds me work of some kind or other to do every day. I can say a word for Him in a letter; or, as opportunity offers, I can speak to the servants; or I can talk of Him, and tell out what I learn of Him, to my sisters or to visitors. This last was one of my chief opportunities at Torquay."

"It *is* often extremely difficult," she adds, "to feel inclined for this one's-self, and perhaps even more so to have courage to introduce it with others; but if you will give me leave to say it, I do believe that all these difficulties vanish and fade away in proportion as 'the love of Christ constraineth us' to live henceforth not to ourselves but to Him. They are wonderfully cleared away for us, too, by prayer—spreading them out before God, as Hezekiah did his letter from Sennacherib. He can and often does, I am sure, open ways for us to speak and act for Him, when we may or may not look out for them—provided only we ask Him each day to teach us what He will have us to do. Only tell Him you wish Him to employ you, and He will soon give you enough to do."

A man in understanding, an infant in heart! The child occupies itself with its father—expects everything from him. "My father loves me:" what more is needed to make the little child—itself so poor—rich in all its father's treasures? This infancy of the heart led forth dear Adelaide daily, with a new simplicity and a new confidence, upon Him who had loved her and given Himself for her. Sending a message, on July 29, to a friend who was "still troubled by looking inwards," she says: "My book on Solomon's Song might cure her of that habit of looking at herself, not by telling her not to do it, but by bewitching her with Christ's loveliness. Don't be shocked at my recommending it; for it just says (without saying so) what cured me of a like habit. Dear —— was the blessed instrument of making me quite forget myself by looking at God in Christ; and I hope God will bless that book to the same end.

'My soul hangeth upon Thee,' are words which I can truly enter into just now. Self is sinking lower, and Christ *is* getting more of His right place, though it is rather through humbling than through happy experience."

On another subject she writes, August 13, thus: "I am enjoying your dear uncle's book, 'The Church and the Churches,' most exceedingly just now. I was reading yesterday his chapter on 'Holiness,' and was more than ever struck with that wonderful doctrine of Reward. How sweet it is to feel ourselves as clay in the hands of the potter, trusting that for His own glory He will fashion us into beautiful vessels—'vessels unto honour!' emptied of self, and filled with all the fulness of God! Oh! how one dreads to mar the beauty of His work, by defiling that temple of God!"

And on Aug. 17: "Let me send you Hos. ii. 19, 20, with the thought especially, that it is Jesus who betrothes you, and not you Him—so that the thing is, to question His love to you, not your love to Him; and of His love there cannot well be any room to doubt—can there?"

And on Sept. 2: "I am certain we need great variety of discipline; and we get it—illness, health, mental trial, family trial, great outward things, and multitudinous tiny, inward, fretting, sort of things—yes, all sorts, to show us what constant need we have of all-sufficient grace, and what innate propensities there are in us to be always starting off from a life of faith to a life of sight. Oh! the power of seen things! I think one of the great lessons I have been learning out is my exceeding sinfulness—not the sin of transgression, so much as the sin of my nature, my leprous state."

Not boastfully, but in humble thankfulness, she writes, Oct. 1: "I thank my God for all you say about my book; and I can't tell you how many encouraging testimonies He has given me of His having spoken through it many a word in season. It has been chiefly blessed, I think, in showing tried Christians how perfect and complete they are in Jesus, drawing off their thoughts from themselves almost insensibly. One, in particular, said that whilst she was enduring the most intense agony from 'tic douloureux' all over her, it seemed 'exactly the cordial she needed.' But I need not multiply instances: if Jesus gets a ray of glory through it, 'tis enough."

And to another: "I have been very deeply interested lately in 'Owen on Hebrews:' it has led me to see beauties and a preciousness in the priestly character and work of Christ which I never thought of before. One short sentence struck me exceedingly—'The want of living up to this truth (His priestly intercession) evacuates the religion of most men in the world.' But after all," she adds, "I find nothing like the Bible itself. There one seems to hear the whispers of God's own Spirit, breathing through His own very words. And it all tells of Jesus; and nothing is put betwixt us and Him. We ourselves, as His peculiar people, are His holy priesthood; and Jesus is our great High Priest; and we go direct to Him with the acceptable sacrifice of a broken and contrite spirit. And oh! how happy the hours and moments are when one seems to draw nigh to the throne of grace!"

Her health had wonderfully revived. "I have been getting decidedly stronger," she writes, Oct. 3, "and have been at church the last seven Sundays, and really am much better." And she adds: "How constantly varying one's feelings are, even towards Christ! Each turn, as it were, in this weary wilderness seems to elicit fresh natural feelings, and to require some fresh application, by His Spirit, of what He is to us." And again: "The tide of nature often seems to roll me far away from the haven where I would be. Still I have a settled persuasion that all I lose from time to time is but the sensible part of religion, whilst the simple faith which looks to Jesus and His unchangeableness, seems rather strengthened than lessened by the loss of all other feelings."

And to another: "To cease from man, and look for our true enjoyment from our God, I am more and more convinced is *the* lesson of the Christian life. We don't know how much we depend on creatures and seen things. I do so feel for Lady C—— G—— in her present fellowship with some of Christ's most painful sufferings: but the Lord will yet light her candle."

The first edition of her work on the Song being exhausted, she was asked to prepare a new work.

"As Mr. Villiers proposed to me two years ago," she writes, "that I should compare Hebrews with Leviticus, and as others have proposed the same thing, I really am thinking of it. But though I have gone through Hebrews on paper, I have a great work before me in attempting to give God's mind about it to others, and it will take much time and thought. I may sometimes send you any thoughts which I particularly enjoy."

One of these thoughts she gives thus: "I have been struck beyond anything with Hebrews lately: I am satisfied that chapters vi. and x. are but a part of a grand whole; and by that I mean that the whole drift of the Epistle is just a warning to be stedfast and not to fall away from Christ. And I think there are passages in chapters ii., iii., iv., and xii., quite as strong as in chapters vi. and x. So many dear good people are in bondage about those passages so very unnecessarily! It is beautifully simple, viewed as a grand whole."

To another friend (the Hon. Mrs. C——), she writes, Oct. 16 (1850): "The subject you mention, of guidance, is one on which I feel strongly. Don't you think that wherever guidance is honestly and simply sought, it is *certainly* given? As to our discernment of it, I believe it depends upon the measure in which we are walking in the light. One indulged sin so clouds the sky that it spreads a mist, so that to see what God is doing is impossible."

And in the same letter: "You have asked a difficult question about sanctification. Its simple meaning involves the being set apart to a holy use, does it not? I think, *in Jesus* we are perfectly justified and perfectly sanctified from the first, but are momentarily needing the Spirit's work to apply and perfect both in us."

Herself living happily on the bright side of the cloud, she was not content to leave any one on its dark, Egyptain side. "I do feel you ought to be praising," she writes, "much more than mourning over your want of better feelings. 'Only let me pant after this one thing, that Jesus may be exalted, and I nothing. It is the Lord's love to me I would see, not mine to Him. I want to look at HIM till I am not. This will not be, when I find myself having more love to God, more holiness, &c., but when I lose myself, and see HIM to be my Wisdom, Righteousness, Sanctification, Redemption.' "

In her Diary at this period we have the following brief entries: "*Aug.* 31. *Sat.* A very precious, happy week, in which I had innumerable proofs of God's tender mercies to me. *Sept.* 1. *Sun.* Went to St. J——: heard a most painfully distressing sermon on Acts ii. 42. Oh, to be in the Father's house above, where Christ 'the truth' will preach (Ps. xl. 9). *Sep.* 12. *Th.* Heard dear Mr. Gell, at All-saints', from Jude 20, 'Praying in the Holy Ghost.' Such a precious word in season! *Sept.* 14. Eliza Radford died about nine A.M. Oh, to win souls! *Sept.* 16. Reached home again from Doveridge, to 'speak good of HIS name' who has dealt so kindly with His child. *Nov.* 24. *Sun.* At home all day. Felt burdened by a sin-sick soul, but tried to tell my case to my Physician."

Her health, again obliging her at times to be "at home all day" on the Sabbath, gave evidence, as winter approached, of being precarious as ever. Alluding to "a bad attack of sickness and of intense pain," she says, Nov. 5 (1850): "It has shown me how soon I may be brought to a very low ebb; and, indeed, one needs to be taught lowering lessons in temporals as well as in spirituals."

And in another letter: "It certainly is the trials of life which makes one cling to Jesus most closely. My Bible is very dear to me just now; and once or twice lately I have felt able to pray again—which is always such a comfort. But I believe it is best of all when we joy only in the Lord. I have so often felt the last few days, that to be covered with Jesus, and to be filled with the Spirit, summed up all my highest wishes."

This winter, like the preceding, was spent at home. "We have had so little real cold yet," she writes, Dec. 28 (1850), "that I have never been made ill by it, so far; and when it comes, if I keep in these two rooms as I did last winter, I hope to get through very well. I grudge the increasing duties which rob me of the time I have so long been permitted to spend in feasting on the Word and its fulness; but I know the field of battle must be encountered, as well as the green pastures and still waters be lain in, for we are not as yet come to our rest."

CHAPTER XIII.

THE family-affections are of God. Antichrist uproots them; CHRIST deepens and sanctifies them. Dear Adelaide is before us in this chapter the dutiful and loving child. Her filial attachment, no longer a mere instinct such as is shared by the lower animals, has been elevated into a 'love in the Spirit;' and the attachment gains immensely.

The occasion which illustrates this feature of her character is her father's last illness. "I have felt it," she writes on Jan. 3 (1851), "quite a tender proof of my heavenly Father's gentle dealing with me, that, through this excessively mild weather, I have been so well as to be able to go after dear Papa and sit with him. I feel every hour as if I were watching his last days on earth. You may imagine, but I could not tell you, what I felt when I said 'Good night' to him last night, and felt his hand so cold—with such a damp, death-like coldness. I had meant to write you a few words before going to bed: but, once alone, I could not utter a thought to any but to Him who could help me to speak them to Him, and, for the sake of my own health, I made myself get into bed, and cried myself to sleep."

And, in her Diary, we have this entry: "*July* 6 Dr. —— and Mr. —— saw Papa, but gave next tc no hope. I asked Papa if I might give him a text, Isa. xl. 28–31; and he said, 'How little, in such a time of sickness, one could think! you might feast on what you had already, but could not follow out anything.'" And, on the 16th, in a letter to the Hon. Mrs. C——: "To Papa death will be real gain. When the fruit is ripe, immediately the sickle will, I know, be put in; and when I remember whose property the field of this world is, and who planted and nurtured each spiritual grain of wheat sown in it, I seem as if I *must* be satisfied to have it cut down when it is ready. It would argue indifference to it in the Husbandman, if He then left it in the field."

And she adds: "I strongly feel how little oneness of spirit there must be with Jesus, when we grudge Him the fulfilment of His share in God's purposes for the sake of our own enjoyment in this stranger-world. We cannot spare Him the spirits He has purchased, because we cling so fondly to their bodies! But, since He has felt the natural feeling of bitterness at parting with a much-loved object, we know He shares our sorrow, just as He did Mary's and Martha's. And what comfort such thoughts give one! You don't know how true 'Treasures in heaven' seems to me now; I think I wrote it for my own profit."

A trial of faith she notes on Jan. 16: "You can't think how precisely you described what I am feeling in that insensibility of soul which kneels before God but utters nothing. I hope it is not altogether sinful, for I think it must be very much physical. I never felt less able to pray; and even the Word of God itself scarcely seems alive, through my own deadness. But I am not unhappy: I think God is just saying in His dealings—'Now you see what *you* are, and how very weak the flesh is, and how everything depends on what JESUS is *for* you, and what it is to have my skirt spread over you.'"

Her triumph of faith is explained, Jan. 24, thus: "Have you marked that passage, Isa. xl. 28–31, and especially the way the verses are connected? Frst of all, in v. 28, we find those two wonderful qualities attributed to 'God, the Lord, the Creator of the ends of the earth'—that He 'fainteth not, neither is weary.' Only conceive the exertion, according to our finite notions, of bearing up a world teeming with millions of inhabitants, day after day, year after year, and never being weary! added to which, each of these inhabitants wants breath every instant, and innumerable other things besides. Sometimes the thought of the infinite variety and number of prayers which are being offered up at the same moment has come across me with a feeling of overwhelming amazement; each separately listened to, and answered—not, probably, all at once, but by a series of events leading at last to the result, which turns out to be the answer to prayers we have been putting up for weeks or months! Fancy God never being tired of listening to all that! it gives one magnificent ideas of the vastness of His power, does it not?"

"Then the contrast to this, in v. 30," she adds, "is very remarkable: 'The youths *shall* faint and be weary;' which I understand to mean, the finest degree of natural strength shall turn out to be weakness; and how true it is! 'But they that wait upon the Lord shall renew *their* strength; they shall mount up with wings, as eagles; they shall run and not be weary, and they shall walk and not faint.' Just those who have 'no might' in themselves, are those who prove the strongest of all; for God communicates His own wonderful qualities to them!"

A little jotting to one of her sisters, suggested by their threatened bereavement, gives a touching glimpse into her tender but strong heart: "For dearest N——. '*I* will not leave you comfortless (*marg.*, orphans); *I* will come to you.' (John xiv. 18.) His offices require His presence with us, and His love secures it. He will not leave us. We never shall be orphans; for our Father ever lives.—Leylands, Jan. 29, 1851."

And, accompanying this, are the following simple lines:

"The place, the things, the persons we love best,
Oft rob us of our place in Jesus' breast;
But He too jealous is the heart to share;
Wherein He reigns, He reigns supremely there.

"The idols He deprives us of shall prove
But as new inlets to admit His love;

> Our present loss shall be our richest gain—
> Therein most likeness we to Christ attain."
>
> (2 Cor. viii. 9.)

Her father growing gradually weaker, Adelaide "took her turn," with her sisters, in ministering to him. "I had a very happy day with him yesterday," she writes, Feb. 3 (1851); "he is so very peaceful, and so tenderly kind. On Saturday morning, very early, he told Mamma he had had a very happy night, thinking of those two lines—

> "'If sin be pardoned, I'm secure;
> Death has no sting beside;'

adding, 'It had but one sting, and that is gone.' I know you will care for these few particulars of one so inestimably precious to me."

And, writing to Mrs. C—— W——, on Feb. 12, she says: "He has been the active servant of God for twenty or thirty years; and God is now polishing the other side of the stone, and making the passive graces of patience, meekness, gentleness, to shine forth in him. May I send you the words which have especially been on my mind lately—'The bondage of corruption,' in Rom. viii. 21? It *is* such bondage. Yet we know that these corruptible bodies are to put on incorruption; and then the bondage will be exchanged for 'glorious liberty!' One longs for the time for one's-self; but it is hard, to my will, to be left behind when others go."

It is a great achievement to "occupy" to-day, and to-day only.

"O! rich banquet of to-day! let me feast upon thee, saving manna!
I have none other food, nor store, but daily bread to-day.
I find none other place nor time than where I am to-day."

Alluding to a tendency to look beyond "to-day," as "*the* grief of her present trial," Adelaide adds: "I feel ashamed to write this; for what have I to do with the thoughts of a future which may never come? How difficult it is to trust practically, that, as our day, our strength shall be; and practically to remember that the Christian has to do only with the present moment.

And the thought is further developed elsewhere, thus: "'Day by day.' The child of God must learn that his heavenly Father maintains his cause on this wise—'The thing of a day in his day, as the matter shall require.' (1 Kings viii. 59, *marg.*) For every trial He sends, He gives sufficient grace for its endurance! but He promises no grace to bear *anticipations* with; and we little know how very large a portion of our mental sufferings arises from anticipation of trial. It is most conspicuous, for example, in Jacob; and in his case his anticipations were, in great measure, positive waste—things turned out so widely different from what he had anticipated. These are the bitterest ingredients of our trials, just because they are self-imposed and must be borne as best we can of our own (*weak*) strength. No wonder they are so hard to bear, if God provides no strength to bear them with! Should not we learn, therefore, how utterly vain it is to anticipate? And more—

should not the fact that God has made no provision for our anticipations, make us shrink from the indulgence of them? 'Day by day,' is His direction to us; and 'no thought for the morrow,' is His gracious, and tender, and positive prohibition."

The closing scenes are given in the Diary thus: "*February* 26.—In the evening, when I was going, dearest Papa put out his hand and kissed me, and said, 'Good bye, dear!' and added, 'It's all joy—all peace—all comfort!' *March* 1.—Commenced my twenty-eighth year on earth. In the morning, dearest Papa called me, stretched out both his arms, and clasped me to him—but I could only hear him say, 'This is your birthday, dear!' *March* 5.—In the evening, he quite opened his eyes and looked at me, as I stood by his bedside—took my hand—and I kissed him. A few moments after, he pushed away the pillow, and again looked up at me, and said, 'It's a long time.' Surely this is God fulfilling my desires! Thank Him! Bless Him! *March* 6.—At a quarter before two P.M., B—— came to tell me how changed dearest Papa was, and I went down. He lifted up my hand in his many times, and begged to be raised—to *go up*—to be lifted up; and his last audible word, we believe, was—'Saviour!' *March* 7.—Again and again in the night he spoke of 'going,' and once said to B——, 'I'm ready—quite ready; I only want to be going.' About two and three he breathed very hard, but became quieter, and breathed more and more faintly, till we could scarcely tell when it ceased—a few minutes after seven A.M."

March 9, *Sunday*.—Dearest Papa's first Sabbath in 'glory everlasting.' *March* 13.—Went twice to look at dearest Papa's earthly tabernacle. This corruptible '*shall* put on incorruption.' *March* 14.—All that remained of dearest Papa buried in the vault at Mickleover, till Jesus says, 'COME FORTH!' Read John xi. It was a day of much tender mercy."

A few days later she writes: "I have grieved to leave your kind letter so long unanswered; but, in honest truth, I have had no heart to write. Numbers of notes of inquiry, which were obliged to be answered, more than used up the little spirit I had for mentioning him who now is set free from the body of sin and death, and, absent from the body, is for ever 'present with the Lord.' It has been a time of deep and unutterable sorrow, yet mixed with countless mercies and multitudes of tender mercies and lovingkindnesses. Indeed, I often feel far more inclined to rejoice than to weep; for, bad as it is to be left behind in a world like this, I know I am following hard after him—and for himself I have not one single feeling but unmixed thankfulness. For above an hour after he went, I sat by all that remained to me of him—the greater part of the time being quite alone; yet not one tear could I shed! No; I was absorbed in thoughts of unseen realities, and so marvellously have they taken possession of me since, that I seldom have felt inclined to weep. He was buried on the 14th—a lovely, bright morning, which filled me full of resurr ction thoughts. 'Lazarus, come forth!' were words I delighted to listen to the Spirit speaking in the Word; and little do we know how soon they may be said to all who are in their graves now."

And to another: "I could not tell you how positively happy I was on the morning of the funeral, after reading John xi. It seemed so impossible to think of the tears Jesus shed over the lifeless body of Lazarus, without going on to the Omnipotence which said, 'Lazarus, come forth!'"

And again: "What wonderful, very wonderful things are reserved for us there! I do feel it so much, when I cannot even tell where my precious father's spirit now is, nor what it is about! 'With Jesus' seems there the only thing: and it is enough; yet at the resurrection we shall also know and be with each other—don't you think?"

Her thoughts were naturally drawn at this season to the intermediate state. "I want to know," we find her writing on March 17 (1851), "whether your mind has ever been called to think much of the state of separation from the body. I have been studying the believer in Jesus in these three states—1. 'At home *in* the body;' 2. 'Absent from the body;' 3. 'Clothed upon with our house which is from heaven.' But I will send you the paper. There is one thing which has occurred to me since I wrote it, on the word 'unclothed.' It gives me the idea that it is a state one naturally would prefer not to be exposed to view in ('If so be, that, being clothed, we shall *not be found naked*'); and how graciously this feeling is met by the hidden, unseen state of spirits, who, so soon as they are 'clothed upon,' will '*appear* with Christ in glory!' I have been reading 1 John i., too, and looking out texts on it; and often have I grown breathless through the rarity of so pure an atmosphere."

And, on March 31, she writes: "I have been thinking very much about the 'unclothed' state; and I cannot but believe, that, while there, each individual spirit is admitted to the fulness of perfected communion with Jesus (which is, after all, what we most intensely long for as Christians while on earth), but that the recognition of saints, and their communion with each other, must wait till they are 'clothed upon,' and have bodies to see, and hear, and speak with. Have you ever much considered this subject? I suppose it is interesting to almost every one, for few can be without some beloved friend or relative who is there. And the chief charm to me of the thoughts I have lately had about it, is, that it really leads one direct to Christ, for it makes Him the everything to the spirits who are now 'made perfect.' Fancy being free from all sin, enjoying all that Christ is, and holding the purest spiritual intercourse with Him, being admitted into His felt presence! Don't you think it must just depend on the degree of our spiritually of mind here, how far we can truly appreciate the 'gain' of dying and going to be 'with Christ?'"

The subject took form and shape ere long in an octavo pamphlet—"The Unclothed State"—which has proved no small consolation to other bereaved disciples.

If the Christian's family-affections are adorned with a new loveliness whilst the objects of them are still here, still brighter and more heavenly is their hue after those objects are away. Then especially do they shine forth as not mere instincts of earth, but as indeed divine. "The real trial," she writes March 31, "is to be left behind. Oh; how do I need Divine grace, to make me content to wait till I am ready to go! Hitherto there has really been such unutterable tenderness and gentleness in each thing which God has done, that silent adoration has been quite the uppermost feeling of my heart."

And again: "I really had not heart to write to you as long as dearest Papa was here; it seemed to weigh me down with such an indescribable weight of anxiety. But since he has been set free from the body of sin and death which kept him so long a prisoner, I have been quite happy in his happiness. I seem only to have to press on to follow hard after him, giving up as much as possible the self-will and obstinacy of my own naturally stubborn character, so that God's will may be done in me and by me."

"Lord, we await Thy glory;
We have no home but where
The unbroken heavenly family
Thy joy with us shall share.

"Our Father's smiles are cheering
The brief but thorny way;
Our Father's house the dwelling,
Made ready for that day."

CHAPTER XIV.

In this new school of trial Adelaide had been learning new lessons. "I feel," we find her writing to the Hon. Mrs. C——, April 21 (1851), "what I had long believed must be the case, that bereavement admits one to an entirely new sphere of sorrow—known only to those who have trodden it. The *isolation* I had experienced from circumstances and from illness is so totally different from the *desolation* of death! But I do believe that the variety of Christian experiences through which we are thus permitted to pass on earth, will add greatly to the depth of our enjoyment in praising hereafter. And when one thinks of spending a whole eternity in praises and thanksgivings, it is a very precious thought to me just now that prolonged life and discipline yield one ampler materials than could otherwise have been turned to account to the glory of God and of Jesus there."

And, alluding to the season, in whose services she had been engaged, and associating with it the scenes through which she had been passing at home, she adds: "I have been especially thinking of the Lord's body, above all, of His lifeless body. Did it ever occur to you to think of the moment of His death, when the darkness which had overhung the land for three hours just passed away, to reveal to the sight of man His dead body on the cross? I was pondering over it so much yesterday; and I think it must have been such a terrific moment when the daylight again burst upon that fearful scene. The subject is so peculiarly harmonious with all that has been so lately passing here, that I have had intense delight in reading over all that is recorded of the body of our Redeemer when he had 'dismissed His Spirit' and left it in the hands of man. It has been so precious to me to notice how God owned and accepted the fond affection which constrained the women to see 'how the body was laid' and where, and to linger about the sepulchre. Don't you think the record of those little things teaches one so very much? And certainly the Father's heart must have yearned over even the lifeless body of His well-beloved Son, or the Spirit would not have said so much about it. I like to believe it; for if Christ's dead body were precious in His sight, so must the dead bodies of His members be, even though they are so different. Don't you think so?"

"I was wonderfully well," she writes, on April 25, "through the winter, and kept up all through dearest Papa's long illness; but I don't feel so well now, and this spring-weather tries me a good deal. People think me looking very well, only thinner. But, oh! how I should like to forget all that is of the earth, earthy, and to think, or speak, or write of

Jesus and His love, so as that others might be warmed, instead of chilled, by coming into contact with me!"

Few did come into contact with her, without being "warmed." Her words were not the prophet's dead staff, but the living, breathing person. "If I could send you one word to give you any pleasure," she writes, April 27, "I would not be silent; and, whilst I would ask God to strengthen you with might by His Spirit in your inner man, I would not forget that His Spirit may speak through others as well as directly to yourself. Only how often He teaches us that it is His own eye meeting ours, or His own voice speaking to us, or the gentle pressure, as it were, of His own hand, which tells the depth of His tender love and satisfies the longings of our hearts. There is such a secret between us and God, that our spirits only, and not our tongues, can give utterance to it. And yet there is the knowledge that, while we can only utter it in spirit to God, it is understood by those who are further on in the road to the city of the living God than we are; so that our hearts may be made to burn while talking of it, even though we could not give expression to it."

The Diary thus reveals the way in which she lived daily on the Word: "*March* 23.—*Sun.* 'HE satisfieth the longing soul, and filleth the hungry soul with goodness.' It must, indeed, be His doing! How often the creature-streams run dry!" "*March* 28.—'My soul, wait thou *only* upon GOD; *for* my expectation is from Him.' It is true of my 'expectation,' that it is from God only; why, then, do I not wait upon HIM *only?* Conduct contradicts principle." "*April* 12.—'Whoso offereth praise glorifieth me; and to him that ordereth his conversation aright, will I show the salvation of God.' How little I see of 'the heights and depths' of the salvation of God, when my conversation is all wrong before Him! Oh, for *rectitude* of heart and life!" "*April* 28.—'He shall not be afraid of evil tidings: his heart is FIXED, trusting in the Lord.' Mrs. Cavendish came over from Doveridge to see me. We went through Daniel together; and I hope 'iron sharpened iron' mutually. Oh, for *fixedness* of heart!" "*May* 11.—Had the Communion—REAL communion with a Triune God!" "*May* 16.—Wrote to dear —— about Prov. xxiii. 15, 16—the joys of Jesus. He is our 'wisdom;' and our words are the breathings of His Spirit through our lips!"

A few such "breathings" occur in a letter, dated May 15, thus: "I suppose I must be thankful to have even this little taste of Christian communion with you, ere we meet in the temple of our God to enjoy the fulness of His precious purchased privileges. But it seems next to nothing—does it not?—and makes one long to be really at home in our Father's house above. I think I told you in my last note how much I had been thinking of the Spirit's joy. This week I have been thinking of the joy of Jesus a good deal. Did it ever strike you in 1 Chron. xxix. 17, taking David as the type of the true David, our 'Beloved,' how beautiful those words are,

'As for me, I have willingly offered all these things in the uprightness of mine heart, and now have I seen with joy thy people which are present here to offer willingly unto thee?' His was the great offering; and we give ourselves and all we have to give, in conformity with His example. Perhaps every cup of cold water given for His sake is an offering which He looks down upon 'with joy;' and, if so, dear ——, how privileged you must have been in contributing to His joy! I often hear of your kindnesses, even at this distance; and how many are known to Jesus, who notices even when 'it was in thine heart' to do them, though perhaps they were not accomplished as you could wish!"

And to a bereaved friend she writes: "I can share in your sorrow, and that not slightly; but I will not (as J. H. Evans so often says) pain you with commonplace remarks about affliction. I know well that no words avail to heal such wounds, except as the Lord the Spirit speaks them. The gathering of the heavenly family appears often to me to be going on very rapidly, and the time of our meeting in the many mansions of our Father's house to be drawing nigh. And what a blessed hope it is! 'Glory!' It seems such a marvellous word. 'The God of glory'—the glory Jesus had with Him from the foundation of the world—His glory, which is the Father's gift to Him, and His gift to us—bodies of glory, like so many reflectors of the glory of HIS body! The whole earth filled with it and covered with it, as the waters cover the sea!—and an exceeding weight of it, being the precious fruit of the light afflictions we have lovingly had allotted to us here! The hope of glory is indeed a bright one, and might well throw the present time into the shades of night, while one is looking for 'the glorious appearing' of the great 'God and our Saviour Jesus Christ,' when 'the day' breaks and the shadows flee away."

And to another: "I have only not written before because I seemed as if I could not—not from want of feeling, but from feeling too much to be able to say it. The lent jewel is returned to its Owner; and Jesus has got it all to Himself—for a little while; but it will not be for long." And to the same, a few weeks later: "I had no idea, till your note reached me, that you had again been feeling as if drawing near the verge of an unseen world; but I am heartily thankful to God for sparing you to all of us. Yet, oh! how delightful it is to walk on fearlessly and happily as if to the river's brink, though it may prove to be only to travel on by the river's side, 'beside the still waters!'"

A retrospect, suggested by the illness of a cousin whom medical treatment had not relieved, occurs in a letter, dated May 12 (1851), thus: "How often I wonder at God's dealings with *me* in bodily things! —how gently He led me, after a sufficient number of years of discipline, down to Torquay, that life might be prolonged, just when I was on the verge of getting past recovery! Then I wonder how long it will be for? But every day I am more satisfied to leave it with Him."

"I have very, very happy intercourse with Him about things very often," she adds. "I did so enjoy the Communion yesterday. I felt I was doing what He liked me to do. Don't you know that sort of feeling? And 1 Chron. xxix. 9 seemed to me so full of preciousness—our joy in doing in our measure what Jesus did perfectly, and what caused Him such 'great joy.' And the thought of contributing anything to the joy of the 'Man of sorrows' is so sweet!"

And again, May 21, to a friend who had paid her a very hurried visit: "This wilderness-world is not the place for home-enjoyments and society. I remember once having it remarked to me, that, in crossing the waves of this troublesome world, the very wave which rolls one towards a friend speedily recedes and bears one away again. But it will not be so in the haven."

And to a friend sojourning in southern Europe for her health, Mrs. C—— W——, she writes (May 23): "I should think you must be feeling a thorough pilgrim on the earth! But still are not the statutes of the Lord emphatically at such times your song? I always feel so strongly that He seems to encompass one about so much more closely, as the absence of others makes room for Him. 'There was no room for Him in the inn,' where strangers were crowding together in numbers—a large, merry, happy party, doubtless. But there was plenty of room for Him in the house where only Mary, and Martha, and Lazarus lived. And don't you think that is just what one realizes sc often now? It does not destroy the desolation which bereavement makes, and which daily grows upon me; but it sweetens it, and so does the absence of friends."

The low state of the Church of God often deeply affected her. Alluding to those words in Amos iv. 8, "So two or three cities wandered unto one city to drink water, but they were not satisfied: yet have ye not returned unto me," she writes: "Does not the literal exactly prefigure the spiritual Israel here? There is such a state of things in Christ's Church militant here on earth, that His showers of blessing are withholden. Here and there a Christian or a congregation is found upon whom the rain descends; and he or it is well watered, while all around is 'withered.' Two or three may wander to that favoured one; but even then they are 'not satisfied,' because they have still not returned to the LORD, the Fountain of living waters."

Another lesson of her discipline she notes, in a letter dated May 28 (1851): "God has been leading me in the valley of humiliation of late; and sometimes my spirit has seemed all but crushed. I keep saying to myself, as I go about like the leper of old, 'Unclean, unclean!' and can truthfully say, 'I abhor myself.' I suppose I may read in it all the answer to my own prayers; for I have so entreated to be laid low and kept humble, because I felt I was horribly self-complacent. And yet I cannot but thank Him that He is chastening me and humbling me; I *know* it is to do me good at my latter end. And this revival of old, secret, unutterable deeps of sorrow, which in their very nature seem unfit to be told to any one on earrh, revives a hope that perhaps God is preparing me to work for Him again."

"Hard thoughts of God," it has been said, "is the death of the heavenly life." Dear Adelaide was ever watching, for herself and for others, against this snare. "I have a text to send you," she writes, June 12, "which is full of consolation to me; it is Ps. xxxvi. 10, with Parkhurst's Hebrew rendering, which greatly adds to its force—'O draw out at length Thine exuberant goodness to them that know Thee.' The word we render lovingkindness comes from a root, 'to swell or overflow;' and when one is made to feel the daily and hourly need we have for fresh demands upon that goodness, is it not sweet to know from Himself that there is such an overflowing exuberance of it, and to know, too, that, if in time it is a stream which overflows its banks, it will but expand into ocean-fulness in the ages of eternity? God goes on teaching me that every fresh ray of light from above does but make manifest some fresh evil within me; but, instead of occupying one's moments with repetitions of the deplorable depravity which *seems* as if it only increased upon me every day, it is a higher and better occupation to try and catch even a glimpse of the goodness which fills the heart of Christ—is it not? I deem it my sweetest privilege to be His messenger at any time, to give you any word from His mouth, or any thought from His heart."

And in another letter, thus: "That passage, Col. ii. 13, has struck me very much, as connecting our quickening with our forgiveness—'You hath He quickened together with Him, having forgiven you all trespasses. Do you not think there is involved in it, that, just as Christ's resurrection proved Him to have been owned of God as cleared from all the load of iniquity under which He died, so, when we are quickened with Him, it is a proof that we are reckoned clear from all our sin and guilt? May we not take the fact of our being alive (out of our death in sin) as certain evidence that the sin which was killing us, is entirely put away from us?"

Speaking of evil spirits, and of their mode of warfare with the saints, she writes, June 28, to the Hon. Mrs. C——, thus: "Should we take Satan's temptations of the Saviour as the example of his ways of tempting us? Did not he tempt Christ by presenting *objects* of temptation—the glory of this world, &c.? And when the angel from heaven 'strengthened Him,' may it not have been by presenting suitable *objects*, such as should predominate over the others (as 'the joy which was set before Him')? If it was so, may there not be a parallel? This is the first thing I have ever got hold of, which seemed to explain Satan's temptations to me."

And she adds: "I have a thought about Eph. vi. 12, which I can't help asking you about. That epistle seems to be full of the deepest truths of any, and for the most advanced believers; and if so, may not their very advance in spirituality lead them into a spiritual wrestling with 'wicked spirits,' which in a lower atmosphere of spirituality Christians are scarcely so much as aware of? Can I give you the idea? Certainly fighting in Canaan is far beyond journeying through the wilderness; and I should think comparatively few Christians come to that reality of conflict. What do you think?"

To another, on July 10 (1851), she touches on the same subject, thus: "My mind is most stirred up just now about 'the working of Satan.' It has been very much brought to my notice lately; and I believe there is danger in 'being ignorant of his devices' and wiles. Have you noticed, in Eph. vi., that there are two distinct ways in which he attacks us—v. 11, by his 'wiles;' and v. 16, by his 'fiery darts.' In such a fearful matter, it is inexpressibly comforting that both these verses teach us that the armour of God is abundantly sufficient to preserve us from all his attacks, if we are but clothed with and standing in it. All his fiery darts may be quenched by faith. The 'good fight of faith!' How much conflict goes on in the inmost recesses of the inner man, unseen by any eye but God's!"

Adelaide was not a mystic, but an earnest worker. "I am as full of occupation as I can be," she writes, July 12, "and all for Him! Is not that sweet, even though much of it may be passive waiting or patient enduring—and that takes up a great deal of time—does it not? I have lately had great encouragement about the Irish work; indeed, God has used me in many ways."

And again: "I never can express the happiness I have in the different ways God suffers me to give up my time and powers to His work and service. You have a work to do which I can never have—and it must be a very absorbing one—I mean the care of your sweet children, and the training them up in the nurture and admonition of the Lord. Oh! that the seed you sow may bring forth fruit, sixty and an hundred fold! What wonderful things we may expect to see in that 'great day!' the seed feebly sown, and perhaps amidst many tears, yet multiplied into a harvest of many sheaves!"

And on July 23: "I have been thinking this week of Jesus as the burnt-offering: it shows the perfecness of His work so exquisitely; every thought, word, and feeling being first consumed, and then ascending up to God as a sweet savour! Don't you think it is a very great help, in realising your own acceptance, to see how abundantly God was satisfied with the offering Jesus presented to Him in our behalf? not only a death for sin, but a whole life of spotless righteousness! God 'takes pleasure' in Jesus and in all that He is doing. Is it not a shame that we should ever go to Him for pardon, either for ourselves or for others, as if He grudged it?"

All her visits she consecrated to the Lord. Writing to the Hon. Mrs. C——, on July 26, she says: "Mamma has kindly arranged to let me have the carriage to-morrow afternoon to drive over. Much as I long to see you, I own I shall come in weakness, and fear, and much trembling. I know by painful experience that more contact with this evil world has most sadly blunted the comparatively keen edge of my spiritual affections; and it must be evident in spiritual communion. But I still hope God may bring good out of my coming to you, and may make it a time of great refreshing from the presence of the Lord."

And to one of her sisters, July 25 (1851): "Did I send you 'A Very Present Help?' Each moment's need through life, and a dying moment's need at last, has made it seem so precious to me lately. As plainly as we can trace the workings of love in every event of Christ's ministry on earth, so it is to be recognised in every event He administers from His throne in heaven. It is a hard lesson to *learn out*—'He hath done all things well,' however fully we may believe it; but we must seek for grace to be able to say—'I am content to fulfil thy will, O my God.' O! the fulness of that word 'fulfil!' to fill up every particle thereof, like a vessel filled to the brim! Who is sufficient? Our sufficiency is of God."

And to another, on August 8: "I have not been able to enjoy Mrs. C—— at all as I hoped; for they have another friend staying here who cannot understand anything beyond the merest A B C of religion, and Mrs. C—— is one of the few who love to read the Word of God with me, and to dig into the hidden treasures of Christ to be found in it. Still, I hope that, however disappointing, I may be learning lessons to conform me to Jesus, especially in bearing the infirmities of the weak, and in feeling what it is not to be at all *understood.* How trying that must have been to Him, must it not?"

Vinet has remarked, somewhere, that the Church has need of our sufferings, because she has need of our services. "As for the inner man," writes dear Adelaide, Aug. 22, rejoicing in that way of the Lord, "I hope that, by this weariness of body, He is strengthening me with strength by His Spirit, though it is rather by a discipline which calls forth His love into exercise, than by leading me by the still waters, or making me to lie down in green pastures, as He has often done. I was struck with the way in which Mrs. C—— often told me it was 'so strengthening to carry the cross.' How delightful it is to know that every stage of our journey is marked out by unerring love! and, as you used often to say, 'divinely adapted' to our weakness!"

And she adds: "I have found that verse very precious this week—'I will rebuke the devourer for your sakes, and he shall not destroy the fruits of your ground.' (Mal. iii 11.) It is so beautiful with that verse in Lev. xxv.—'I will command my blessing upon you.' I think the great enemy of souls so often mars and corrupts our fruits by causing pride to bud, or by sending some secret sin to eat at their root almost unperceived by us. And is it not very precious to go to God with His own Word of promise in our mouth that He will not suffer our fruits to be destroyed?"

And again: "I have liked Ezek. xxxvi. 29 also very much, in connexion with Mal. iii. 11. It is not only that He will cleanse us from all our filthiness (Ezek. xxxvi. 25), but He adds—'I will also *save* you from all your uncleannesses; and I will call for the corn and will increase it, and lay no famine upon you.' The restraining grace of God is so exceedingly precious, in all that He saves us from—is it not? I think, sometimes, that it will be one of the many *reserved* subjects of thankfulness and praise which we shall understand hereafter. 'I, the Lord, do keep it, and I will water it every moment: *lest* any hurt it, I will keep it night and day.'"

She devoted many of her hours this summer and autumn to the study of Hebrew. "It is so intensely interesting," she writes, Aug. 30, "and seems to lead one to so very much fuller a knowledge of God's thoughts in His Words—those precious Words which have come forth out of His mouth! I do long," she adds, "to dig deeper and deeper into that mine of sanctifying wealth. I cannot tell how I enjoy searching out the idea which each word is intended to convey. It runs away with many an hour of my time—I hope not unprofitably."

A "weight" which hinders many a pilgrim's race she exposes in the same letter, thus: "How slow we are to learn that our portion in this life, as ordained by God, need be no hindrance, to our onward, upward, heavenward course! I am so fearfully irritated and provoked by others, that clouds are ever and anon hiding from me the heavenly sunshine which is beyond them. Oh! what a den of iniquity one's evil heart of unbelief is! How precious the spotless robe which covers it!"

It was no incapacity to enjoy the world's pleasures which had separated her from its ways. Before her illness, she had lost all relish for them; and now, when comparative health was giving her "opportunity to return," she still "chose the better part." "I have written a note," she says, August 31, "to send, through you, to Mrs. ——, as I have no idea where she is. I try to urge her to be more decided for God. God has wonderfully helped me not to give in at all about becoming more worldly. I am resolved, by His grace, to be as openly given up to the 'one thing' needful now, as when I was too ill to attend to other things. He is very good to let me bear this testimony for Him. I feel it to be a great privilege, though each day it is more difficult."

The self-reproach which continued to sting her so often, was the result only of a conscience more sensitive to sin by reason of a closer fellowship with God. "I see plainly," she writes, Sept. 5, "that half I suffer arises from a desire to be comfortable and able to enjoy myself in this life. I know but little of taking up a cross. How the life which Jesus lived shames me! You cannot believe how little I have of that charity which is 'not easily provoked.' I need not multiply words to tell you the delight it would be to me to see you and hear you talk of Jesus—our dear, precious Saviour, and of our better and abiding home. I might be, with God's blessing, an opportunity of much recovery and restoration to my sin-sick soul."

And, on Sept. 10, revealing the secret of her bereaved heart's consolation, she writes: "The emphatic silence of Scripture as to any meeting together of believers before the resurrection, and then the constant and direct assurance of it at the resurrection, seem sufficient ground for believing that there will not be recognition in the state of absence from the body. Of course, I would not affirm that there *may* not be recognition. Every single passage, however, where the subject of the unclothed state is spoken of, makes the 'being *with Christ*' the fulness of their joy. And do you think it in the least likely that the hope of seeing our beloved ones again would have been deferred to the resurrection-time (as it is in 1 Thess. iv.), if it had been to be realized after death?

"To my own mind," she adds, "there is something intensely solemnizing and unutterably precious in the thought of being (if one may so speak) *shut up to Jesus* during that season—so filled with the bliss of being with Him as to need and desire nothing more —and yet capable of such an expanded increase of enjoyment, when that waiting state is ended, and when we shall all be gathered 'together' to Him, and all see His perfect image in one another, both visibly in our bodies and spiritually in our souls!"

And, led into a kindred region of Christian experience, she proceeds: "That sympathy of spiritual feeling which we must believe to exist in a perfect degree between the spirits made perfect, exists also, imperfectly, betwixt us on earth and those with Jesus. It seems only our earthiness which makes us realize it so very little in general. The more I think of the whole subject, the more strongly I am made to feel the absolute oneness of the whole family of God, in whichever of all our varied states we may be. God's eye must look upon each and all as members of the body of Jesus; and don't you think that, in proportion as His Spirit dwells in us, we feel ourselves united to all in Him—the whole family in 'heaven and in earth?'"

And in the same letter: "'Lord, all my desire is before thee, and my groaning is not hid from thee.' Each word has been full of comfort to me lately. 'Desires' and 'groans' *all known*, even when one can scarcely utter either! And the particular feeling which that verse had so fully expressed for me is, that when a whole day, or perhaps many days, have slipped away, and I could scarcely say that I had prayed at all, the very groanings of one's spirit have been heard and heeded in the upper sanctuary of our God. You will understand what I mean, though I don't know how to say it."

Referring to some new tracts which she was publishing, she writes, Sept. 18 (1851): "Perhaps I am too cautious and fearful, but I never dare take any step in the way of printing, unless I see what I believe to be indications from God that He 'has need' of my attempts to serve Him." And she adds: "Mr. Gell said in his sermon last week, that no one should think himself of no use to Christ, for He never says to any of His members, 'I have no need of thee.' He has need. What an insignificant animal it was said of originally, 'The Lord has need of it.' So I thought that He might have need of me, though perhaps He does not need my tracts; and then I hope I shall be hindered from thrusting them in His way."

Like the oak which strikes deeper its roots by reason of the winter's blast, dear Adelaide's heart was, by reason of her manifold trials, fixing itself day by day more stedfastly in CHRIST. "My mind," she writes, whilst on a visit to a not very congenial circle, "is very much distracted here; but I really believe it is good to be shaken out of dependence on or rest in outward circumstances in all ways. It makes me feel how firm the ground is, in resting on the Rock of Ages."

"O Lord, we happy children,
Whilst yet on earth we roam,
Find in our Father's bosom
Our spirits' present home:

"For where thou art reclining,
By faith we too repose,
In thee all rais'd to heaven,
When thou, our Head arose."

CHAPTER XV.

Ritualism is not Christ. Writing to a schoolfellow whom the prevailing ritualistic tendencies of the day threatened to ensnare, she writes: "I grieve to hear so poor an account of the place you are staying at; but, do you know, I don't think reformation would be half so effectually brought about by repairing the church as by visiting the people. Don't you think it is a great mistake in these days to make so much of church-architecture and outside things, instead of real, downright, earnest prayer for the work of God's omnipotent Spirit to change the stony hearts of the unconverted amongst both rich and poor? I think it is a great snare. I greatly fear T—— is slightly poisoned with the High-Churchism of these days; though he denies it in words, his letters have betrayed it to me. Oh, how almost universal it is! My book on Solomon's Song is full of the Church; but it is the Church as Christ's Bride, not as an ecclessiastical body. 'The Church which is His body,' is my notion of the Church."

On another occasion, addressing the same correspondent, she writes: "I hope the clergyman you mention is not the same as a friend of ours heard when she was at A——; for he was far from preaching the truth as it is in Jesus. Oh, how sadly in these days the Church is exalted, and JESUS left out! To look at things, as *I* cannot fail to do, more in the light of eternity than others who have not felt on its brink, makes everything which will last only whilst time lasts, appear comparatively unworthy of thought; whilst the things which are unseen—the Spirit working in us (like the wind, which is heard, though unseen), Christ who is our life (though now hid within the vail), the sustaining vital principle of God's strength made perfect in our weakness—all these truths are forgotten or not to be talked about, because they are too sacred! and we live very unlike those who are sojourners only in a world which must itself soon pass away.

"But," she adds, "there are many who are arousing from such a life, and devoting themselves as servants to do their Master's work, sowing seed now to reap the harvest hereafter. This seems to me the only true value of life. Were it not for this, it would be far better to depart so soon as the soul is won to Jesus. But, in the bearing which each moment has upon eternity, the saint is sowing 'to the Spirit' as truly as the ungodly are sowing wind to reap the whirlwind! Dear ——, do pray for me, that what yet remains to me of life may be each moment spent for God: I ask it for you—I feel it to be of such eternal importance."

One day Henry Martyn, after preaching in Calcutta on the cross of Christ as the only way of life, was publicly charged with "driving men to mopishness, melancholy, and despair." Starting soon afterwards for Dinapore, he was met on his way by some brethren who had assembled to commend him to God. "My soul never had such Divine enjoyment," he writes, contrasting the pleasant fellowship with the heartless ritualism which he had left behind in Calcutta; "I felt a desire to break from the body, and join the high praises of the Church above. May I go in the strength of this many days!" Dear Adelaide also had select hearts in whose sympathies she found a congenial home. "I do so feel," she writes, "that very spiritual thoughts can be expressed in spirit to God, but not in words to man, except as His Spirit makes two minds to receive the same thoughts, and then they are mutually understood, though scarcely, perhaps, expressed at all."

Does not this account for that mysterious communion of thought and of feeling which pervades, like one electric wire, the saints who dwell in the secret of the Lord's presence? And does it not account also for that not less mysterious incapacity of other saints to receive certain truths which their brethren discern on the sacred page, written as with a sunbeam?

Like Martyn, she often longed to "join the high praises of the Church above." "Frequently I wish," she writes, "to be gone to my real home, and to be with Jesus." And, on Sept. 19 (1851): "It is singular that you should have been reading the seventy-first Psalm lately. There is such precious intercourse in it betwixt one's own soul and God! I was thinking last Sunday how very partially it could be realised by us in this short life, and how greatly we needed an eternal day, such as we shall soon have, in which to show forth the now unknown numbers of the salvation, and victories, and righteousness of God. Will it not be blessed with an incorruptible and immortal body, to have our 'lips' and 'tongue' and 'mouth' filled with His honour and praise, literally and uninterruptedly 'all the day long?' and our souls, too, will then so '*greatly* rejoice' in the perfection of our Redeemer's work!"

Brainerd in his Diary speaks of being so occupied with God and His perfections, as exhibited in the Gospel of His grace, that his own personal self ceased to have a place in his thoughts. "There is something," writes dear Adelaide, expressing a like experience, "in the very love of our hearts towards God's 'salvation,' which in itself is quite inexpressible. This Psalm (seventy-first) gives vent to so much of it to God, in a way which one feels He can appreciate, though almost no one else could tell what our own secret experience means when it praises Him for His glory, and beauty, and righteousness, and truth!"

One of her trials and triumphs of faith she notes in another letter, Oct. 1, thus: "The text which has been given most emphatically to me lately is

Ps. xxxi. 20. The word we render 'pride,' means 'rough, proud, untractable, vexatious in temper and action, which are in life like rugged knobs in a road,' being the same word as in Isaiah xl. 4, 'rough places, or rugged, difficult to pass; a chain of mountains.' Does not this give a marvellous fulness of meaning to that precious promise—'Thou shalt hide them in the secret of thy presence from the pride of man'—from those who are ever vexing one's temper, whenever one meets with them, by the rugged knobs which they lay in our way, so very difficult to pass? I am not sure whether you are tried by people as I am; but I feel certain that you will enter into the comfort of a promise like this. Just to feel, when the trial is pressing hard upon one, that now is the moment when God is hiding one in the secret of His presence! Oh! it is inexpressible relief. What wonderful training God's is," she adds; "it is so much of it unperceived, not only by others, but even by one's-self at the time! I so very often forget that He is concerning Himself about me in each momentary occurrence of the day. 'The Lord thinketh upon me'—'with great exactness' (according to Dr. Wilson). I must be intensely provoking to Him! Nothing astonishes me more sometimes than that He never wearies of me."

And to another: "I am sure that you have had some very blessed communion with Jesus in His Word; and I hope that you will have no silent moments even, but that the Spirit may be speaking peace to your soul continually. May I send you these two words, 'Meat indeed,' with a heartfelt wish that you may be richly fed and feasted with all that is in Jesus? 'let your soul delight itself in fatness.' 'I sat down under His shadow with great delight, and His fruit was sweet to my taste.' How sweet that repose may be in this life, as a kind of foretaste of the rest which remaineth! 'Many shall come from the east and west, and shall sit down.' Did you ever think particularly of the *rest* from warfare, and journeying, and weariness, which is implied in the words?"

A solace for the sick chamber she puts thus: "I comfort myself with that wonderful promise that God Himself will be strengthening you upon the bed of languishing, and will Himself make your bed. Don't you like the marginal reading there—'Turn your bed?' the word meaning, to 'turn or change the condition of a thing.' I think it must be meant to teach us God's minute knowledge and care about our earthly tabernacle, showing that He can adapt His omnipotence as well to the least thing in a sick-room as to the greatest thing in a kingdom."

The Word grew daily in preciousness. "I have been looking out," she writes to Mrs. Carus Wilson, Oct. 6 (1851), "all the different meanings to the Hebrew words for prayer, and have found nearly thirty, each having some rather different idea attached to it. One, for instance, signifies 'a low, whispering sound' (see Isa. xxvi. 16, *marg.*, 'secret speech'); another, 'words set in order before God, like the shew-bread' (as in Ps. v. 3, 'In the morning will I direct my prayer unto thee, and will look up'): there is also the pouring out of the soul like liquids: and there is the opening of the heart, like a cloud of incense expanding itself, &c., &c.; all showing, I think, most wonderfully the minuteness with which God has taught us how well He knows all our varied ways of approaching Him."

The issues of this momentous NOW! who shall fitly conceive them?

"Each breath is burdened with a bidding, and every minute has its mission."

And what a mission! "Mr. Stowell was lately quoting," she writes, Oct. 19, "a remark from some old writer, of the necessity for the judgment to be passed on individuals being delayed till the end of time, because their works do not end with their death; for instance, parents, in training their children, might not reap the fruit, perhaps, for many years after they were dead—and so on. In thinking of this, I began to see such wonderful heights and depths in the judgment of God, that I have been lost in adoration. To think that a word spoken or written may be like a grain of seed cast into the earth, to be multiplied a thousand-fold, and re-sown perhaps again and again from one to another! and yet that each will have exactly his own measure of reward in the great day of reckoning—oh! is it not amazing?

"Don't you think," she continues, "that it will glorify God very exceedingly then? We could not determine what share we have had in the good which has been wrought, if one person wrote a book, another gave it away, and another lent it—or, to go further back, how much the writer of it may have learned from books he had, and from thoughts he had gathered from others! One seems lost in a labyrinth of which one knows next to nothing; and yet each link of the chain must be so clear in the eye of God, that He will be able to give to each precisely what their thoughts, and words, and actions will have produced in all their varied and multiplied results. Did you ever exactly think of it in this way? it seems to have opened up such a field of wonder to my mind! And while, on the one hand, it seems to fill every moment of time with immensely increased importance, giving us an interest in it not only during our own short span of life, but until time shall be no more, it also gives one an idea of the boundlessness of God's knowledge and of the rectitude with which He will come to judgment, which fills one with adoring wonder and delight! Of course, you will not misunderstand me as meaning anything of merit in this."

Luther used to say that "justification by faith alone," was "the article of a standing or of a falling Church." Dear Adelaide felt it day by day to be the article of a standing or of a falling Christian. "What a glorious subject the atonement is!" she writes, referring to Lev. xvi. "The perfect remission of our sins through the one offering, the Lord Jesus Christ, once and for ever! No works, no repentance, no services needed for our acceptance with God; for all was wrought for us in Jesus. How this relieves the anxious, burdened mind of the poor sinner! He comes to God in the imputed righteousness of Him who stood in his place as a sin-offering.

And in another letter: "I am glad you are interested with the subject of the priestdood—it is immensely wide. Think of the 'spiritual sacrifices' we are to offer as God's holy and royal priesthood, rendered acceptable as they are 'by Jesus Christ,' our 'great High Priest.' 'Present your bodies a 'living sacrifice'—is not that a remarkable expression? A lamb, when once offered, was dead; but we are to go on offering our bodies, to be consumed in the flame of love continually—the sacrifice of one's whole life! And don't you think we are to offer our talents, and time, and money, and affections as 'spiritual sacrifices,' to be burnt or consumed on the altar of Christ's body, *i.e.*, His members on earth, that they may daily ascend as a sweet savour to God by Christ Jesus?"

One of her anxieties she calmed thus—the words occur in a note to the Hon. Mrs. C——, dated Nov. 3 (1851): "I have been gathering comfort lately from a marginal reading the 139th Psalm. I don't know whether it may have struck you; but, in connexion with a view which is sometimes taken, that verses 14–16 refer to the mystical body of Jesus, it is very interesting, I think. 'Thine eyes did see my substance, yet being imperfect; and in thy book all my members were written, *what days they should be fashioned*, when as yet there was none of them.' Is it not a nice verse to think of, when one is anxious about any one as to their spiritual condition, if their conversion seems to be very long delayed? each member of the body being fashioned *in the day* which is written in God's book!"

And she adds: "I do indeed feel, as you say, that such thoughts are overwhelming to our finite minds, connected as they are with regions unexplored almost by the most matured faith. Yet the little glimpses of heavenly light which come down, like the rays of the sun behind a cloud, upon our earthly hearts, are very sweet. They seem to tell of a light which we are not yet 'able to bear.'"

This life's brief hour is our infancy; our manhood is in the age to come: but the sapling is now receiving its bent.

> "Character groweth day by day, and all things aid in its unfolding."

Feeling the overwhelming weight of this fact, Adelaide writes, Nov. 17, thus: "Has it ever struck you, in reading Revelation, how each of the songs which are there recorded as sung by the saints in glory, refers to their own specific characters and discipline on earth? For example—the song of the twenty-four elders and four living creatures, in Rev. v. 9, 10, on the opening of the seven-sealed book (which must, I think, refer to some part of Christ's redeeming work; and the context leads me to conclude it must be the redemption of this earth). Then the song of the countless multitude, in ch. vii. 9, 10. And the song of the 144,000 'redeemed from the earth,' in ch. xiv. 1–5. And the song of the victors over the beast, in ch. xv. 2–4. And in ch. xix., the united voices of the heavenly throng, 'saying, Alleluia.' Don't you think it gives immense interest to each day's existence here, to see how the character of our praises hereafter will be connected with it? May Jesus be ever present with your spirit, and give you sweet foretastes of the fellowship which you are to enjoy with Him through all eternity! And may His mercy, peace, and love be multiplied to you moment by moment till you 'enter into peace'—the desired haven!"

The person of Christ continued to be the centre of her heart's desires. "I was so delighted," she writes, Nov. 28, in allusion to Ezek. i., "with the way it ends, pointing to 'the appearance of a man' as the very centre of all the glory, and Himself the 'brightness' of the glory! Are you not delighted when you catch a fresh glimpse of Jesus in a passage of the Old Testament where you had not seen Him before? It seems as if the Spirit were actually engaged with us in showing us something more of Him."

And, indicating another of the Lord's ways, she writes: How long it sometimes takes to answer prayer! and how unlikely the several steps seem to be, by which it is answered! It was the case of Israel in Exod. ii. and iii., which struck me so much

They cried, and their cry came up unto God, at the very time of their distress (Exod. ii. 23–25); and He seems at once to have spoken to Moses about it, saying, 'I have surely seen the affliction of my people which are in Egypt,' and I am come down to deliver them.' (Exod. iii. 7, 8.) And yet, in the first instance, they could not have had the least idea that God was answering them; for He only spoke to Moses, and Moses was in another land. Then Moses caused a delay by his unbelief, so that the Israelites did not get the assurance that their cries had been heard until the end of the fourth chapter. Then after that, instead of immediate deliverance, their bondage was actually increased; and when God again assured Moses that He would fulfil all His promises to them, in ch. vi. 1–8, they were so bowed down with 'anguish of spirit and cruel bondage' that they could not believe it was true. It gave them no comfort whatever, and their misery altogether seemed immensely increased. Then Pharaoh was another great hindrance, and again and again God gave him 'respite'—all which must have been exceedingly difficult to the Israelites to understand. Surely it must have been a very great trial of faith, and one which must have lasted some months, as far as I can make it out, though the number of days is not always specified as to the length of the plagues, &c. And yet God was in fact answering their prayer all that time, was He not? And at last the deliverance really came, and at 'the set time'—'at the end of the 430 years, even the self-same day.'"

To a fellow-pilgrim who seemed near her home she writes, Dec. 4 (1851): "I do not feel as if I could bear to think of losing you; but I would like to lose my will in God's. The thought of your being 'with the Lord' is too bright to make one wish to detain any one down here in such a world of darkness, ruin, curse, and death. But to know the sovereignty of God's unalterable purpose silences many wishes. Each link in the chain has its own right place. Those words in Joshua i. 11 are so precious—'Within three days ye shall pass over this Jordan!' The limited, fore-ordained, fixed time; the safe passage over; the certainty of entering Canaan; and the fact of its being God's gift—are all so sweetly brought out; and I like the thought too so very much of the three days' preparation—lodging on the borders of Canaan in such composure, whilst, in leaving Egypt, they had to be in such haste."

For some time back, she had forwarded to a dear friend fortnightly a paper of "texts for each day." Writing, on Dec. 12 (1851), with the texts for the two last weeks of the year, she says: "Sometimes I hope I have been permitted to bring you daily food in the desert, as the ravens fed Elijah; and if so, I am thankful for the privilege, and shall be more thankful if I am allowed still to minister to you as long as you are in an earthly tabernacle to need it. How different it will be when 'the Lamb which is in the midst of the throne' feeds you, and leads you by the living fountains of water in heaven! Then it will be indeed true that our 'warfare is accomplished' as well as that our iniquity is pardoned. And I am sure you must often look forward to the day when the fight of faith shall be over, and you shall 'sit down with Abraham, Isaac, and Jacob, in the kingdom of heaven.'

"I have seemed so weary of the conflict of late," she continues; "I am sure I should have fainted had I not believed to see the goodness of the Lord in that land where all is life, and light, and glorious liberty. The humanity of Jesus has been very comforting to think of; His calling us 'brethren,' and partaking of our very nature, owning us as His 'children.' I have done some texts on His 'trust' in God, from Heb. ii. 13; and it seems as if it helped one exceedingly to see how He was upheld by the Spirit just as we are. 'Behold my servant, whom I uphold. I have put my Spirit upon Him.'

"I met," she proceeds, "with a new thought the other day. I found it stated that the word rendered 'bruise,' in Gen. iii. 15, is literally, 'to overwhelm with darkness, or with a tempest.' It is the same word that is rendered 'darkness' in Ps. cxxxix. 11; and it scarcely occurs anywhere else. If that prophecy were a looking forward to the darkness which covered the earth at the crucifixtion of Jesus 'for three hours,' how wonderfully it was fulfilled, being such a comparatively light thing to the 'outer darkness' into which Satan shall be cast for ever and ever!

The one a bruising of the heel, but the other of the head! The 22d Psalm shows so very beautifully how the darkness passed away from Jesus—from His soul as well as from external nature. And do you not think that the darkness—the 'horror of great darkness'—which fell upon Abraham before the burning lamp passed between his sacrifice, was a striking prefiguring of the horrible darkness which fell upon Jesus, ere His soul was poured out unto death (He being Himself the sacrifice)?

'I think, if one may understand Gen. iii. 15 in this way," she adds, "it suggests a very precious thought also for all the members of 'Abraham's seed.' For it tells—does it not?—that our bruising, our times of darkness, are but the sufferings of 'a little while?' They shall pass away, and our songs of deliverance shall mingle with those of Jesus, when, in the midst of the congregation, He sings praises unto God. Do you remember a beautiful sentence of Owen's on Heb. ii. 12—'In the midst of the Church will I sing praises unto Thee?' He says: 'These words are taken from Ps. xxii. Most of the Psalm containeth the great conflict He had with His sufferings, and the displeasure of God against sin declared therein. As He lands upon the shore, from that tempest wherein He was tossed in His passion, He cries out, "In the midst of the Church will I sing praises unto Thee."' "

Too real to be imitative, she yet was drawn to certain saints by a very peculiar affinity. "Have you seen the Memoirs of Hewitson?" she writes,

Dec. 26. "I never read a book which I enjoyed or entered into so thoroughly. My mind is full of it. He so longed for close dealing with God." And, uttering her own soul's longing, she adds: "Oh! it is indeed His own self I pant after. Fellowship—living, constant, intimate fellowship—with Him, is the cry He often hears from the desolate void of my unloving heart. How I do loathe the sin which makes the atmosphere so misty, the clouds so thick and dark! I am now reading Deuteronomy, to see more of God's holiness and of the necessity for not sparing the darling lust. That is where I suffer such loss."

Another feature of her own maturing life, she describes thus: "Oh! I do so intensely enter into what you say of the deeper experience of riper years as so much more abiding than the brighter experience of the babes of Christ. Lambs frisk and play; for they have nothing to do but enjoy themselves. But how different when they become sheep, and have to travail in birth and to feed their young? Is it not a true picture of Christ's fold? I could not at all tell you how I have been made to feel lately that this later and riper experience is coming upon me, and the earlier and former and more lightsome kind passing away. I have so felt other people's sins, and seemed so identified with my family, the house, the parish, the congregation! I feel as if I must make confession of all their sins for them. I believe it is precious experience; for it is Christ-like, is it not?"

Her health this winter occasioned her not a little

inward conflict. "Oh! to be more swallowed up and absorbed in Jesus!" she writes, Dec. 26; "then I should be more content with His dealings, of whatever kind they might be. I do so much feel the truth of all you say about our personal and individual dealings with God alone—the work hidden from every eye but His. My body often keeps down my spirit. Well as I now am to all appearance, I have many a weary day or night, and frequently such restless uneasiness, without actual pain, that it is no wonder to me that the inner man is often greatly burdened and oppressed. But it is all so 'well,' that I cannot be thankful enough."

Another year closes upon our pilgrim, and leaves her still in the wilderness. Labouring like one who feels the preciousness of the short hour, she writes, Dec. 29 (1851): "I esteem it such a privilege to minister to the members of Christ's body militant here on earth, especially as the time shortens. I have been so stirred up with the state of this large parish, that I have got a poor man to go about among the poor in the evenings for me, hoping to lead some at least to Jesus. If you can lift up one prayerful thought for me and him and Christless souls here, I shall be most grateful. His ear is 'not heavy,' but 'open to our cry.' Go when we will and where we will, we find Him ever listening."

And on Dec. 31, writing to the Hon. Mrs. C——, she says: "May I send you Deut. i. 30, 31, for this season of the year. It has struck me so much, that New-year's day seems like a time for the Christian to strengthen himself for the future by the review of all the past—of all that took place 'in Egypt,' and 'in the wilderness,' until 'we came into this place.' What confidence we are exhorted to place in God—'Dread not!' (v. 29)."

"Our times are in thy hand,
Father, we wish them there;
Our life, our souls, our all we leave
Entirely to thy care.

"Our times are in thy hand,
Why should we doubt or fear?
A father's hand will never cause
His child a needless tear.

"Our times are in thy hand,
Jesus the Crucified!
The hand our many sins had pierced
Is now our guard and guide.

"Our times are in thy hand;
We'd always trust in thee,
Till we have left this weary land,
And all thy glory see."

CHAPTER XVI.

"How I should like her portrait," writes one of Adelaide's most intimate friends, "with her open Bible in her hands, as it always used to be, and all the energies of her penetrating mind digging deep for its unsearchable riches—now bringing up a bit of the precious ore with such delight as another bright addition to her store, and now surveying with increasing joy all she had already got! No Memoir could be in the least faithful which did not throw a strong light upon the peculiar way in which she *lived upon* the Bible. And this resulted, I think, from that feature in her character which led her to sift so indefatigably every subject into which she cared to inquire. Grasping the whole plan of salvation, and settled and established in it immoveably, she fixed her eye steadily on God; and to know Him was all her desire. On that subject she was insatiable—ever exploring His word to find Him out, ever tracking His mind; and thence arose those ardent longings to be wholly absorbed in Him. The study of Jesus—His thoughts as perfect man, His mind as God—occupied her almost continually; and so richly was she repaid in these researches, that there were seasons when her soul was so filled with adoration at the discoveries opened up to her, that, for a time, they seemed to extinguish temptation and leave her free to delight herself in God.

"Then, again," continues her friend, "there was a reverse side to this picture—when this very study would open the flood-gates of temptation and raise strong conflicts within. She could not bear to feel she had any thought which did not seem to harmonize perfectly with the mind of Him she worshipped. She was not satisfied to assent, to believe, and to *leave* deep matters; she felt assured it was the privilege of the child of God to enter into full, unrestricted, entire conformity of thought, wish, will, and purpose to the Divine mind—and this through union with Christ and the indwelling of the Spirit. She seemed so well to know when He was taking of the things of Jesus and showing them to her, or when her own mind was at work. Her spirit could find no rest when she found herself in a state only to acquiesce in any word of God: she wanted to go along with it; and, if the hindrance to her doing so arose from imperfectly understanding it, she ceased not to ask, to knock, to seek! Oh! how diligently did she spread her sails, how patiently did she wait for the precious gales of the Spirit, to carry her into that presence, without which existence was really a burden to her!

"You can understand, then, I am sure," her friend adds, "how this world—this life, in the common acceptation of the word, was nothing to her. Nor was it any temptation. Her's was, if I may so express myself, altogether a spiritual warfare; and she found hardly any one who could understand her. The conversation of Christians generally was a positive trial to her. She used to say to me, 'While they are talking around me, I am occupied with singing and making melody to the Lord in my heart. I can talk to Him, and I can hear His "still, small voice."' But, equally, when she did meet with those whose sympathies were in unison with hers, her communion with them was of the purest, most elevated description, and her enjoyment of the highest degree. Her method of searching the Scriptures will be seen in her papers, and will show how she loved to harmonize all the plans of God and bring out their wisdom, beauty, and glory, as a faint reflection of Himself. This appears to me to have been the leading turn of her mind."

The writer of these lines (the Hon. Mrs. C——) was one of the very few by whom dear Adelaide felt that she was understood. "Mrs C—— is my *prime* friend," she writes; "I could not tell how I *delight* in her. I have spent nearly three weeks with her at D—— both the two last summers. She is such a Bible-Christian! We used to talk about it for hours together."

In her brief Diary the year opens thus: "*Jan.*, 1852.—'The poor committeth himself unto thee.' (Ps. x. 14.) What better can I do with myself this year? 'I am *poor* and *needy*.' MY WHOLE SELF I would commit into my Father's hands, whether for life or death. His promise is, 'The expectation of the poor shall not perish for ever.' (Ps. ix. 18; Isa. xlix. 23; Ps. lxii. 45.)"

And again: "*Jan.* 1.—'Who, then, is willing to consecrate his service this day unto the Lord?' (1 Chron. xxix. 5.) And 1 Chron. xxix. 17: 'Is it not *my* "Beloved" who speaks? has He not seen a willing offering in His servant?' *Jan.* 4, *Sab.*—'Thou hast avouched the Lord this day to be thy God.' (Deut. xxvi. 17.) I have, at His table—owning myself His, and that He is mine, before a great congregation on earth, and before angels—good and bad—and before the Triune Jehovah. *Jan.* 19.—The opening day of the school at Mickleover. Oh, that it may be the letting down of the net to catch a multitude of fishes!"

And, later: "*Feb.* 1.—Again fed at the Lord's Table, remembering Him who is still absent. *Feb.* 8.—Heard Mr. —— on Gen. i. 2. Alas! the waters of baptism spoilt it *all* to me! *March* 15.—Vestry meeting from St. Alkmund's Schools; we each sent £50. May Jesus own and bless it! *April* 3.—Saw dear Maria W——. She spoke of Jesus and the Father making their abode with us, and told me Dr. M'Neile's sermon was a blessing to many Christians. 'Bless the Lord, O my soul!' *April* 9, *Good Friday.*—Heard Mr. —— on John xix. 30. A precious service. Did not Jesus rejoice to be so remembered on earth?"

These jottings indicate not uncertainly dear Adelaide's daily life. "She fixed her eye," as her friend so truly says, "steadily on God; and to know Him was all her desire." Rarely has any one more "ardently longed to be wholly absorbed in HIM." But it was not a mystic pietism. Her life, as we have seen, was one unceasing "living sacrifice." Poor Herbert once sighed—

> "Oh! that I were an orange-tree,
> That busy plant!
> Then should I ever laden be,
> And never want
> Some fruit for Him that dressed me."

Adelaide Newton did more than sigh. Life was with her a business—a business for God.

Her "strength" in doing and in suffering was "the joy of the Lord." Gazing not on the sun as reflected in the ever-varying waters, but on the sun in His steady march in the heavens—not on God as seen in the fitful surface of her own feelings, but on God as seen in the unchanging expanse of His Word —she learned to rejoice in Him continually, even amidst unceasing trials. "Did you not feel," she writes, for example, on Jan. 9 (1852), "as you looked at those texts, how much the past year's experience had deepened your interest in all that GOD is to you? I seemed to feel it so much, as I was doing them—above all His long-suffering, and constancy, and unwavering loving-kindness. How truly in Him there is 'no variableness, neither shadow of turning!'"

Alluding one day to the words, "Prepared as a bride adorned for her husband," she said, "Yes, it is that 'preparation' which is now detaining us down here; for no hammer can be heard in 'the city'—the preparing is done now."

And another day, following out the same thought, she said: "I have been so struck with the Greek word in James v. 11, which we render 'patience.' It is literally 'to remain under.' Does it not give the exact idea of prolonged suffering? How much we have to remain under—have we not? Such a load of daily crosses and trials from which there is no escaping! It often comforts me to think what it is preparing us for. Do you not think our work as well as our places in heaven will depend very much upon what we have been here educated and trained to do? Every day I think I connect earth and heaven more and more together, each event here being linked in with our happiness there."

Her own "preparation" hastened forward. "The last few months," we find her writing at this period, "have made the greatest difference in me—I feel more than so many years older. I feel this so much, that I have sometimes wondered whether I was living my life in a small compass; but it may not be so, and I am content to leave it."

And again: "How little we know, when we begin to use the little talent or power we think we have, what use God intends to make of it! I often think what wonders will be revealed in the day when all the links in the chain become visible."

Adelaide "overcame," not by going out of the world, but by witnessing for Christ in it. "I felt sure you would have to go to —— to dinner," she writes; "and I can well understand your preferring to be alone with Jesus; but His 'go to my brethren, is a word of command which must often send us as well as Mary, *in a sense*, away from Him—must it not? But soon He will have us where He is for ever."

Sending to a friend a new tract, she writes: "You see my pen cannot be still. I do hope this word may lead some Christless souls to get ready, ere the day shall banish them with all their works of darkness into the gloom of eternal night."

And she adds: "I send you the report of the Hospital. I have some hope of getting some good ladies about here to contribute. I don't like Mrs. ——'s way of writing; how can she call it 'the dear Hospital?' My Bible is very precious to me just now. I have not seen Trench's book; but I am sure I should like it. I am more rivetted by *words* in Scripture every day."

Krummacher somewhere says, that if there be a spirit within us which can be at ease in the midst of defilement and can bear sin, we may be sure that that spirit is not the holy Dove. A dove has been known to flutter and tremble at the very sight of a hawk's or of a falcon's feather. "Nothing strikes me more," Adelaide writes (Jan. 12, 1852), "as year after year rolls on, than the wondrous forbearance of such a God of holiness with such a world of sin. Oh! how intensely of late I have groaned under this world's sin and ungodliness! Words could not tell it." And again: "I have another tract which I think of printing ere long, on the 'Purging of the Floor.' (Matt. iii. 13.) What a prospect that is to look onward to—'He will *thoroughly* purge His floor!' I cannot tell how deeply I have entered lately into passages which show how the earth will be cleared of all its abominations when Jesus comes—swept with the besom of destruction."

Growing in sympathy with Him who wept over sinners, she writes: "My heart is often so heavy that the wheels drag slowly over the ground. I seem quite unable to forget the unpardoned sin which is sinking so many into hell, and the unconfessed sin which keeps so many believers at such a distance from peace and joy in Jesus."

And sympathizing also with Jesus in His joyful anticipation of the coming "rest," she writes, some days later, thus: "Yesterday I did so enjoy Heb. iv.—the 'rests' of God and of His people. What a sweet subject for a Sabbath down here—a pledge and foretaste of the Sabbath which 'remains!' I am sure Owen's explanation of the 'rest' stops far short of the truth, because he sees in it nothing beyond the Gospel-rest for Christians. I have been reading a good deal of Horsley lately, and was so struck with one passage, where the Hebrew word for 'rest' occurs in 2 Sam. xxiii. 7. Our translations says, 'They shall be utterly burned with fire in the same place;' but he says it should be 'In the Sabbath (the 'rest') they shall be utterly burned with fire'—referring not to the end of that which is burned, but to the end of all things, when they shall be utterly consumed out of the earth."

And in another letter she says: "Did you ever notice how beautiful the meanings of the two Hebrew words are for 'rest' quoted by St. Paul in Heb. iii. and iv.? The one in the ninety-fifth Psalm is 'Noah,' which Parkhurst defines as rest from toil and weariness—as the ark rested on Ararat after its tossings to and fro on the waters, or as the land had 'rest from war' in the days of Joshua. The other word, quoted from Gen. ii. 2, is 'Sabbath,' literary cessation—*i.e.*, rest (not from labour, but) because the work is finished. God rested, or ceased, because all was done. Does not this give an exquisite view of rest? The two together seem to me to present such a perfect prospect for faith to rest itself upon. We shall have rest in the desired haven from all the toil of life; and we shall enter into God's own rest, when He shall have made all things new; and nothing will remain to be done to break His Sabbath of rest to all eternity. This latter kind of rest does seem so inexpressibly perfect—the whole creation sharing in it, as it did on the first Sabbath-day in Eden, and Jesus bringing into it all the blessings of His Sabbath-day (if I may so express it) when all His new creation work was ended, and a Triune God finding perfect and eternal satisfaction in that keeping of a Sabbath which remaineth to us His people."

The "man in the picture" had his eyes lifted up to heaven. "After suffering dreadfully for a while by restraint in prayer," Adelaide writes, Jan. 24 (1852), "for many weeks the constraint upon me has been to pray; and much time has been spent in the attempt. As to the expression of prayer, it has been a mere nothing; but I have found the greatest strength in those words, 'He that searcheth the heart, knoweth what is the *mind* of the Spirit,' which, I suppose, refers to the groanings which could find no vent in utterance or outward expression. If so, are not these inward 'groanings' (for no other word half expresses it) the very things which the Spirit is working in us, and which, after all, constitute the truest prayer? The grand point where I fall short is, that I go away so often without any consciousness of getting what I ask for. Hewitson said he never went to bed without knowing with 'absolute confidence' that his sins were forgiven, because he believed in God's truthfulness when He said, 'If we confess our sins, He is faithful and just to forgive us our sins.'"

And, somewhat later, she writes: "It is remarkable, that, since I wrote to you, two very dear friends have been dreadfully tried of late, in not being able to *express* anything in prayer. This restraint is very painful in one way; but, do you know, just very lately I have seemed to feel as if my groanings spoke more than my words. Words are not needed *to God*. He reads the mind of the Spirit in us;—how much that means! I only want to be filled with desires, and they shall be fulfilled. I have been thinking how every wish of our renewed hearts is summed up in those words, 'Thy will be done!' What is not included of good in our Father's will?"

And again: "Do you enter much into prophetic study? You will see what a sweetly refreshing and sustaining subject it was to Hewiston. It is so much more the thought of seeing Jesus, than of any of the accompanying circumstances, which I love to think of, that I value my tract as likely, I hope, to call attention to the subject. I know it is 'the living Person,' as Hewiston so often says, that we need to come in contact with, if we are to be lively Christians. Don't you often pant for better fellowship with Him?"

A lesson of her maturing heavenliness she notes graphically thus: "Deuteronomy strikes me most as the book which instructs the true Israel of God as to their condition 'in the land.' I take it to be a stage beyond the wilderness—beyond even the conquests of the book of Joshua. It is not the first taking possession, so much as the unflinching yielding up of the whole heart and life to God in after-experience. It does so condemn me, dearest ——, from page to page, that I almost shrink from saying what I seem to see in it: nought of the 'cursed thing cleaving' to one's hand—the cities of the enemy burnt to the ground, and all the spoil, every whit—the diligent, careful hearkening to God's words, and the holy obedience and truthfulness required—and then, too, the rejoicing even before the Lord, and the intense holiness which the whole atmosphere of the entire book seems to breathe. Altogether it makes one breathless, if you understand me, to be in so pure an air. I think it is not studied by Christians as it deserves. We should be saved out of such mixture with the unholy and unclean, if we saw our true standing 'in the land.'"

And, writing to one "very near the entrance into glory," she says: "How beautiful Deut. i. 25 is—the spies going into the land, and bringing some of its fruits, to show to others what a good land it is! May not this be great reason why you have been detained so long in the body, that, having spied much of its fruitlessness, you might tell of it to me and to many, many others?" And again: "Don't you think the 'garment of praise' is a very essential part of a Christian's clothing, and becomes so more and more as he draws nearer to the society of those who stand around the throne with harps of gold and cease from anything but praise?

"'Then we shall sing more sweet, more loud;
And Christ shall be the song.'"

And to the same, some weeks later: "I scarcely imagine you look much at the waves of trouble now. Are you not occupied with Him most, who walks *upon* them and whispers in your ear, 'It is I?' I feel, more and more, that it is in proportion as we come personally and individually into contact with the living person of Jesus, that the work in the inner man grows in depth and in reality. I often think of you as just on the borders of the heavenly Canaan, receiving the finishing strokes of the great Architect's hammer."

A similar experience she indicates in another letter, thus: "I have been struck to-day with Mark vi. 48—Jesus looking on whilst His disciples were 'toiling in rowing' on the sea, and He Himself was on the land; and, though He saw them, yet He went not to them until the fourth watch of the night. And even then He would have passed by them. Don't you think we may gather from incidental remarks of this kind how much less our mere enjoyment or relief from trouble is His object than it is ours? His thoughts are so very much higher than ours in all these ways; He seems so often to be represented as looking on while His people are suffering, yet not bringing relief for some time, like Israel in Egypt—'I have seen, I have seen.' It has occurred to me lately that these words could almost convey the impression that his own heart of love had been wrung with anguish with what He had seen (if one may speak of Him in language so human), as if He could not speak strongly enough of what He had seen. And yet how long it was, after that, ere they were finally rescued! It often wants David's kind of waiting in 'waiting,' does it not? (Ps. xl. 1, margin.) But they who wait on Him shall not be ashamed.

Some interesting touches of character come out indirectly in a letter to another friend, dated Jan. 26: "I own I should be glad if the —— could leave ——; it is evidently so utterly unsuited to

——. What a very singular experience theirs has been in the Christian life! I felt greatly interested and truly sorry for Mrs. ——; for her whole tone of mind seemed to me so unhealthy. I think both sisters want Christian society to call them out of themselves; and that they cannot have at ——. They want spiritual vigour and spiritual strength; but there is much to love in them, and they were most kind to me."

"I have heard no more of Mr. ——," she adds; "but I am sorry if I slandered him. He is one of the Lord's chosen vessels; and I would not be guilty of breaking off even a little bit of the ornamental chiselling, by throwing even a small stone at him. I need not throw stones at others. Enough—oh, how much more than enough!—for me, if I look at the beam in my own eye. And how it blinds and distorts my powers of seeing others aright! One thing I do hope my heavenly Father is teaching me, and that is, to loathe and abhor myself. I would sink deeper and deeper still, that Christ may get all the glory of what His grace does in and by me, and that 'yet not I' may ever be my motto. I have been more and more delighted with 'Hewitson' each time I have read it—and I have gone through it three times, and read the greater part four times. Oh, how closely he walked with God! His *mind* so exactly suits mine; it is more interesting to me than even M'Cheyne's Memoir. I grieve to hear of your illness, though I am sure it is a token of your being led more alone with Jesus. I cannot give you the least idea how I have been dragged out of my happy 'solitude of experience,' as I called it long ago, not so much by going amongst strangers again, as by being made to feel identified with those around me, and with 'the Church (which is His body).' Do you know much of confessing sin for others? It has been my constant occupation lately. Oh, how sin does afflict me! I need only hear of it or see it, and my own spirit is wounded and darkened."

Some other features are given elsewhere. For example, on February 4, she writes: "Your kind note did me great good, because it was so full of Jesus. I am so thankful you are so happy in Him. Surely you need not fear to indulge in enjoying Him with joy unspeakable. He is leading you into green pastures, and making you to lie down beside the still waters; and he means it to be a sweet time of refreshment, does He not? I suspect we should enjoy those opportunities while they last; for we are soon enough called back into scenes of conflict."

And to Mrs. C—— W——: "I value all your experience so much, when you review your long life and tell me how you feel now. It is deeply, deeply humbling to look back on what we have sought to do to Him; it is, as you say, so spoilt with sin, even in our holiest things. I have deeply felt it lately; and I suppose it must be my experience, more and more, as I go onward. Dear Mr. Evans! how he felt it! But he had naturally one of those very powerful minds which feel everything in an intense way. It makes the 'Memoir' exceedingly precious to me. His deep views of sin, and his proportionally deep appreciation of the efficiency of the blood of Jesus to wash it away, give such fulness of meaning to his words. I am so glad you have got 'Hewitson;' it has been a precious book indeed to me. He walked in the secret of the Lord's presence, under the eye of the same holy God as Evans did; and his faith was so very simple that he did not linger about the threshold, but entered into Jesus (as he expressed it) and lived upon His breath!"

"I cannot tell you," she continues, "how much and often I think of you, dearest Mrs. W——, in that foreign, distant land. But

"'What are distance, time, and place,
To the God that fills all space?'

I am most thankful, if you are suffering less bodily and enjoying much of the felt presence of Jesus. I love to believe that He has accepted all the unripe fruit of earlier days, and now looks to the 'fruits of the valley' in His ripening children. I often wish that advanced believers were less cast down by their views of what they are; but I suppose this is a part of those fruits which belong to 'the valley,' which I am still too young and too unripe to yield to the Lord. May He find in His gardens fruit which is sweet to His taste, whether we admire it or not."

Her health this winter continued stationary. "I am keeping up very wonderfully," she says. "I don't suppose people can see any difference in me;

but I keep up outwardly at great cost sometimes. However, the trials I have I cannot ask to be without; for it is through them the gold is purified from its dross."

Her friend has remarked, in the paragraphs quoted in the beginning of this chapter, that "she seemed to know so well when the Spirit was taking of the things of Christ and showing them to her, and when her own mind only was at work." An illustration occurs in a letter to the Hon. Mrs. C——, Feb. 2: "I am so glad you have enjoyed part of Heb. ii.; it was very sweet to myself in doing it, for it seemed to be *given* me—and *you* know what that is. I think I am now getting into the third chapter a little; but it often seems to me as if God kept me waiting now, until He has made me feel entirely without one thought, before He begins to teach me. It is exceedingly humbling to feel that I have made this necessary."

And she adds: "How very, very different Christian experience is, when acted upon by different outward circumstances! It seems to me impossible that one's friends should be able to know and make allowance for these changes: and that makes the omniscience of God so unutterably precious; for He can—and one can go to Him with such confidence in this knowledge far exceeding even our own! He knows the mind of His Spirit in us, when all seems to us in a maze."

In the same letter another thought occurs, which throws not a little light upon her own intense friendships. Alluding to Mr. Evans, she says: "I scarcely think his letters equal his sermons; but they reveal to me much of the secret of his being so useful and so beloved—at least, *I* trace much of it to his intense way of entering into the specific circumstances of his friends. He does not deal in general, commonplace remarks, but enters with minuteness and touching sympathy into each person's peculiar state of mind or body. And don't you think this tells powerfully on a man's ministry, as well as in more private life? It is a faint reflection of that individual contact with God in each and every circumstance of life, which makes the reality of religion so precious. I think the only person I ever knew carry it out as Evans seems to me to do, is Dr. ——. He never lets you feel that he is indifferent about you. I marvelled once at his sympathy with a weak-minded friend of ours at Torquay, who fretted about the death of a pet bird till every one else laughed at her. And Jesus condescends to sympathize in all our tiny daily vexations, as well as in our great troubles. O! for a heart of love like His!"

Each saint in glory, as he remembers all the ways of the Lord towards him, shall exclaim, in adoring thankfulness, "Thy gentleness hath made me great!" Dear Adelaide keenly felt the so-frequent lack of this Christ-like gentleness. "He preached a sermon on Sunday morning," she says, alluding to a preacher whom she had heard, "on 'How long halt ye?' It was very powerful—I might say overpowering, for I could scarcely bear it. Had it been combined with the tenderness and gentleness which such a subject required, it would have been enough to break the hearts of many: but there was a *hardness* about it which made it very painful to me. Oh! how unlike Jesus we are in our feelings towards hardened sinners!"

Amidst the langour and fatigue of "many a weary hour," she still resolutely laboured for her Lord. "Don't think any more of my outer man," she says, Feb. 3 (1852): "it is intended to perish in due time; and I really try to do my duty towards it while it lasts. We are but strangers, at best, down here; and often earth seems desolate to me, though I have so much to be thankful for and to make me happy. My time is very fully occupied; and that forbids the indulgence of sad and gloomy thoughts. I love to think that we are here for a little while, with precious opportunities of sowing seed which may hereafter add immensely to our harvest of joy in glory. This is often a great motive with me, to stir me up; for I feel that I am losing not only present comfort, but eternal enjoyment, when I trifle or sin away my time. You have two precious little souls to train for eternity, which must occupy most of your time. I have only to work in other ways as best I can; but I never find lack of work to be done in the Lord's vineyard."

CHAPTER XVII.

TERSTEEGEN describes, as "a real stratagem in the inward conflict," the "occupation of the heart with GOD." It is like a child (he says) which, at the sight of a dog, flees to its mother, and, instead of fighting with him, hides itself with confidence in her lap

Dear Adelaide was daily learning this "stratagem." More and more intensely her soul went out upon God. "I do so love," we find her writing, Feb. 15 (1852), "to think of each day's events as just the developement of His eternal plan, all coming to pass in perfect order, perfect harmony, and not one thing hurried over or out of place. Don't you feel more and more that it is Jesus Himself, His own glorious Person, that is everything and everybody to you? Now we truly see through a glass darkly; yet glimpses, through the lattice of Him we love, are very, very precious on our way Home."

"To think," she adds, "how soon we may see Him—'see Him as He is!' and then be like Him! 'One thing have I desired of the Lord, to behold the beauty of the Lord.' HIS beauty! what a sight it will be then for us to gaze upon! and what a sight it is to faith now! I am sometimes discouraged 'because of the way,' and sometimes because of inward conflict and innate depravity; but one sight of HIM, or one sensible grasp of His hand, quite seems to lift one up. Is not that wonderful—'Thou hast holden me by Thy right hand?' like a friend taking us by the hand, or like a father holding his child by the hand! 'His hands are as gold rings,' enclosing us!"

And in another letter, she says: "There has been something wrong about me lately; I have not enjoyed the fellowship I have sometimes done with the Father and the Son. I think it must have been 'the lust of other things entering in,' which has choked up the avenue, as it were, betwixt my soul and Jesus, and has hindered the soft whispers of His Spirit from falling on my ear. I am trying to confess and forsake the sin, whatever it is, and to return unto my resting-place in the bosom of Jesus."

It may be imagined with what feelings one who thus lived upon the kernel regarded the teaching which exalts the shell. "Never can I forget yesterday," she writes, Feb. 9, to Mrs. C—— W——: "You can scarcely conceive what I felt, in the midst of what would otherwise have been a very good sermon from Mr. —— , on the Spirit moving upon the face of the waters (Gen. i. 2), to hear him come out with the waters of baptism, and, while he strongly denied baptismal regeneration, yet to as strongly affirm that, where there was no conversion, there was still a great benefit conferred in the doing away of original sin ! ! ! This he also partly unsaid; but I really don't know how, for I felt so stunned that I retreated behind a pillar in the corner of the pew, and only entreated that the stream of deadly poison might not flow on through the congregation, and that the dishonour done to the BLOOD, which alone can take away sin, might be forgiven. I don't know what to do; it has wounded me to the quick. I feel, do you know, just as if I had been thrown into a dungeon like Jeremiah, surrounded with filthiness in this fallen world, from which there is no escape until the word is given, 'Come up higher!'" Do Christian men, whose trumpet, in this matter, gives so uncertain a sound, know how grievously they wound some of the holiest of the saints? It is no light matter to "offend one of these little ones."

Knowing how "tender" are the "grapes" of the living Vine, she was ever on the alert to "take the little foxes" which "spoil it." "The very fact of doing HIS work," she writes, "is often a great snare. I do so intensely feel the need of incessant *watchfulness*. You know my thoughts upon the difference betwixt this and self-examination; and I cannot tell you how experience deepens them. I would be always watching: then I should be perpetually looking, and walking 'in the light.' I want to be as an empty vessel, ever being filled from above with the rich droppings of the showers of God's blessings. I suspect my great success in the Lord's vineyard has tended to make me feel and act as though there were a spring of living water in myself, instead of every drop being to be derived from the Fountain of living waters above. Don't you understand the sort of thing I mean? It is to be self-emptied, self-abased —it is self-renunciation and self-denial which my soul now seems to need, in order that Jesus may reign there and fill it."

And, in the same letter, she adds:—"You still speak of wanting to know more of the liberty of God's children; and I believe my danger has been from feeling it so strongly as to be tempted by the ever-busy Evil One to abuse it by a less careful walk. Oh! dearest L——, what a straight and narrow way it is! and yet how inconceivably rich, and free, and complete, and satisfying our portion is 'in the Lord!' To plead His blood, and have not a single stain of guilt imputed to us; to plead His righteousness, and be clothed in raiment so white and pure, that God's eye admires our beauty; to stand, in fact, 'complete in Him,' and 'accepted in the Beloved;' what can be more blessed?".

Earnestly alive to whatever concerned the Word, we find her writing thus: "Have you met with Forster's work on the 'Sinaitic Inscriptions'? How intensely interesting it is! To think of Israel's wanderings being read upon the rocks, after the lapse of so many centuries! Do you not think that it is very remarkable that the decypherment should have taken place just when Infidelity is growing so formidable? And how very fearful the growth of Infidelity is! I am sure the only safety, in these days, is in keeping close to the Word. I scarcely think a greater work can be done in the Lord's vineyard than in leading people deeper into its treasures. The pure gold makes the world's dross useless."

And, alluding to one of her own Bible-searchings, she writes, in another letter: "Have you ever particularly studied the 10th of Genesis? It is so interesting, as givin gone a key to much of the ending of things in Revelation. In Genesis, we have the buds of those blossoms which in Revelation have ripened into full, ripe fruit. For example, the meaning of the word Babylon, or Babel—'confusion, or mixture'—throws such meaning into Rev. xvii. 1, 2, 15–18, and xviii. 2, 3. How plainly it shows that God's mind has read the chapter of its history with but one opinion, from the beginning to the end!"

On Feb. 20 (1852), she writes to another, thus: "I have been able, of late, to say very little to any one but God. In that verse—'My soul, wait thou only upon God, for my expectation is from Him'—what remarkable solitariness there is betwixt God and the believer, is there not? May I send you 'I will be to you a God'? N—— read your letter to a very nice, poor man, who is dying, and he seemed quite to drink it in, saying, in the middle of it, 'Yes, Jesus is very near—quite close to me.' It is, indeed, when earthly stays are taken from us, that the Lord becomes, as you say, everything to us. Will you sometimes breathe a thought into the ear of Jesus for me?"

To a "beloved Persis," in humble life, whose fellowship was very pleasant to her, she writes: "Will you get your half-holiday on Thursday, and give as much as you possibly can to me? You can't come too early; and, oh! may Jesus bring such a blessing with you as shall make us both cry out—'Stay me with flagons, comfort me with apples, for I am sick of love!' My text for you is John vi. 57. How full of life it is! 'As the living Father hath sent me, and I live by the (living) Father, so he that eateth me (the living Bread), even he shall live by me.' I do so love to think that Jesus is no longer the crucified One, no longer buried in the grave; but, 'rather,' that He is risen again, exalted, seated at the right hand of the Majesty on high. Dear M——, does it not raise you above the level of earthly trials, to feel your life hid in Him up there—'in God?'"

And to the same, on Feb. 25: "Will you oblige me by using the enclosed to give yourself fires in your bedroom during this severe weather? For the sake of your dear brother, do be persuaded to take care of your own body, remembering that it is dear to Jesus, for He has bought it at no small price. A new house is so dangerous in such weather: but there is One who cares for you, who will doubtless take care of you in it. My wish for you shall be what dear Mr. C—— asked for us one winter at Torquay—that the rooms may be always lighted up with the sunshine of His presence. I can't tell you how I enjoy seeing you, dear M——. What will heaven be, to have Jesus Himself, and all dear to Him and dear to us, to be around us for ever!"

Another of her maturing experiences she indicates,

March 3, thus; "Pride is peculiarly devilish, and it is where I think Satan gets great advantage over me. But there have been times, lately, when I sank into the most abject nothingness before God. No words can utter the feelings of moments like these; they are lessons which, as you most truly say, one must learn for one's self. I do feel how much there is to learn: it seems to be a feeling which grows very much on Christians, I think; one seems so increasingly to pant after more intimacy with Jesus—and that must, of course, involve oneness of mind and feeling with Him. And, oh! what a suffering life His was down here! Nothing has been more impressed on me lately than this: and all *I* have to learn out of suffering I feel more and more comes so infinitely short of what He felt. His experience in the Psalms is truly marvellous; and painful as one's own experience so often is, when one really feels what the Psalms say, I still do think it is positively comforting to know it is 'fellowship' with Jesus."

And still another feature of that deepening experience she notes: "I have been peculiarly tried by the sins of others. At every turn I see or hear something which I know must grieve 'the Spirit of holiness,' and am for ever joining myself in doing the same things along with others; and sometimes the sins of believers, and sometimes the sins of those who quite set our Lord at nought, seem as if they would crush me, Oh! is it not like going under a wheel full of iron spikes, to be made to hear unholy things said of One so dear as Jesus? But if we feel it, how infinitely more cutting it must have been to Him! Oh! what words those are—'I am the song of the drunkard!' To think of Jesus hearing Himself on the lips of a drunken man, whilst He had come down from the realms of eternal purity to rescue us sinners by His blood! But I cannot say in words what such thoughts as these lead one to—language seems to fail one completely."

One day, in conversation with a deeply tried friend, she said—"Don't we fail, as Christians, in not seeing all our sufferings to be a faint reflection of Christ's? I don't think we half believe that He really had the feelings of sadness, of distress, of inward desolateness, which He had and which we have. And yet I believe that when we are tried, the truest comfort and strength are derived from seeing our trials to be a participation of His."

And, writing to another, she says: "Have you ever read 'Payson's Memoir'? I don't wonder at Hewitson's love for it. Is it not very interesting to you to watch the different ways in which the Lord trains His plants, especially those which are to bear much fruit? I like looking through memoirs, just to see this. The Memoir of J. H. Evans suits me exactly just now: his was such deep experience; but I feel throughout his memoir the lack of that brightness which the hope of the Lord's coming gives, and which lights up Hewitson's Memoir with such brilliancy."

And she adds: "How kind it is of you to think of me! It is the love of Jesus running through you from His own heart. All you have told me of Mr. Krause is most precious. I do increasingly love to hear of God's dealings with His children; it has seemed lately to tell me so much of Himself. How suddenly he was admitted into the presence of his long-loved Master! I wonder how soon all the Lots will be taken out of Sodom. A closer walk with HIM is what I want so much. I almost always seem at a little distance from Him. Oh! when shall the clouds of sin be for ever dispelled by the unclouded sunshine of His presence in glory everlasting?"

In her own genial and touching way she writes, March 9 (1852), to her humble friend, thus: "Truly my heart often longs for communion with yours; and I believe I should often have written, had I not been so sad. I am certain it is chiefly bodily depression; but do pray for me, will you? that the light of the beaming countenance of Jesus may shine on me and gladden me. I hope He shines on you. Will you accept this little hyacinth? It does not smell so sweet as it should do; but I think it will shed a sweeter fragrance in your house than in our's. It is white, and I know you like white flowers—they remind you of the spotless purity of Him in whose 'white raiment' you are arrayed. Oh! how we feel the need of our being clothed in our white, blood-washed robes, when we would enter into 'the holiest' to appear under the very eye of our heart-searching, rein-trying, holy, holy, holy God!"

The "sadness" here named she alludes to in another

letter: "I have felt so unable lately to think, or read, or love, or pray, that it has been rather a dreary time with me; but how thankful I ought to be that I have had no doubts about being a child of God! Don't you think a negative state toward God is far better than anything positively evil, in contact with the Evil One? At least, when one is feeble, it is very tender dealing to be shielded from the attacks of the 'roaring lion'—is it not? I should be very unhappy about myself, only that I am really sure it is physical infirmity which makes me so unable to feel; and I believe it is a thorn in the flesh which is sent expressly to humble me, so that I almost value it whilst it grieves me."

Turning from herself and her experience to Christ and His experience, she writes, March 19: "Reading Mark xiv., and comparing it with Luke xxii., I have been so exceedingly struck with the way in which thoughts of 'the Kingdom' seemed to fill His mind, as He drew nearer to His greatest sufferings. In this, Psalms xxii., lxix., and cii. are perfectly parallel; the extremest sufferings and the brightest glory seem brought close together. And has it struck you how increasingly 'the Kingdom' seemed to occupy Him as He drew near to it—so that He spent the forty days after His resurrection chiefly (I suppose) 'in speaking of the things pertaining to the Kingdom?'"

A kindred thought is given in another letter, thus: "Do you remember that day when dear Mr. C—— first gave us the Lord's Supper together, and H—— B—— was with us? It has struck me lately, in thinking of Melchizedec, that his bringing forth 'bread and wine' to Abraham after his victory is a remarkable foreshadowing of the day when Christ will, *in a certain sense*, exchange His priestly work for His royal character, and, when all His enemies are put down, He enters on His reign of righteousness and peace, and fulfils His word in Luke xxii. 16–18: 'I will not any more eat thereof, until it be fulfilled in the kingdom of God,' and 'I will not drink of the fruit of the vine, until the kingdom of God shall come.' Do you not think that the typical character of Melchizedec throws light upon those difficult words? Until this connecting them with Melchizedech's royal priesthood struck me, I never felt to have a glimpse of light as to their true meaning."

Another of the experiences of the Man of Sorrows she alludes to elsewhere: "How intensely wonderful the sympathy of Jesus is in all the varied sufferings of this life—is it not? How wonderful the tears He shed over Lazarus, the inward groanings of His troubled spirit, the bitter trial of finding no one who could go all lengths with Him in what He felt! Have you noticed in Luke xxii., that it was in the supper-chamber, on His last night on earth, and when they must have been round the very table where they had just been partaking of the outward symbols of His lowest degradation, that the disciples began to contend and strive about which should be the greatest? I think it must have been so deeply painful to Jesus on that last night to witness it, and so trying to Him to hear their 'strife.' To me there is something so exquisitely painful in hearing a sharp contention about anything; so, what must it have been to HIM?"

Once more in the sunshine, her face again shone. "Have you noticed," she writes, "those four wonderful words (Exod. xxxiii. 21)—'A place by me?' Is it not, of all places on the earth, the place one would choose to be in above every other? And I think there is something so striking in the thought of the Holy One placing the sinner by His side! But it is all explained by its being 'in the cleft of the Rock'—'that Rock is Christ.' I am thankful to tell you I have been permitted to spend many happy days lately, as if with Jesus—His Word has been so precious to me, and Himself so dear. I shall never be near enough to Him till I am actually with Him. I am so glad you are feeling these intense desires after Him: is it not like the parched earth waiting on Him for showers of rain? And it shall come, 'in its season.' But we have surely got the earnest already in our desires for it."

In a house she was visiting one day, she met a German governess, to whom she spoke kindly of the "great salvation." "I found her," she writes, April 28, "a simple-minded young creature, anxious to be a Christian, yet hardly knowing how. She had been with a clergyman at ——, before she came there: but when I asked her if they were Christian people she had been with, she said she really did not know

—they were called so, but they did not seem to live as the Bible would make Christians live, and she could not well understand who were Christians and who were not! Oh! how it did make me feel ashamed of our traitor-like character!"

And to another: "Thinking this morning of you and your troubles, that verse occurred to me—'I will bring the blind by a way which they know not.' (Isa. xlii. 16.) I was supposing a father with several blind children, leading them through the streets of London. Is it not a fit illustration of our heavenly Father's leading of us through this trackless world? and does not everything depend on the confidence we feel in the hand which is leading us? Oh! how safe we are, though blind and utterly unable to see our way through the crowd of harassing events surrounding us!"

And to an old schoolfellow: "One thing lately has so pre-occupied my mind that I have left nearly everything for it; it has been a craving after intercourse with God Himself, which nothing less could satisfy—and I like to spend my time on my knees as much as I can. I can't call it praying, but 'waiting upon God,' as it were: and then, with the Bible open before me, it is almost as if He Himself were personally present, saying the words—they seem so really to come from Him. Oh! to be present with the Lord! what bliss it will be!"

The Bible's adaptedness to our manifold necessities she was ever delighting to exhibit. "Is it not very beautiful," she writes, "to see Job (chapter xix.

25–27) taking that particular view of his Redeemer which was most exactly suited to his own case? His body being so afflicted, and so much the cause of his suffering, it seems to me as if he were given to look onward in faith to the 'day' when it should be 'redeemed,' and so purified that in it he should see God! Paul, again, in writing of 'redemption' when one might imagine him to have been in health, speaks of 'waiting for the redemption of the body' rather in connexion with the renewal of 'creation.' Don't you think there is an interesting distinction betwixt the two states of mind, just arising from the different outward circumstances?" And she adds: "How wonderful it is, dear ——, that I may call myself your sister in and through that 'Redeemer,' our kinsman—is it not? May you enjoy much sweet intercourse with Him, in holy *intimacy* with Him, in that character!"

And, on May 27 (1852), she appeals to another thus: "You say you are 'in wretched spirits:' what, then, shall I say to comfort and cheer you? Why, of all things, I know nothing so comforting or so delightfully cheering as to look up above all the changing scenes of this changing life, to the serenity, and beauty, and exquisite glories of the world to come, where nothing needs change because all is perfect and satisfactory, and so good that it cannot be made better! Look up there, till your eyes are so rivetted that you forget the toil, and tumult, and din of London; and, what is better still, look till you are 'changed from glory to glory.' Has it ever struck you that transformation of character actually takes place by 'beholding glory?' I don't believe we have any idea of the effect which 'looking' with the eyes of our mind has upon us. May you experience the relief of such a 'look,' for the cure of all the wretchedness of your spirits!"

And, on July 8, she writes: "I have had some long and happy talks lately with Mr. G——: he is like one who has nearly passed through his Sionward journey. It is seldom one can meet with such ripened and matured Christians; and I found 'a rest in my spirit' with him which I have not known since I was at Torquay; no, nor even there, for I was comparatively young in experience myself then. You will say, So I am now; and it is true: and yet I often feel as if I had been long enough on the borders of eternity to have learned a good deal since then. Oh! what a difference that makes! Was your illness dangerous? I am so interested in knowing how others feel when they think they are near Home, especially if they are turned back again a little longer to sojourn in the wilderness."

CHAPTER XVIII.

In a garden near Milan, in the spring of 372, a young man lay one morning under a fig-tree, moaning and bathed in tears. "Take and read!" cried a voice to him from a neighboring house—"Take and read! take and read!" A neglected Bible flashed upon his soul; and he hastened to a friend with whom a short while before he had left a roll of Paul's Epistles. "I seized the roll," says he, describing the scene, "and read in silence the chapter on which my eye first alighted, the thirteenth of Romans. 'Put ye on' it said, in closing, 'the Lord Jesus Christ, and make not provision for the flesh, to fulfil the lusts thereof.' I did not want to read any more; nor was there any need—every doubt was banished." Augustine, from that hour, was on the Lord's side. "A passage of God's Word," says Gaussen, alluding to the occasion, "had kindled that glorious luminary which was to enlighten the Church for ten centuries, and whose beams gladden her even to the present day."

The same Word was Augustine's daily joy. And in the measure in which he was a Bible-Christian, he grew in the knowledge of God and in the graces of the life of God.

Adelaide Newton also owed to that Word her daily growth in heavenliness. Talking one day about the words, "Whatsoever He shall hear, that shall He speak," she quoted the passage—"The Spirit searcheth all things, yea, the deep things of God," and added: "Don't you think there is not a truth of God He cannot lead us into, if only we were able to bear it? I have been so struck with the thought of His searching out these things. And the word," she continued, "seems to imply it: it is, 'to trace, to investigate, to explore'—as if He delighted to explore the infinite depths of His own eternal mind, and then reveal them to us!"

Here is the Bible-student in her chamber. "I often feel inclined to smile," she writes, July 15 (1852), "at my sofa, with a Hebrew Bible and Lexicon at one side, a Greek Testament and Lexicon at the other, and one or two English Bibles always about it, too. I long only more and more to make my Bible the study of my life. Precious little volume! what wonders it reveals!"

And a farther glimpse into the chamber is given elsewhere: "I am left alone just now. I enjoy the quiet solitude so much, often not seeing any one for hours together—

"'His Omnipresence my sweet company.'

I am fancying you all solitary and bereft of visible creature-society. But you are at least surrounded by three Friends, who can look at you, and converse with you, and make your heart burn with intenser joy than ever you felt with a creature-friend. Like Shadrach, Meshach, and Abednego, and the Son of God, you may be in the furnace; but you have three Divine Persons with you there! they were—three human and One Divine."

And in another letter, she writes: "Is your mind enjoying any special portion of the Word just now? I am like a bee, gathering in something which is very 'sweet to my taste,' as I roam about in the Lord's rich pastures, yet knowing nothing of the science of the plants I am feasting on, nor able, during my short span of life, to explore the yet unknown fields of delight which even the Word of God could reveal to me. Still I am almost entirely occupied with it; and I think I can truly say, 'His fruit is pleasant to my taste.'"

An attack this summer, when on a visit to D——, again reminded her of the frailness of the tenure which kept her on this mortal scene. It came in the form of an overwhelming prostration. "I cannot say I am much better yet," she writes, on her return home; "nor do I at all understand myself. No one has found out here that I am not as well as ever; and I cannot tell them."

Dear Adelaide's religion was not an exotic, living in the solitude and in the sick-chamber, but unable to face the world's rough winds. Before her first illness, and again during the last two years of comparative health, it had proved itself a hardy plant. And if, in the sequel, we find her, amidst the privacy and the sharpness of new sufferings, adorned with a new holiness, it is only a new phase of that inner life which had already been nurtured so abundantly and so tenderly by the divine Husbandman.

> "Such sharpness shows the sweetest Friend;
> Such cuttings rather heal than rend;
> And such beginnings touch their end."

On Aug. 7 (1852), she writes: "My body is a very great burden to my spirit. When shall it be changed for one like that of Jesus? May He reveal much of Himself to you hour by hour! Hebrews has been interesting me exceedingly. I am thinking just now of chap. ii. 10: there is such a depth of meaning, that I am utterly lost in it; but if it were fit in God to perfect our Leader through suffering, of course His followers must be led along the same pathway." And again: "Oh! how I long for a near place in the Body (of which we are the members) to the heart of Jesus! that every pulse might beat in close unison with His! that I might always move in that precise direction in which the Head designed!"

And a few weeks later, she says: "I am so delighting just now in those precious words—'Surely, I come quickly.' Does it not make your heart throb with holy joy to think how soon Jesus may come, and fetch us all to be His bride for ever? There will be no more little irritating vexations, and no more of these greater tribulations, then. And God's estimate of the time which has to elapse first is so comforting. Seven times within four verses (John

xvi. 16–19), the Lord repeats the words, 'A little while.' And then that text (Rev. xxi. 6)—'And He said unto me, It is done!' does it not convey the idea that God Himself was rejoicing in the completion of His work? and if so, don't you think it is a great source of sustaining comfort to a tried believer, to see each day's trials as the successive steps leading on to that blessed consummation?"

Alluding to two friends who had visited her, she thus delineates God's "manifold" grace: "I am sadly afraid you did not get the spiritual refreshment or strength which you hoped for. I never like those large parties; and you had not even the quiet hour with him which I had. He was, beyond anything, delightful when I was alone with him: he talked to me of Christ, and gave Him such true pre-eminence. He was so calm and subdued, and yet so brilliantly happy; it was like sunshine to have him in my room. In fact, he so perfectly enchants me, that I am glad to have the disappointed feeling in him, that in some of the deepest feelings of my heart he has no sympathy. Just where —— sympathises so deeply he seems a stranger to the path I have, in my measure, trodden. And the reverse is equally true—where the one is depressed and unable to soar, the other calmly, yet with the truest magnificence, seems to me to dwell. Is not this the creature dwelt in by the Saviour, who shines forth in each through different mediums? And are not we deeply taught by each to love Him in them as streams of living water, yet not the Fountain?"

The Jew and his vacant Land could not fail to engage the thoughts and sympathies of one who so earnestly pondered the Word. "I really do not wish to trouble you to write," she says, in a letter to Colonel G——, "unless you can tell us anything about the chosen people, so dear to the heart of God that they ought to be dear to us. All you tell me of their present state and feelings is deeply interesting. I am glad, too, that you still purpose to publish your Tour. I cannot express how my heart responded to your remark, that God ever checks human impatience and keeps us waiting. Sometimes 'an horror of great darkness' creeps over me, when I think of all that is involved in Israel's restoration; but the 'end' is 'peace, and not evil,' and we must keep our eye fixed on that."

Another subject also occupied her thoughts at this period. "Egypt," she writes, "has rather been dividing my thoughts with Jerusalem. I felt that Forster's decypherments, if true, were so important in the cause of truth, that, having Egyptian hieroglyphics within reach at the Derby Museum, I resolved to test them, as far as I could, for myself. I studied Forster's 'Pharaonic Alphabet' very carefully before I went to look at the mummy; and you may readily imagine my delight on instantly recognizing the identical characters upon its back, in two long inscriptions. I copied them on the spot, and afterwards sent a copy to Mr. Forster, with each letter of the inscription put side by side with what I believed to be the corresponding English letter. Mr.

Forster says I have 'read the characters with the greatest accuracy, and enabled him to give a full decypherment of them.' "

And, some months later, writing to the Rev. Mr. Forster, she says: "The eager interest with which I read your most kind letter, with its accompanying decypherments, you can probably imagine, but I could not attempt to express. I never anticipated so much success in my endeavours to ascertain for myself the truth of your decypherments. I hope you were satisfied when you saw the bustard. But the point which has most weight with me is, that I should have fixed upon the only unknown hieroglyphic in either inscription which was not a letter, as the one which thoroughly puzzled me. I think this is immensely conclusive, in favour of the truth of your alphabet. You do not need such proofs for yourself; but, for a stranger to have met with such success, is an important, independent testimony—is it not? You are perfectly at liberty to make any use you like of my drawing, provided you say nothing of me."

In the same letter, she gives another specimen of her researches, thus: "I was looking out some words in Exod. xxviii., when I came to the 'pomegranate,' and when I saw, to my great delight, that the Hebrew word is רמוו—so like *raman*, that I hoped I might find something agreeing with your decypherment in the tablet from Osiris. Is it not singular, that Parkhurst should give this definition of the root רמה—'To cast, throw, project;' in Kal—'to cast or throw into some calamity or evil;' 'to throw into some disagreeable situation or circumstances, by deceit and fraud. *In fraudem impellere aut injicere*, to deceive, cheat, throw, or fling'? In that inscription you gave the word 'wahar,' as 'casting a man into something from which he cannot get out;' and the words immediately preceding the word *raman*, were 'dissembling,' and 'an accuser, or deceiver.' So that the Hebrew root suggests the very ideas actually to be found in words surrounding the pictorial representations of the 'pomegranate tree!'"

And, a few days afterwards, Mr. Forster replies: "I have to thank you very cordially for your last letter, and for its highly valuable confirmation of my renderings of the inscriptions surrounding the picture of the Fall. The sense of the root רמה, which you adduce from the Hebrew lexicons, is indeed most important; for, while it independently corroborates my versions of the adjacent terms, it shows anew the close affinity betwixt the Hebrew and Arabic, and supplies a valuable correction of a grave error of the lexicographers."

And, in April, 1853, she writes: "I need scarcely say with what pleasure I am anticipating the third part of the 'Primeval Language.' The subject grows in interest every day; but I have regretted my inability through illness to pursue my own investigations of it."

These scattered fragments of a very full correspondence are given, not for their subject-matter, but as another specimen of Adelaide's earnest zeal in prosecuting any inquiry which engaged her. The hieroglyphics we find her "studying almost day and night, the subject taking entire possession of her." It was not, however, to indulge a mere intellectual taste, but, as she tells us, "because it bore upon God's truth," and because she was "convinced that these are days when everything connected with the East is of vast importance."

Meanwhile she grew in heavenliness. "The stream runs past," she writes to an afflicted friend at Torquay; "and, I dare say, you often come within sight of the harbour now. But if you, and I, and others, are bid to tarry here to dispense the food which Jesus would give to save the lives of those who 'perish with hunger,' we may well do so with gladsome hearts. To be hid in God with Christ seems to me the very highest possible pitch of exaltation!—and yet this is our privilege now; and hereafter, when Christ 'appears,' so shall we 'appear,'—to display to angels, and principalities, and powers, the manifold wisdom of our God! They shall see why your life is still prolonged—don't you think?—and wonder and adore the depth of the riches of His wisdom and knowledge."

And her eye was still fixed on God. "May I send you to-day," she writes, "this verse from the 139th Psalm: 'How precious also are thy thoughts unto me, O God! how great is the sum of them!' There is such a striking contrast in that Psalm betwixt the felt poverty of our thoughts of God and the rich profusion of His thoughts of us! And just the same of His knowledge of us, contrasted with our inability to know Him. 'Thou hast known me; thou knowest my downsitting and mine uprising. THOU understandest my thoughts afar off.' 'Such knowledge is too wonderful for me; it is high, I cannot attain unto it.' This only we seem able to say; and don't you think there is felt relief in saying it—'Marvellous are thy works, and that my soul knoweth right well?' We know and feel how little we can know of the unsearchable greatness of our God. But is it not indeed 'precious' to be assured that His thoughts of us are more in 'number than the sand?' How 'very great' it makes one feel He is! I often feel now so overwhelmed with thoughts like these, and how impossible it is to say anything to Him or of Him, that I am quite dumb."

And in another letter: "I had a very happy, solemn time last night. Only I am almost overwhelmed with the immensity of God's greatness and the sense of my own insignificance;—all that I can do seems such child's play! I am such a mere speck—such an infinite atom—in creation! Surely Christians must be driven soon to make greater sacrifices in doing the Lord's work before He comes."

The conversation turned one day upon "the very close connexion betwixt the joys of heaven and the joys of earth."

"Will not there be," said a friend, "a distinct calling to remembrance there of the things done in the body? Every one is said to 'receive the things done in the body!'"

"Yes," said dear Adelaide; "and don't you think it seems the great principle on which God has ever acted, to produce an increase of good through the permission of evil or trouble? I was so struck with this last night," she proceeded, "in looking for the Hebrew of Isa. lxv. 17, 'new heavens,' and the Greek of Rev. xxi. 5, 'I will make all things new.' In both the word has the sense of 'renovation;' and our glorified bodies coming out of these bodies of humiliation—life out of death—glory out of afflictions (as in 2 Cor. iv. 17), all seem to tell the same thing—do they not?"

Another day, talking with a friend who was cast down by seeing little fruit, she said: "But in the broad daylight of eternity you will know (what you cannot well know now) how often God has spoken through you words in season to the weary—the very work which He instructed Jesus how to do! (Isa. l. 4.) Oh, how precious it is," she added, "to have any kind of fellowship with HIM!"

And on another occasion, conversing with a much-tried disciple, she said: "Don't you find the feeling grows upon you, that very few words are necessary in speaking to the Lord? He reads each thought; and as one realizes this more, don't you think it takes off very much of what, in earlier experience, one might call the burden of prayer? Does not it turn it rather into fellowship and continual breathing in the spirit of prayer?—and that, you know, is so different from the set speaking of certain seasons. I can't express exactly what I mean; but it is like thinking all one's thoughts aloud in His presence.

Oh, for more of it! Oh, to have no silent moments towards God!"

Martin Luther, in his Will, wrote: "Lord God, I thank thee that thou hast been pleased to make me a poor and indigent man upon earth. I have neither house, nor land, nor money, to leave behind me." Dear Adelaide was enabled, with a like "thankfulness," to rejoice in her peculiar discipline. "I have just been reading," she writes, "'Sickness; its Trials and Blessings,' by ——'s recommendation; and I have been telling her that, sound and useful as the practical advice is, I cannot like the general tone of the book—it breathes so little of the glorious liberty of the children, and so much of the hard and severe bondage of obedience, making the 'will of God' a thing to be submitted to rather than loved. The writer seems to me to have sought support more through the Church than through Jesus. Oh, how tenderly HE sympathizes! and how completely it is in fellowship with Him that we learn to bear, and suffer, and endure unto the end!"

And she adds: "I do so feel the truth of what you said in your last, that it is the secret guiding of His eye, and the discipline of one's spirit moment by moment, which seems the reality of the work of grace. This has been very much brought to my mind by Ps. lxxi. 17, which is, literally, 'O God, Thou hast disciplined me from my youth.' The Hebrew word is the same as that used for 'a goad' for breaking in oxen. He has been unweariedly training us from our youth until now: most truly you and I can feel it has been so, can we not? And may we not well repeat the constant prayer, as David did, 'Teach me Thy statutes,' go on training me? for it is the same word all through Ps. cxix., except in verses 33 and 102, where teaching means rather guidance or direction in a right way or course of action. Then we need not complain or bemoan ourselves, like Ephraim, as bullocks untrained (or unaccustomed to the yoke), undisciplined, and wayward. The verse I should like to send you especially is Ps. lxxi. 5, 'Thou art my hope, O Lord God' (signifying, as in Rom. viii. 20, and in Phil i. 20, a stretching forth the head and neck, with earnest observation, to see when the person expected shall appear). Oh, for this longing after Jesus! and surely it arises out of the words that follow, 'Thou art my trust from my youth.' The object we have been clinging to, trusting in, and relying upon! must we not long to see Him whom unseen we adore?"

And, in another letter, she says: "I grieve for your uncomfortableness; but I am sure it is a proof of love. And that is a furnace which will do you no harm. Some time ago, I remember thinking that God was teaching me to *justify* Him in all His trying dealings; but really of late this feeling has been changed for one of real *thankfulness* for each and every sorrow He sends me. It is the family-rod; and I dare not ask to be the child that is not to have its waywardness crushed and its will broken. So I thank Him for doing it; and I thank Him for enabling me to kiss the rod."

She continued to "watch for souls." Writing to a young friend who seemed to be "halting between two opinions," she says: "I did not know, till after you were gone home, that you were to be 'confirmed' to-morrow, or I am sure I could not have seen you without giving you a text, and telling you how very earnestly I wish that it may please God to draw you with the cords of love, and to make you 'His child' to all eternity. A very dear girl, whom I knew at Torquay, was 'confirmed' a few weeks ago; and writing to me beforehand, she said, 'Oh, what a happy day it will be, when I publicly declare my determination to be a follower of that precious Jesus who gave Himself for me!' And when she wrote again to give an account of the day, she added, 'I was admitted to the privilege of partaking of the Lord's Supper. I seemed so fully to realize my acceptance in "The Beloved." In the midst of the pleasures I am expecting this summer, do pray for me that I may

"'Remember, in my gladness,
'Tis HIS love gives me all.'"

I only quote from her letters, instead of writing myself, because she says exactly the things I should like to say to you, and they come so much fresher in that way than if I were to seem to sermonize! She lives with a young cousin who is very, very gay; and therefore it is no easy thing for her to determine to be a decided Christian. But she loves Jesus heartily; and what we love we find means to follow. This makes me earnestly desire for you that the love of

Jesus may take possession of your heart, and be what Dr. Chalmers called 'the great expulsive principle,' which drives everything else but Jesus out—the world, self, and everything. The text I should like to send you is Jer. l. 5, and especially the words, 'a perpetual covenant.' I shall only add to all this, that, as far as my knowledge of religion goes, I can truly say I owe all my happiness to it, and believe it to be the happiest thing in the world. So I can honestly recommend it."

Her onward journey brought with it new sorrows and new joys:

> "Like light and shade upon a waving field,
> Coursing each other, while the flying clouds
> Now hide and now reveal the sun."

Writing to one beloved friend, she says: "Those words, 'The sorrows of my heart are enlarged,' have struck me so much this week as so truthfully giving expression to the experience of the advancing Christian. Don't you think that each day seems to open up some new avenues of sorrow, as if it were continually finding some fresh channels in which to flow through our ploughed-up hearts? And the far advanced Christian must find, both in the deeper views of his own sin, and in the fresh calls for sympathy with each new sinner he meets on the Sionward way, that the sorrows of his heart are enlarged and enlarging with every onward step he takes." And to another: "This morning I have been thinking of those words in Ps. cxiv. 2, 3, 'Judah was His sanctuary, and Israel His dominion. The sea saw it, and fled.' When the sea saw God in His people, it fled before them! Does it not tell us that it is God in us which clears our way through the most impenetrable obstacles, and that seas of trouble will flee before us when the presence of the Lord is manifested in us?"

And as she journeys onward, she is found clinging with a very peculiar love to certain fellow-pilgrims. "It is interesting to me," she writes to Mrs. C—— W——, Oct. 25 (1852), "to hear you speak of your experience now. I am so struck with the humbling experience which those Christians who have lived actively for God get in the autumnal stage. There is something to me perfectly exquisite in the chastened and subdued spirit of an aged Christian. I wonder that I like it, when I am so unsubdued myself: but I do; and I only long to make them feel how 'the glory of the Lord' is seen upon them. (Isa. lx. 2.) I wish you knew how much your self-renunciation teaches me—you would scarcely mourn any more."

In this region where she now journeys, another experience comes. "I have felt much more," she writes, Dec. 21 (1852), "of the Devil's presence and working of late than I ever did before. I seem to feel so much, especially, that he is fighting with God, in every case of a sinner's resistance of Jesus." And in another letter: "I had a sharp conflict, some days ago, literally with the powers of darkness, but I can't help telling you how one text helped me

—it must have been given to me—'Take the shield of faith, wherewith ye shall be able to quench all the fiery darts of the wicked one.' It did seem to me so wonderful at that moment, that the fiery darts which one might almost say are lighted at hell's unquenchable fire, should be quenched, one after another, as they touch the shield of faith."

And again: "The state of the world is painfully interesting. I cannot tell you how strongly I have felt lately the contest which is carrying on betwixt God and the devil, and the broad line of separation between the travellers to the One in heaven and those to the other in hell—the great end which everything is tending to. I seem as if I had no middle ground left me to stand upon; and the realizing of this is immensely helpful in making you feel that you must act as on the Lord's side."

Entering on a new year (1853), she writes in her Diary: "Began the year in the Lord's house on earth: is it a pledge of ending it in the house above? Began it by commemorating Jesus' dying love. May that love be realized daily till time shall end!

"'I want as a traveller to haste,
Nor forethought nor anxious contrivance to waste,
On the tent only pitched for a day.'"

And, writing to a friend, she says: "May I send you the words I have chosen for myself, as expressing my earnest longing for nearer communion with Jesus during the new year—'Let Him kiss me with the kisses of His mouth'? That is His drawing near to us—is it not?—and in such a way as to make us feel His love, and know that He is manifesting Himself unto us as He doth not unto the world." And to another, on Jan. 7: "Oh! that the victory which Jesus hath wrought over death may banish every painful thought, and enable you, in holy fellowship of mind with Him, to make the present a time of triumphant joy to you!"

Lighter occupations also were consecrated to God. "I have been painting in oils a little lately," she writes, "for a rest to my too active head, which cannot bear such constant thought. Yet it is very, very tempting to be always mentally at work." And, another day, she writes: "I have actually spent seven whole days on oil-painting, which I find easier to me than water-colours. The first day I painted one pretty little picture of the Garden of Gethsemane. Then I did the Sinaitic Inscriptions, which took two days; and I have done two others since. If I can only paint without self-gratification and self-exaltation, I think the talent may be turned to account." The talent was of no common order; and the account to which she turned it, was to aid the Irish Missions and other Christian enterprises.

As the season advanced, the weather "tried her a good deal, giving her such sleepless nights." "I cannot help looking on with adoring love," she writes, "at all God's dealings with me; there is such an unfolding of His manifold wisdom in the mingling of joy and sorrow in them all. I can truthfully say, that I would not now be without one needed stroke, or one hour of preparation for my place and work in the heavenly temple.

"'As hour after hour passeth by,
Mark'd by its own peculiar joy or woe,
Which Jesus means should tell upon the heart;
Behind each hour, O may some stroke be left,
Made for eternity upon each living stone!'

How miserable one would be rendered throughout eternity, if it were possible for us to escape some trying part of our discipline here, and so be admitted there with some hideous deformity which should mar our symmetry for ever! But the house will be finished in all its parts—is not that comforting? even though years of preparation be still needed."

In her Diary she writes: "*Feb.* 27. *Sun.*—'The blood of Jesus Christ His Son cleanseth us from all sin.' Another Sabbath at home; read Job xix. I feel more sure than ever that the right thing is, to take each sin, the moment the conscience feels it, to the blood of Jesus, and, there having it 'once purged,' to remember it 'no more.' I don't think of one scriptural example in which a forgiven sin was charged upon the conscience a second time by God; and I suppose that the year's sins were never expected to be *again* brought to mind after the scapegoat had borne them away into the land of forgetfulness. Oh! for grace to plunge into the ocean of Divine forgiveness!"

And, somewhat later, she writes to a friend thus:

"I have had no time for any drawing since I wrote you, save hieroglyphics; but I hope to return to it some day, if I live still on this lower earth and have more time given me to trade with. If not, I will gladly bid it all farewell, to go to Jesus. The world is in a most critical state; yet how sleepy Christians are! I almost ventured last night to ask for the 'north wind' to blow upon me; but, at all events, I do exceedingly want the 'south wind.' I'm afraid Jesus gets no sweet fragrance from His garden."

The holy Rutherford once remarked, that "we might beg ourselves rich, if we could but hold out our withered hands to Christ and learn to seek, ask and knock." Dear Adelaide was not a stranger to this heavenly art. "I have had such enjoyment," she writes, "in that Psalm (the ninety-ninth)—'Worship at His footstool;' exalting Him, prostrating ourselves; and then His holiness the great theme, thrice over 'for He is holy!' Is it not like putting into our mouths on earth the very song which is sung in glory—'Holy, holy, holy?' I cannot imagine any feeling so sweet as that of adoration; it seems so to imply

"'A soul at leisure from itself,'

to think of God; His holiness filling, as it were, our souls, so as to banish, for the time, the bitterness of a view of our own sinfulness, and giving us the most intense happiness. It is but transient tastes of it which I get; still I hope they are earnests of the fulness of it when God 'fills His temple' so that sin can never enter to interrupt His worship."

And the result was a calm self-possessedness, even amidst increasing trials. "I must tell you," she writes again, "a word which was lighted up to me the other day by what you call

"'The light of affliction's fire.'

It was a dark night-season with me, through some painful outward circumstances; and oh! how exquisite that word of Jesus did seem to me, 'I am the bright and morning star!' I looked to the Greek word, and found it defined—'lustrous, dazzling, shining, resplendent;'—the very darkness added to its brilliancy. And is it not so with Jesus?"

Meditating one day on those words, "When my spirit was overwhelmed within me, then Thou knewest my path," she poured out her soul in these plaintive lines:—

"My God, whose gracious pity I may claim,
Calling Thee 'Father,' sweet endearing name!
The sufferings of this weak and weary frame,
All, all are known to Thee.

"From human eyes 'tis better to conceal
Much that I suffer, much I hourly feel;
But oh! this thought doth tranquillize and heal—
All, all is known to Thee.

"Nay, all by Thee is ordered, chosen, planned;
Each drop that fills my daily cup Thy hand
Prescribes, for ills none else can understand:
All, all are known to Thee.

"The fittest means to cure what I deplore;
In me Thy longed-for likeness to restore;
Self to dethrone, and let it rule no more;—
All, all are known to Thee.

"Nor will the bitter draught distasteful prove,
When I recal the Son of Thy dear love;
The cup Thou would'st not for our sake remove,
That cup He drank for me!

"And welcome, precious can His Spirit make
My little drop of suffering for His sake:
Father! the cup I drink, the way I take;
All, all is known to Thee."

CHAPTER XIX.

Wordsworth, in his "Excursion," speaks of a child, living on "a tract of inland ground," who applied to his ear "the convolutions of a smooth-lipped shell."

> "In silence hushed, his very soul
> Listened intently; and his countenance soon
> Brightened with joy; for murmurings from within
> Were heard, sonorous cadences! whereby
> To his belief the Monitor expressed
> Mysterious union with its native sea."

Dear Adelaide is now approaching her heavenly home. And as she nears it, her utterances sound in the ear of faith more and more accurately as the "cadences" of her "native sea."

In her Diary, she writes: "*March* 20 (1853). *Sun.* Meditated on the land of Beulah—so sweet to pilgrims on the Sionward way." And in a letter: "Oh! I do so want some more vivid piercing glances through the lattice! Those words have been much on my mind for some days—'The eyes of the Lord run to and fro throughout the whole earth to show Himself strong in the behalf of them whose heart is perfect towards Him.' They 'run'—from Madeira, to Torquay, and to Derby, watching each person; and 'to and fro,' backwards and forwards! it almost annihilates the sense of distance, does it not?"

And writing to another, also nearing home, she says: "I have been growing up into your experience. I knew very little of conflict when I saw you, and very little comparatively of sin. The last year or two have taught me much; and, painful as it has been, I see the value of learning it. The struggles of the inner man are so real—so entirely God-ward (for man sees them not), that one seems by degrees to learn out the value of life as it brings one into contact with the living God! Oh! how blessed it will be when it is all life, when death has 'no more dominion!'"

And, in the same letter: "I have thought that hell and heaven don't occupy us enough. It does strike me so very much, in the experience of the few Christians I see and of the many I hear from, that there is such a tendency to rest in present experience and in all the daily fluctuations and variations, sins and infirmities, sorrows and trials, which, after all, acquire their real importance only through their connexion with eternity. There is, for the most part, comparatively little realization of the unseen—the ultimate carrying out of all these 'seen' things to their certain issue. I suppose it is experience one must come to by degrees, just in proportion, indeed, as one nears the eternal realities themselves. The nearer one gets to heaven, the more vividly one sees what holiness is, and, as a natural result, one feels the more what sin is and what it leads to in hell; in short, it just comes to this, that we have more of the mind of Christ and see more in God's own light. And how entirely oneness of heart with Him is what one sums up every desire of one's heart in, is it not?"

To another friend she writes: "Oh! how I do long to live and walk in real personal fellowship with Jesus all the day long! It comforted me very much some days ago, in reading Matt. xxvi., to see how, even when Jesus was personally present, there were the very same interruptions to communion which we have now in spiritual things. Did it ever strike you how remarkably this was the case in the Supper-chamber, when, in the very midst of that solemn, sacred feast, they were interrupted by Judas getting up and going out of the room? Such breaks in seasons of retirement and communion seem to me to say, how can you expect to go through any service of prayer or praise without interruption? How often, when Jesus went to be alone, He was interrupted! and we are not greater than our Lord."

The holy Bolton once said—"Oh! when will this good hour come? When shall I be dissolved? When shall I be with Christ?" Another holy man once wrote—

"Should not the exile, Lord, desire
His own sweet realm to see?
The bride to greet her absent Lord:
The prisoner to be free?

"When we, amid this stormy world,
 Feel like the homeless dove,
We would in spirit spread the wing,
 To flee to thee we love."

Dear Adelaide was beginning to long more and more intensely for her Home. "I was thinking last night," she writes, April 13 (1853), "of the words—'Humble yourselves under the mighty hand of God, that He may exalt you in due time.' There is no such 'exaltation' as going to be with Him. I do often wonder if the time is near for that. I shall not mind this humiliation, if it is the prelude to that honour. I most fully agree with what you say about 'time.' I believe waiting is quite as much a part of our serving as any active work might be, and that it is the acting of the Spirit, and not of the flesh, which tells."

And, in another letter, she says: "Every one seems to think me well or nearly so, except myself; but I don't feel it, and therefore don't believe it. Perhaps I am unwilling to believe. Indeed, I cannot be contented to be down here, though I do try to say 'As thou wilt' about it. And God chooses to exercise me by keeping me abiding still here in the flesh. One thing I know—Jesus will have me, whenever He chooses, to be with Him where He is. And you, too!"

Other pilgrim-experiences she gives thus: "I do long for some face-to-face communion, if the Lord Jesus will sweeten it by filling us both with His Spirit, and then drawing near Himself to share our joy." And, alluding to a visit from the Rev. Mr. T——, of Rugby: "I saw very little of him; but that little was enough to excite mutual interest on various subjects. I can't tell you how strange these momentary catches at Christian intercourse and friendship seem to me. How they explain that this is 'a time-state,' and that we are finite creatures, 'pilgrims and sojourners,' meeting only to part again—everything, in fact, being only 'in part.' I do long for this 'in part' state to be 'done away,' and the 'perfect' to come. And yet how many enjoyments peculiar to itself belong to it!" And again: "I do so like the ups and downs, and all the sudden transitions, in the Psalms. They used to trouble me, as if they disturbed the beauty of the passage; but now I seem so to enter into them." And elsewhere: "Lately I have found such comfort from the type of the 'red heifer,' as the special provision made for our wilderness-journey when we get continually defiled and want re-admission (if I may use such a word) into holy communion in the holy place. Amidst our unceasing re-commission of sin every moment, should not we make instant application afresh to the cleansing blood of Jesus, and so keep our conscience purged moment by moment?"

The seraphim—those emblems of redeemed sinners in glory—use two of their six wings in service; but with four of the wings they cover their feet and their faces. Writing to Mrs. C—— W——, Adelaide says: "I have been sent down into the valley of humiliation lately, in a way which makes me feel for you. I have just seemed to go from one depth to another, till I have felt sometimes ready to lay me down 'as the ground and as the street' for others to walk over. How little young Christians know of self-abasement or 'self-sacrifice!' Those are tremendous words, are they not? I often feel like a sacrifice, bound indeed to the horns of the altar, but shrinking from the flame which comes to consume the sacrifice. However, Jesus will take care that His Father is glorified, in spite of all our crying while the rod is in His hand. That thought often comforts me. And I was thinking this week that it is really a privilege to be in *His* furnace at all; for it is not intended for reprobate silver, but only for choice gold; and if we were not His choice gold, we should not have been put in there."

This "house-devil," self (as Rutherford calls it), was exorcised, not by melancholy mopings over her own heart, but by a steadfast contemplation of Christ. "I want God," she writes, "to have quite entirely His own way with me, and to be uninfluenced in wishing anything for myself. I have been thinking to-day of Jesus as the 'burnt-offering.' Mr. Jukes says, 'Everything He did or said was for God. From first to last, self had no place; His Father's work, His Father's will, was everything.' There is no joy so great as sharing the Father's delight in Jesus. How wonderful it will be hereafter, will it not? 'My beloved Son, in whom I am well pleased.' 'Mine Elect, in whom my soul delighteth!' and *the* Offering in which God could and did find pleasure. What a very sustaining thought it must have been to Jesus, to feel so sure as He did that He always did those things which pleased the Father! I think it must have been that which carried Him through those hours of tremendous endurance on the cross; for He would know, even then, that He was doing His Father's will in enduring His Father's righteous displeasure. And, though it could not alter the agony, or create joy, it could sustain Him. Oh! how delightful it must be to Him now, to look back and see how perfectly He pleased His Father, and how beautifully He executed His work as His righteous Servant!

"Don't you think," she adds, "we might be much happier, if we pleaded all Christ's holy obedience as our own, and learned to know ourselves as really welcome and well-pleasing to our Father in Him? I was struck with this in the texts I am sending on Rev. iii. 18—that He would have us clothed, so that the shame of our nakedness 'do not appear.' Does it not mean that He would have us lose the consciousness of that nakedness of soul which sin brings with it, just as, when He clothed Adam and Eve with skins, they would not need any longer to hide themselves through shame? And, if we were 'hot' and zealous, instead of cold and lukewarm, we should really get all those blessings which He offers us —riches, clothing and eyesight;—wealth to traffic with spiritually; beauty which Jesus could admire (as He so often did in Solomon's Song, when even one chain of the neck could ravish Him); and eye-sight for ourselves to see the King in His beauty? I cannot wish you more precious things than these, can I? But I try to pray that they may all be yours abundantly."

Another interesting glimpse into her hidden life is given elsewhere, thus: "Lately I have felt such an indescribable apathy come over me; but I believe bodily debility has a great deal to do with it. However, in spite of all these clogs and hindrances to fellowship with the Father and with His Son, I often get such precious foretastes of heavenly realities as only make me impatient to 'be swallowed up of life' (how strange that that should be 'death!' but I suppose, in 2 Cor. v., it refers rather to the resurrection-morning). And I have a more realizing feeling of nearing the haven, by every passing hour, than I ever had before. But do pray for me, that this natural self may die and Christ live in me."

And she adds: "Have you read the 'Memoir of Emma Maurice?' I have been so struck by her prayers that she might be 'crushed' and Christ glorified. Could you ask that? I like many of her letters and prayers so very much, especially one on '*Freeness* of grace'—like a crown set upon its 'fulness.' Free, in spite of all our coldness and desperate sinfulness as Christians! I have learned to prize the 'searching scrutiny of God.'"

The summer brought with it only increasing weakness. "The main feeling I have had for many months," she writes, May 20 (1853), "is as if I were worn out by lengthened illness. I have none of the energy I used to have; and I find it very, very humbling." And to another: "I often weary to be gone; and the 'little while' seems long. But, as Mr. Stowell was saying to me, the thing, after all, is, to be brought to say, 'Not my will, but thine be done.' I suppose seven years of illness must wear one out, in some measure, and damp one's spirits; but 'the joy of the Lord' can soon raise one up again, if He sees one can bear it. I trust you are full of peace, and joy, and hope."

And some weeks later she says: "I have been feeling how unreasonable it is for me to wonder that, after seven years of illness and so much joy, there should be now that wearing down of one's energies which I have felt so much. However, I am better of this; and I think I shall soon be able to look back upon it as a very valuable passage in my wilderness-journey. I had a precious glimpse within the vail on Saturday. I could only think of the words, 'The King hath brought me into His chambers;' and these words came home to me as full of sweetness, 'Sing unto HIM, sing psalms unto Him,' as if it were enough for the soul to sing for Him alone to hear. Can I give you the idea I had about it? like singing for Jesus, as one would do for some very dear friend who took pleasure in listening to one. He does say, 'Let me hear thy voice.' I want you to pray that I may have the joy of His salvation fully restored to me, or, rather, more than restored. I want to have it so as I never had it before. I want to be a burning light—a sacrifice ascending up with a brilliant flame of fire."

And again: "I have been a-begging to Him; but I should like to take you with me, and let us urge each other on to grow bolder and more urgent, and to vie, as it were, with each other, and see which can get most—to be more Christ-like—to see how much we can get for each other. Oh! my precious L——, how my heart clings to the remembrance of days when we have had Jesus with us, warming our hearts whilst we talked with Him. I was thinking last night of Enoch—how like a 'burnt-offering' he was, his whole life consecrated to God, 'walking with God!' and then, how literally an ascension, being 'translated!' God 'took him'—himself—his whole self! How beautiful, is it not? I don't think there is anything like it in the Bible, save his Master."

Like "Christian" emerging from the "Valley of the Shadow of Death," she now could say, "His candle shineth on my head, and by His light I go through darkness." And, like the Pilgrim, looking back upon "the dangers of her solitary way," she writes: "I never had gone through anything like this before. Hell-deserving I had indeed often felt myself to be; but this was as if I had hellishness in my very nature. I seemed as if I could not love; and the only words which suited me were those of Peter, 'Depart from me, for I am a sinful man, O Lord.' I could only be thankful that, in spite of it all, I could not but continue on my knees before the throne of grace, expecting deliverance in due season, and that I never seemed able for a moment to disbelieve my adoption and my right to call God 'my God.' How precious the very struggle is betwixt the new man and the old! It at least proves that the 'strong man armed' is not keeping 'his goods' in peace. And such abasing of self, too, is the means God has used for preparing me to 'see greater things.' It is just the way He dealt with Daniel and with Isaiah, is it not?"

And, in another letter, she adds: "I was in danger of being 'exalted above measure;' and, in answer to my own prayers, I was laid low, and have been kept low. I have found out many precious things by it, which I know I could not have learned in a happier state of mind; and I am really and honestly thankful, though one cannot help longing to be full of light, and life, and love."

And again: "My greatest trouble has been from going on day after day without any of what Dr. Chalmers calls 'conception;' for faith may be in strong exercise whilst we are all in the dark, as it were, from want of conception—not being able to realize the countenance and smile of Jesus, though knowing assuredly all the while that it was there unchanged if we could but see it. The idea I found in the forty-third Psalm one day, greatly to my delight. You remember how David calls God there his 'exceeding joy,' at the very moment when his soul was so 'cast down.' He was fully conscious that God was that to him; and yet at the time he had no happy consciousness of the truth in his own experience. Is it not so exactly what one often feels one's-self?"

Bishop Ridley once remarked that the walls and trees of his orchard, could they speak, would bear witness that there he had learned by heart almost all the Epistles, and that of the study he should carry the sweet savour with him to heaven. "To get deeper into any of God's thoughts," writes dear Adelaide "is so sublimating. You can't think what longings I have had for a sight of Jesus lately; faith does not in the least satisfy me. I know, indeed, there is a heaven of communion to be enjoyed even on earth. How very beautifully one sees it in Cant. i. 4 and iii. 4 taken together—Jesus bringing His bride 'into His chambers,' and she bringing Him into hers; both unlocking, as it were, the innermost recesses of the inner man, to admit each other into the very closest intimacy which language can convey an idea of—Jesus entering into the soul, and the soul entering into Jesus! But if we can taste such exquisite sweetness of delight when we get into His chambers now by faith, what will it be to be with Him bodily and for ever?"

And, again looking back along the way by which she has been led, she writes: "I am so glad to hear you say you have had more rest in Jesus of late. It is just the one thing that I think I can say I have had. It has certainly not been resting in enjoyments, or in outward ease, but just simply turning from all these to seek and find it in Jesus only. It is not any one thing which has tried me; it seems to me more the living over again of David's life. I am so exceedingly struck, in reading through Samuel, with the complication of his trials, the one folllowing so upon another, and so little peace between. Such a picture of our experiene, don't you think? I was thinking yesterday how remarkable it was that through that experience he was enabled to write the Psalms, a book which one like Solomon could never have written. So there must be Davids now; and I believe we who know most of the reality of such experiences, will enter most deeply into the praises of eternity."

And the same letter, thus: "What lessons we may learn in the 'Potter's house!' (Jer. xviii. 1–6.) I have taken the re-making of the marred vessel, in reference, first, to our bodies, then to our souls, and then to the earth. It is very striking to my own mind, that the word used, in Gen. ii. 7, Isa. xliii. 7, xliv. 2, 21, or Ps. cxxxix, 15, 16, of the forming or fashioning of the body, is the very same word which describes the operations of a potter; and the same is true of the spirit in Ps. xxxiii. 15, Zech. xii. 1; and also, I think, of the earth, in Isa. xlv. 18—'formed' it. All three are 'marred' by sin; yet all three are renewed or re-made by the Heavenly Potter. And I was struck with the expression, 'the vessel was marred in the hand of the potter,' as if Jesus lets nothing fall out of His hands, but simply keeps the vessel, even when marred, until it is re-made. Oh, how I long for a yielding, clay-like spirit! 'Learn of me, for I am meek and lowly in heart, and ye shall find rest.' How fully one knows, that so soon as a real lowliness of spirit fills one's heart towards God, a calm steals over one, in place of the agitation of the troubled waves of rebelliousness of will! Oh, how my will has distracted me these last few months!—but I believe God could detect the 'new man' ever saying 'Not my will' even when I could only discern the workings of the 'old man' in myself struggling for the mastery."

A thought on Resurrection she gives to a bereaved friend thus: "I cannot tell you how I have delighted in the thought of every seed having 'its own body' lately. I never liked what some people lay so much stress upon—each particle of dust which forms these vile earthly bodies being gathered together and raised: the expression, 'Thou fool! thou sowest not that body that shall be,' seems quite to contradict it, to my mind. But every seed will have its own body, and be instantly recognized, just as each plant now is known from the seed that was sown. And is there not food for precious contemplation in that?"

The Lord's "appearing" she watched for with a new longing. "I have many times," she writes, "thought of your question, 'What are the signs now which warrant the expectation of the immediate coming of our Lord?' I always feel that the peculiarity of the signs of the present day consists chiefly, if not entirely, in the movement amongst the Jews. But do you not think that, in order to a real expectation of Christ's coming at any hour, we must give up the idea of not seeing Him until all the signs are accomplished and He stands on the Mount of Olives in the Holy Land, as in Zech. xiv.? I have been driven to this."

CHAPTER XX.

THE poet Spenser, himself not a stranger to the mysteries of the inner life, once wrote—

"The soul's dark cottage, shattered and decayed,
Lets in new light through chinks which time has made."

Dear Adelaide's "dark cottage" was gradually decaying. At the end of August (1853), her cough grew worse; and we find her physician "warning her that it would be serious if not checked." "Of this," she herself writes, "I feel perfectly conscious; I am very low and poorly." But a new joy filled her soul. "Perhaps," she said one day, to a friend who was leaving her, "the next time we meet, it may be with Jesus." "I never shall forget," says that friend, "the heavenly smile which beamed in her features as she spoke."

And writing to the Hon. Mrs. C——, she says: "I have seen more of Jesus lately than ever before. There is something overpowering beyond expression to my mind in seeing anything of His intense holiness and perfectness. I could not endure it, I am certain, if it were not for knowing that that very life was lived for me, in my stead, and as my righteousness and sanctification. One passage which has come with special power to me about Him is John xvii. Up to that hour He had gone on in uncomplaining silence, except as from time to time He had let drop expressions which plainly told all He was feeling, as in Ps. xxxv. 17, 'Lord, how long wilt thou look on?' or in Luke xii. 50, 'How am I restrained?' But no sooner was the time come, than His delight broke forth as (in ver. 1) He 'lifted up His eyes and said, Father, the hour is come!' Who can imagine the depths of untold satisfaction with which He must have burst forth with those words towards His Father? as if His spirit were ready to bound towards Him the instant it might! And then He goes on to say (v. 11–13), in His own most exquisite way, 'And now I am no more in the world'—'and now come I to thee.' Is there not something exquisite in that? Oh! I think God the Father must have listened to it with such supreme delight (as in Prov. xxiii. 15, 16).

"And then," she proceeds, "if one looks at Him in John xii. 27, 28, and for one single moment hears Him ready to say, in the anguish of His soul, 'Father, save me from this hour'—how instantly He sets aside the wish with the words, 'But for this cause came I unto this hour;' and then quite, as it were, triumphing over self altogether, He makes this His real prayer, 'Father, glorify thy name!' learning, through that very experience, to be able at last to testify, 'I have glorified thee on the earth.' I can't write down what this reveals to me of what

He felt; but you will understand it all for yourself, and I know you will enjoy it as I do. Oh! the comfort I have found in using His words! it has been so very precisely what I wanted. You can imagine how precious it has been, though it has cost me many bitter tears. How, without such bitterness, could one long to say with Him, 'Save me from this hour?' but when 'the hour' is really 'come,' won't it be glorious? to be 'no more in the world!' to come to the Father!"

And she adds: "Another passage is Matt. xvi. 21–27. The margin of verse 22 struck me first, 'Pity thyself, Lord.' It was such a natural outburst of kindly feeling from Peter's affectionate heart; and yet, just because it was natural, and savoured of man, it was so offensive to Jesus that He could not bear it. Does it not wonderfully reveal the quick discernment of Jesus? Knowing that it became God to make Him perfect through sufferings, He would not tolerate the idea of evading those sufferings for one moment. 'The cup which my Father hath given me, shall I not drink it?' Don't you think there is a wonderful unfolding of His perfectness in the shrinking He had from pitying Himself? and then, with all these thoughts and feelings fresh in His own mind, how one seems to understand what He meant when He turned and said that if any man would follow Him, so far from pitying, he must deny himself! I suppose you had often traced out the connexion between these two things. I never had seen it before. And I have just been so much struck with the Transfiguration following it. Did it ever strike you that the very subject Peter so recoiled from was the very theme which Moses and Elias talked over with Jesus?—they 'spake of His decease.' Probably that was the only time on earth that He was ever able to speak freely of His death to any one who understood about it; and can't you imagine it to have been exceedingly comforting to Him?"

Other vails, besides the "dark cottage," hide the glory of Christ. "I know," she writes, Oct. 13, to one who had been smitten with a sore bereavement, "you will be finding out some fresh recesses in His heart of love, now that this vail of flesh is rent asunder which hitherto has been as a curtain to conceal them from you. Oh! that both of us may be enabled to penetrate deeper into Jesus, and learn all the beauties which our tear-dimmed eyes can discern, while we seem drawn within the very threshold of that glory into which the happy spirit has entered."

And another veil is a ruffled spirit. "I never remember," she writes, "having felt so irritable before. How trying it is! I have been exactly what Cant. i. 7 (marg.) says, 'as one that is vailed.' How characteristic of the book that expression is—is it not? The Bride not imagining for a moment that Jesus is changed, but truthfully owning that she cannot see Him rightly!"

And another vail is external ease. "It does me good to be made at times uncomfortable outwardly—

it unsettles me from my earthly home, where one is so apt to settle so unconsciously." And she adds: "Don't you think there is such a difference in the very way one says 'O Lord,' at one time and at another? One day, it may be with a vague and general assurance that there is a God to whom one speaks and looks. At another time, one's very heart seems to go forth to the Person one looks to, as to one's dearest and most intimate of friends—a Father, a Maker, or our Jehovah."

In her Diary, she writes: "*May* 14 (1853).—Cocker died about seven A.M., to enter into the presence of Jesus. The first-fruits (to me) of the Ragged School. Oh, to pray for a large harvest to follow!" "*June* 5, *Sun.*—Was very, very tired all day, and only felt at the Lord's Table what a miracle of mercy it will be for me to be found in heaven!" "*June* 22.—M—— was transplanted to the garden of Jesus in glory. From the very commencement of her illness she used to speak of going to Jesus, and seemed quite aware she was going, saying, 'M—— going to the blue sky.' She liked of all things for H—— to talk to her about it, and would smile sometimes at this when nothing else moved her." "*July* 14.—Sent Dr. Bonar 'Terrible Things in Righteousness'" (article for "Quarterly Journal of Prophecy"). "*Aug.* 6.—Finished the rough copy of article on Solomon's Song for Dr. Bonar."

And again: "*Aug.* 15.—Dr. Bonar came at seven P.M. He promised to read my 'Hebrews' if I would do it, and bade me consider myself pledged to do it.

Is this God's certain token to me of His will?" "*Aug.* 29.—Dr. —— said my cough was becoming serious. Mrs. B—— and the Rev. C—— B—— came; he talked of Solomon's Song, and prayed with us." "*Sept.* 27.—Mr. B—— came, and stayed nearly two hours with me: he talked of JESUS; Cant. i. 5; ii. 17, 18; iv. 6, 7; vi. 11, 12." "*Nov.* 15.—Irish Church Missions Meeting. Saw Mr. Bickersteth." "*Dec.* 11, *Sun.*—Mr. Dallas preached at St. A—— on Rom. viii. 26, 27, and afterwards gave it to me alone, and prayed with me."

At the end of October, her illness so much increased that she never again was out of doors. But, with a singular energy, she devoted herself during her remaining months to her work on the Hebrews. And the Lord seemed to use it for teaching her new lessons as she hastened forward to her home, "Hebrews has shown me so much," was her remark one day towards the close, "what sin is, by what it cost—I owe it so much! Oh! it has been well worth any suffering, to learn out of it the need of Christ's salvation by what sin is. There is no reality in your religion, at least no depth of reality, till you have learned in this way for yourself. It makes me feel that we don't enter into the hundredth, nor the thousandth, nor the millionth part of what there is for us in Christ, or we could not live as we do."

And another lesson which it taught her, she indicates: "I cannot do Hebrews—I am so humbled over it still. I seem to have no power to touch it. How dependent we are upon God—are we not? I have not a word to say till He opens my lips; and I feel as if He had laid me down with my face on the ground, and as if I must wait till His hand touched me, and set me on my feet again. It is worse than useless to try to do anything in my own weakness (I need not call it 'strength.')"

And again: "Solitude and isolation drove me to Jesus as my Beloved One, at the time I did Solomon's Song. And bitter lessons of sin in myself and in those about me, which deepen almost every day and hour, seem to be my necessary portion, ere I can understand what Jesus is as my High Priest." And elsewhere she adds: "How intensely interesting the later discipline of God's people is—that self-prostration! It is the thing I feel youngest in, of any in the Christian life."

Her sympathies with the afflicted, too, were kindled into a new vividness. "I hope ere this you are really better," she writes to one tried sufferer. "These poor, frail bodies, how full of infirmity they are! I am constantly made to feel it, and therefore can feel for you. For how differently sympathy is felt when it arises out of felt experience, from the mere sympathy of kind fellow-feeling! I have had this strongly on my mind lately, from those words in Heb. ii. 18: 'In that He himself hath suffered, being tempted, He is able to succour them that are tempted.' And I think one sees the opposite of this so strongly in the Book of Job, where his three friends actually aggravated instead of lessening his miseries, from their want of understanding of his trials. 'Miserable comforters are ye all!'"

And she adds: "How often one is shut up to look for sympathy and help from Him who alone can know the peculiar texture of our minds, and who only can have largeness of heart enough to comprehend all the variety of trials which distress all His 'many sons.' Did you ever find comfort to yourself from that expression, 'largeness of heart?' I remember once its being made such a word in season to me, as I was reading 1 Kings iv., and saw in Solomon the type or figure of the 'greater than Solomon.' It says: 'God gave Solomon . . . largeness of heart, even as the sand that is on the sea-shore.' And taken in connexion with the promise to Abraham, that his seed should be as many as the sand on the sea-shore for multitude, I think it is inexpressibly comforting to feel that Jesus has 'largeness of heart' enough to take in every smallest grain of sand—every feeblest child in His family, and to care for every one!"

To a bereaved mother, Mrs. C—— W——, she writes, on another occasion, thus: "I felt for you not a little. I knew how your heart was bleeding, and I hoped you felt the hand of your tender Heavenly Physician binding up your wounds. For dear E——, I could, of course, only rejoice. She has made her escape from her clay prison, and is at liberty to bask in the full sunshine of Christ's own presence—not one sin grieving her! I could almost envy her."

Borne upward on the wings of faith and of hope,

we find her longing at times after Christ with an intenseness of desire almost more than human. "Oh! I have such intense, unutterable cravings," she writes to the Hon. Mrs. C——, at one of those seasons, "after a real seeing and handling of the Word of Life Incarnate, that I am only conscious of the most intense emptiness and longings after the real, real thing. I wonder if you will understand, what I cannot express;—it has been, as it were, such a sense of immortality which I have had—the immortality of my own soul, and its inability to find rest in anything finite. I can't understand why the indwelling of the Holy Spirit is not more enough to me than it is, unless it be that I have so little of it; but it is CHRIST I want to see; and nothing but being present with Him seems the least to give me any idea of being satisfied."

And to another: "The character of Christ, as given in His own words in the Gospels, is such a study! Its marvellous perfectness—how it astonishes me and fills me with wonder and admiration—I may say, with awe! I am downright staggered by the exceeding riches of His grace sometimes—how He can go on pardoning day after day, and hour after hour! Don't you often feel ashamed to go to ask it? really I sometimes cannot get the words out for shame. Do you remember how Hewitson used to feel this? he does so suit me. G—— has just got his 'Letters and Remains,' and I have been feasting on them again to-day. I never knew any one whose experience came home to me like his: he attained to such closeness of walk with God. No words could describe the unutterable longings and cravings of soul I have had after Him lately, and intercourse with Him. I quite like to spend my time on my knees, whether I can pray or not; and often I have not a word to say. Oh! to be fed by the Lamb before the throne from those living fountains which will quench our thirst!"

The "Great-hearts" of the wilderness stimulate other pilgrims on their way. "Slow-pace" and "Short-wind" and "Linger-after-lust" and "No-heart" bring up an evil report of the Land, "saying it is not half so good as some pretend it is;" and they "persuade people that the Lord is a hard task-master;" and they call the bread of God, husks—the comfort of His children, fancies—the travel and labour of pilgrims, things to no purpose." But Great-heart "takes sword and helmet and shield," and, facing "Giant Grim," boldly says, "These women and children are going on pilgrimage, and this is the way they must go; and go it they shall, in spite of thee and the lions." And Great-heart is not bold in vain. "Come," said he to the pilgrims, "what think you of the pilgrimage now?" "Sir," said the youngest of them, "I was almost beat out of heart; but I thank *you* for lending me a hand at my need."

Dear Adelaide was a Great-heart. "I feel so sorry for you having to go from place to place," she writes to a friend travelling on the Continent; "but this comfort, at any rate, I have, that in all your wilderness-wanderings the Lord walks with you from place to place in the tent or tabernacle of your body (2 Sam. vii. 6, 7); and that sanctifies all. The joy and peace of 'walking in the light' is something so unutterably blissful, is it not? and surely it is our purchased privilege in Jesus—'They shall walk, O Lord, in the light of Thy countenance: in Thy name shall they rejoice all the day.'"

And to a friend in Edinburgh, Miss G——, she writes: "Many thanks for your note to me. Those words of Mrs. Barbour's are truly wonderful and God-glorifying. What an idea it gives one of the immensity of God, that He can be giving so abundantly to such numbers of His people all at once, and be none the poorer Himself! 'The Lord will give grace and glory'—the one for time, the other for eternity, don't you think? Are you freed yet from all the dark clouds you spoke of? I am wonderfully brought up out of the depths. No words can say, in the least, what unutterable cravings of heart I have had after a sight—a real, satisfying sight—of Jesus. I can't understand it, when I ask to be filled with the Holy Ghost. Is it His indwelling which creates these longings after heaven's own bliss in what Mr. A—— described yesterday as 'union with God?' Oh! how sweet a Refuge Jesus is in every storm! I do believe He grows dearer to me now every day. As to health," she adds, "I am just ready to be finished with at any moment if it pleased God, and yet in that state that, if He chooses, He may keep me going for a while still on earth."

And to the same friend: "I have just read through the two books of Samuel. Poor David! what a life he led! I can't say what a feeling his history has given me. I grew so weary of his incessant miseries, and did seem so to sympathize with and understand the endless variety of them, that one thing, and only one, helped me through; and that was, the realizing how exactly that discipline fitted him for writing the Psalms. One sees how exactly one's own path is chosen by God to fit us for doing the particular work He designed for us from eternity, and how no other path could do so well; and does not that give you a great feeling of contentment and of being satisfied to have things as they are? A little patient endurance will bring us where we shall admire each step of the way with such admiration! Oh! what intensity of happiness there is in casting in one's lot with Jesus! I have so much felt lately that it is less the particular enjoyment of the present hour or moment that I care for, than the settled assurance altogether that I am His and that I am going along the Zionward way which leads straight to His presence. What privileged beings you and I are, to be under His own hand—His own training, and to know it!"

In another letter, her strong heart encourages a fainting fellow-pilgrim thus: "I am very, very jealous of any vagueness of thought respecting the real personality of the Spirit. I don't believe we half realize it, or we could not talk of His 'influences' as we do. Oh! to be filled with God the Holy Ghost!

Then how strong we should be! how holy! how Christ-like! in short, everything we want to be. I have so rested on those words lately, 'I am persuaded that He is able.' Shall I send them to you? What does it matter how weak *we* are? Rather may we learn to 'glory in our infirmities!'"

Do not the thoughts which follow strike a chord in many a pilgrim's heart? "I am reading Hosea," she writes. "How fearful our tendency is to be ever dealing treacherously with Jesus! I am so tired of my heart. How wonderful Jesus is, that He can 'love us to the end'! I have been so much struck with the picture He Himself has drawn of our wilderness-life, in calling it by those two emphatic words, 'The provocation.' One feels it is so true that each fresh stage only calls forth fresh murmuring and rebelliousness, until, from beginning to end, one literally seems to look back upon one series of provocations. And then, too, the bitterness of it is so aggravated by the remembrance that it is all against that loving God who has already 'many a time' forgiven our iniquity. Oh! how great it makes His love to forgive and pardon all those forty years' provocations!

"But the text," she adds, "I had thought of sending you to-day was this, 'Ye are they which have continued with me in my temptations.' (Luke xxii. 28.) It has been made very precious to me in two ways—one, as showing how Jesus prizes and appreciates the constant love of His people and their protracted endurance of suffering for His sake; and the other, as showing the preciousness of protracted life, when it is viewed as a continuing with Jesus in the fellowship of His sufferings. It seems to be only in advancing experience that one can at all enter into the deep meaning of His words; but when continuance amidst temptation is felt to be very trying, they are precious words indeed, are they not? and if I can feel them so, how much more can you! But I must stop—only wishing you great grace to enable you to rejoice greatly in the Lord, and to make your boast in Him continually. Don't you like to give vent to your feelings in those three words, 'Blessed be God?'"

William Cowper has beautifully said of "Contemplation," that

> 'Her power is such that whom she lifts from earth
> She makes familiar with a heaven unseen,
> And shews him glories yet to be revealed.
> Not slothful he, though seeming unemployed
> And censured oft as useless. Stillest streams
> Oft water fairest meadows, and the bird
> That flutters least is longest on the wing."

Adelaide Newton makes little noise; but, on her eagle-pinions, she soars higher and higher into the regions of the heavenly life. "I have just finished reading through Kings," she writes, in the autumn of 1853; "and one thought has impressed itself very strongly on my mind, as I have gone from chapter to chapter;—especially in contrast with the subject I lately sent you on Christ's character, as given in the Gospels—He always doing what His Father did

(John v. 19)—always keeping His Father's commandments, without turning aside—always maintaining such entire and universal regard to all that was holy, just, and good. How very, very seldom we come upon very thorough Christians! A great many are sincere, and do a great deal that is right; but a Caleb, a Joshua, a David, a Moses, or a Daniel, are very rare. And how striking is such a testimony as this—'He did that which was right in the sight of the Lord; yet not like David his father'! (2 Kings xiv. 3). It was altogether a much lower standard; and it is added, 'Howbeit the high places were not taken away—as yet the people did sacrifice and burnt incense on the high places.' These are the words which have so especially struck me. Again and again we read—'he did that which was right,' save that 'the high places were not removed, the people sacrificed and burnt incense still.' (2 Kings xv. 3, 4, 34, 35, &c., &c.) Oh! dear ——, is it not a solemn thing to hear the Searcher of hearts ever saying that there is 'still' some idolatry indulged; 'still' some secret sins spared; 'still' some reserve in our obedience? If there had been no exceptions amongst the kings, we should naturally feel that it was a kind of impossible thing to reach a higher standard. But don't you think such cases as Josiah and Hezekiah quite prove the contrary? Of both it is said, that they did that which was right in the sight of the Lord, according to all that David did (2 Kings xviii. 34; xxii. 2); and they did remove the high places, and cut down the groves. So that altogether it tells of the low state in which, for the most part, we are, as Christians, content to live; so unlike Jesus, who had respect, literally, unto all the commandments!"

And she adds: "The text I have chosen to send you this week is such a precious one—'Let them shout for joy, and be glad, that favour my righteous cause; yea, let them say continually, Let the Lord be magnified, which hath pleasure in the prosperity of His servant.' Is not that raising us immensely high, to make our joy to consist so largely in God's joy in the prosperity of Jesus? And is it not beautiful to hear Jesus praying that His Father may 'be magnified' for taking pleasure in His success? I feel, dearest ——, that I can wish you no higher enjoyment than much of this gladness, and that you may really be able to 'say continually,' 'The Lord be magnified.'"

And in another letter, she says: "I always think it is the highest kind of joy we are invited to indulge in—to be sharers of God's joy! And it is a joy so wholly independent of ourselves and of our own feelings, that it seems as if it might be possible that it should be realized, as Christ prays it may be, 'continually.'"

It is well to touch "from behind" the hem of Christ's garment, for even such a touch brings "virtue out of Him;" but it is better to come up in front of Him and look into His face. "I want," Adelaide writes, "the felt 'kisses of His mouth.' R—— seems to get 'close up' to Him in prayer. Did you ever connect the words, 'Be not silent unto me,' in

Ps. xxviii., with the grand description of 'the voice of thė Lord,' in Ps. xxix? May He bless you every moment with His love, watering you (as Hewitson would say) with the silent dew!"

And again: "I am sure we are not half enough alone in prayer. I do so long for a closer walk with Jesus. I seem so very often in a kind of mist, as if I knew He was in the room but I could not see Him. Do you understand this? Pray that I may have a greater spirit of prayer, and of praise too. I have been reading of the singers 'day and night' in the temple: how little we know of such constant praise now!"

A visit which "a Free Church minister, Mr. C—— B——," had paid to her, she sketches in the same letter, thus: "I greatly enjoyed it, because he seemed so very happy in God and in His Word. When he was up with me in this room, he appeared as if he could scarcely sit still sometimes for delight, especially when speaking of Ps. lxxxv. 10—'Righteousness and peace have kissed each other.' He clasped his arms and *looked* all he seemed as if he would like to *say* of the exquisite beauty of God's own joy in the perfection of His own attributes. It is impossible to put it into words; but perhaps the idea may strike your mind, as it did mine, in a way it never had before."

And, in another letter, she says: "It strikes me more and more every day, how much people dwell upon their own feelings and experiences and duties, rather than upon all that Christ was and felt and did for them;—I mean practically. Do you not think one chief part of the Spirit's work is to testify of Christ and, by revealing Him, to conform us to His likeness? I think we often begin at the wrong end (if I may so express myself), trying to copy Him and to follow His example, instead of studying Him and expecting to be changed into His image 'while beholding His glory.'"

A threatened bereavement drew forth the following: "I know what it is to lose a father; and I seem instinctively to shrink from the thought of any one I love having the prospect, even 'afar off,' of passing through those deep waters. But let me not lead you, for a passing moment, into the sin of anticipating the unknown future. Do you know those lines:—

"'I'll spare all useless thinking,
Nor shall my mind be shrinking,
Concerning what *may* be.
I'll follow thy kind leading,
Dear Lord, in each proceeding:
That thou art all, sufficeth me'?

I don't know that any precept in the whole Bible has been more invaluable to me at times than this—'Take no thought for the morrow;' but it is hard to carry it out into practice. In fact, each day and hour make me see more and more how amazingly slight our understanding of the mere words of Scripture is. Its heights and depths seem reserved for Him whose understanding is infinite."

Towards the close of the year, she speaks of "having within the last few weeks been really ill, though still going about the house and pulling through all the outside-work of daily life." And she adds: "I have been compelled to give up nearly all my letter-writing. I have thought of your approaching confirmation-day many times lately, seeing it marked in my 'daily food.' It is now thirteen years since I took those vows, and said I renounced the world, &c. Badly enough have they all been kept; but I thank God for having taken care of me, when I might have broken loose from Him so often if He had not held me in with a somewhat tight hand. Did it ever strike you what a solemn view it gives of what our separateness from worldliness should be, that we are in Christ even in His character of 'Nazarite'? It almost overpowered me last week, when the idea first struck me. How false a representation we give of Him to the world—do we not?"

The fruits of this new discipline she notes in another letter, thus: "What has tried me most is, that I have felt so utterly unable to exert myself, especially in reading or writing. It is very humbling discipline; but, oh! E——, I do feel so increasingly that that is just what we most need. We do live so very much to please ourselves; and it will not do. God will not suffer it, if we are really His; and, in one way or other, self must be abased now, if we are to be exalted hereafter. The thought of this reconciles me to it all; I may say, it makes me thankful for it, even when it is trying me most."

And elsewhere she says: "He keeps me in very 'great peace.' I can't often speak of joy; but even that I have sometimes—and I feel every day how the items for praise are being added to, which will give me full employment for eternity when I know all."

Another feature of her inner life was developed into new prominence. "I do wish I loved Jesus more," she writes, "in those who have no comeliness outwardly (or mentally) to attract me." And to another: "She is a friend of ——; and seeing that she and you are no longer 'strangers and foreigners,' but of the household of God, I hope you will not feel it strange to be thus introduced to her. As 'daughters' of the Lord, you are sisters to one another: will you treat her as a sister and write to her yourself?" And again, on Nov. 11: "I suppose you have been very busy, not to have let me share your trials and sorrows all these months. I won't suspect Christian love—it would be wronging Him who dwells within. Oh! ——, what a marvel 'godliness' is! 'God manifest in the flesh,' not in Jesus only while He was on earth, but in His body mystical, still dwelt in as we are by God the Holy Ghost! Oh! the wonder of this!"

Some other thoughts are given elsewhere thus: "We were so agreed upon the bliss of getting away from self to God. One of the things which struck me most in Mr. P—— was his strong feeling of distress at the dishonour we cast on God by our unbelief of His grace. Is it not very remarkable, in John's first Epistle, how every unholy thing is resented, as if he would instinctively have shrunk from it—as if he really would 'touch no unclean thing,' 'no lie,' 'no sin.' It is such 'walking in the light'—is it not? in fellowship with Jesus, the 'holy, harmless, undefiled' One—so 'separate from sinners!' I was so exceedingly struck with those words in 1 Sam. xvi. 1—'How long wilt *thou* mourn for Saul, seeing *I* have rejected him from reigning over Israel?' as if God looked in His people for such oneness of mind with Himself, and such an understanding of what He was about, that it was a strange thing for Samuel to be in the dark concerning it and to be in such useless grief. Oh! E——, what untold sorrow we should be spared, if our minds were more at one with God in all the things He is doing!"

And to Mrs. G——, on Nov. 18: "Have you had your mind led to the subject of the 'meetness for the inheritance,' stated in Col. i. 12? Mr. —— was preaching on it lately, and took the 'meetness' as the sanctifying work of the Spirit wrought in the heart. But it is properly, I think, neither the Son's work nor the Spirit's, but the Father's—'Giving thanks unto the FATHER, which hath made us meet.' And it seems to me that there is a very peculiar beauty and preciousness in this; for, if I mistake not, the idea of the passage is, our being put into a new position or standing, even that of children—our 'sonship-position,' which is the literal rendering of 'adoption;' in other words, our being translated into the kingdom of His Son (v. 13). The Greek word for 'meet' assuredly signifies, not inherent qualification, but rather meetness of position. How much cause *I* have for 'giving thanks unto the Father' for what He has done! 'The Lord Jesus be with your spirit' night and day, with light, and peace, and gladness!"

And to the same, on Dec. 6 (1853): "The subject which has been on my mind this week is, the way in which our sufferings have been made to unfold the character of God. Formerly I had always thought of suffering as appointed or permitted of God for our good; and I saw little or nothing more. But now I can see, in His choice and arrangement of it, and in His methods of dealing it out to each single believer in the countless multitude of the redeemed, the most magnificent display of His own character. And I cannot tell you how altered a view it has given me of it. His wisdom so exercised and exhibited in always selecting the right kind of trial for each individual character; the right quantity; the right time for sending it, so as that it should not clash with any other's; the right duration! And then His power, almightiness, tenderness, and patience—how wonderfully they are developed in sustaining and comforting us under them! Do you like the thought? To me it is most precious, and takes me off self so much, and fixes the eye on God, which is just what I need when suffering presses somewhat sore."

An interval of renewed elasticity was given in

the month of December. "This intense cold," she writes to the Hon. Mrs. C——, on Dec. 8, "has suited me better than the damp; it has quite restored my faculties to me (if I may so speak), and has wonderfully cheered me up, and filled me with thankfulness for this unspeakable boon. I just contrived to finish Heb. viii., that it might go to you in the parcel, and have since been thoroughly delighting myself in the three next chapters, which, after much thought, I seem to see my way into."

An interesting glimpse into her sick-chamber occurs in a brief note from one of her sisters, dated Dec. 12 (1853): "Dearest Adelaide is shut up here, living chiefly in her own two rooms, but coming down stairs for a change every day. She has failed ever since last March, and was apparently altering fast in October, when the idea which had been entertained of going to Torquay was abandoned, because the medical opinion was that she was unable to travel. She was beautifully acquiescent in the decision to remain; indeed, her state of mind may be called 'heavenly:' it is so far above any that I ever saw in any other dear Christian friend, that I cannot but feel it is possible she may be thus rapidly maturing for an approaching removal to a holier atmosphere—this is so unlike all she is and all she feels now! But lately she has seemed to rally, and to employ herself so diligently, that perhaps she has yet more work to do for Jesus; and if so, she will have strength to do it. Her light is most clear and beautiful amongst us: she only seeks Jesus' glory in life or in death."

CHAPTER XXI.

"This," said a dying saint, "is heaven begun. I have done with darkness for ever, for ever. Satan is vanquished. Nothing now remains but salvation with eternal glory—eternal glory!"

"The celestial city," said Payson, on his deathbed, "is full in view: its glories beam upon me; its breezes fan me; its odours are wafted to me; its music strikes upon me; and its spirit breathes into my heart: nothing separates me from it but the river of death, which now appears as a narrow rill that may be crossed at a single step whenever God gives me permission."

We are now to enter dear Adelaide's dying chamber; and we shall find it, not sombre, but illumined with a shechinah-glory.

"What have I left, that I should stay and groan?
The most of me to heaven is fled;
My thoughts and joys are all pack'd up and gone,
And for their old acquaintance plead."

One of her sisters writes: "For four or five months, she might almost be said to be dying."

The last day she ever got downstairs was one morning (January 3) when she hurried after a friend with a parcel which she was anxious should not be forgotten. "The effort," says her sister, "was to her very great; and the exposure to the cold on that bitter day, as she passed down the staircase into the hall, was a real sacrifice. She regained her room only with distressing difficulty—her breathing was so painful, and her whole system so affected by the cold air."

In her Diary we find the following brief entries: "*Jan.* 1 (1854). Very ill. 'Lord, I believe;'—my text for the year (?)" "*Jan.* 16. Dr. —— told me all the acute symptoms were much increased." "*Jan.* 23. Saw Dr. ——. I asked him if it was right to let them think I was dying; and his reply was, 'There is active disease now,' adding that he did not think my having rallied before, any pledge of my doing so again, but the contrary, because, each attack, it became more difficult. Solemn to be really told it!" "*Jan.* 31. Was enabled to write out Heb. ix. 11–14. G—— promised to undertake my Scripture-reader! 'Begone unbelief!'" "*Feb.* 2. Saw Dr. ——: felt much better; and he said I had gained some ground." "*Feb.* 11. M—— came to see me. How much happier we both seemed than the last time! God be praised for it, and for leading us on, even though it be through the great and terrible depths of the wilderness."

And again: "*Feb.* 17. Wrote to Dr. Bonar, consenting that Hebrews should be begun to be printed immediately." "*Feb.* 19. Was enabled in the afternoon to write Heb. ix. 15–20. May God accept and bless it! A very bad night." "*Feb.* 23. Very poorly; could do nothing all day." "*March* 1. My thirtieth birthday." "*March* 6. Saw Dr. —— again; he said I was not so well: a very poor day." "*March* 9. Saw Dr. ——; but he could do nothing more for me." "*March* 28. Saw Dr. ——, who evidently thinks me going off very decidedly." "*March* 31. Received the first proof-sheet of Hebrews. The Lord make it all His own!" "*April* 12. My difficulty of breathing very great all this week, day and night." "*April* 13. Received third proof-sheet, to chap. ii. 3." "*April* 14. Received fourth proof-sheet, to chap. iii. 1."

Lord Bacon has remarked that "there is no passion in the mind of man so weak but it mates and masters the fear of death. Revenge triumphs over death; love slights it; honour aspireth to it; grief flieth to it; fear pre-occupieth it." In a sense which Bacon did not personally know, dear Adelaide "mastered" the last enemy. "I feel," she writes to Mrs. C—— W——, "as if it would be quite impossible to express the change which is come over me in thinking of death. It used to be my favourite subject. But now it seems not worth a thought. Indeed, I quite dislike it, not from any fear of it, but from a kind of feeling that it is one of the things a Christian has left behind. No—that does not express it, for it is still to come. But I mean that we have actually got the victory over it in Jesus. And I think, as one realizes union with Him, one feels to have done with it in Him, and that the circumstances attending death need not be anticipated one whit more than those of any other trial which may or may not be 'on the morrow.' And there seems to me such extraordinary liberty and happiness in this. I would anticipate nothing, but rejoice in the present privileges of my inheritance, so far as I am enabled to do so, from moment to moment."

Meanwhile, she left not an instant unused in finishing her work of service. "I have thought of you very often," she writes, for example, to one whom she felt she had not tenderly enough warned, "since the few words I had with you the last day I saw you. If you remember, you were just telling me how afraid you were to die, when I was called away. Have you ever closely asked yourself what makes you afraid? I can remember the time when I was so much afraid of dying that I often dared not go to sleep at night lest I should not live till the morning. But during the last five or six years, and often when I have been apparently on the very brink of the grave, I felt no fear at all. Quite the contrary; I longed to die! Now you can surely guess what made this change in me. Once outside, now in Christ! There is no real happiness until we have gone and told God all we feel and all we are, and asked Him to cover our nakedness and to wash us in the blood of Jesus. I long for you to be truly happy. Pray to be hid in Jesus. You have beautiful time for praying, when you sit alone with God in that nice little room. Oh! what a happy room it might be to you, if Jesus were with you there! I pray that He may be. Join me in praying yourself also; then, if two 'agree,' see Matt. xviii. 19."

And to another she writes, in a different strain: "You cannot think how much I prized your visit. We thought and spoke together of Him whose name we love and fear; and I have not a doubt He looked on, and loved to be so remembered in this God-forgetting world. You know I always like to think of His pleasures, and rather to draw mine from them than to make mine the chief thing." "Is not the Potter and the clay," she adds, reverting to a figure formerly named, "a comforting thought, in all ways? for not only does it put us in our right place as helpless clay in the Potter's hand, but it gives one such confidence in all He does with us; because, of course, He will fashion us so as to get Himself most glory by us. And with such an object in view, one feels so sure that His designs for each vessel must be so full of exquisite beauty, displaying such exquisite skill. And there is something so very sweet in the feeling that we can be made use of to exhibit the beauty of His workmanship. May you often be enabled to pray for your poor, weak, worthless friend, and *yet* a sister in God's family, where all is royalty, splendour, and might!"

Her bodily weakness became at times so oppressive to her that she could scarcely even bear to be prayed with. "I can sink into Christ," she said on one of those occasions, "though I cannot rise to Him."

And another day, when she had not strength to pray alone, she whispered, "Yet it comes to me!"

And again, one night, as she was suffering great pain in her chest, and was almost overwhelmed by nausea and a "distracting headache," she mildly whispered—"But you know JESUS prays."

"The way," says one of her sisters, "in which she used at this time to name His name, conveyed to me far more than I had ever heard her say about Him before; she seemed always conscious that He was close to her—almost abstracted from every one besides—in some unknown way (to me) filled with Him, filled by Him, and that so continuously that literally she 'lacked nothing.' The impression on my own mind is most vivid, though I know I cannot in the least convey it to others;—it was not that she spoke about it, for literally she had not breath to speak with, it being only occasionally that she talked whole sentences at once—but she really seemed entirely absorbed with HIM—Jesus was her 'all in all.'"

A new radiance, quiet and still like the setting sun, appeared to rest now upon passages of the Word which before had been wrapt, even to her eye, in a kind of mist. "Bright," they seemed,

> "As the glimpses of eternity,
> To saints accorded in their dying hour."

"Oh! how very, very little," she said, one day (Jan. 19), "friends are to us in the matter of dying! It is so exclusively betwixt God and the soul. I am so enveloped just now in that bright 'cloud'" (alluding to Heb. xii. 1)—"so realizing the being 'encompassed' by it—so enjoying the thought that Jesus is the SUN which sheds on it all its brightness!"

And, on another occasion: "I have been thinking of the Melchizedec priesthood, and have found it such a rich 'feast of fat things!' That word—'which passeth not from one to another' (*marg.* Heb. vii. 24) —is so dear to me; it shows that our tale, being once told to Jesus, has never to be told again to a stranger!" And then, after a pause, she added: "It is always the same heart of love which listens and intercedes. And, of course, the oftener we go to Him, the better we can appreciate the value of the assurance that His priesthood passes not into other hands."

The Pilgrim, in his struggle through the "black river," "cried out to his friend Hopeful, 'I sink in deep waters.'" Dear Adelaide, during these months, was not without tasting this trial. "I cannot help telling you," she writes, in a brief note, "how despondency has been trying me; for I know you will ask that the temptation may be taken away. I think it is plain that Satan has been taking advantage of my weakness; and I feel as if I could not help turning to you, as the only friend to whom I can unburden this particular trial, to ask your kind help in prayer. I always feel that to be spoken for to God is more than all besides."

When the Pilgrim was trembling, Hopeful exclaimed, "Be of good cheer, my brother; I feel the bottom, and it is good." Dear Adelaide was never without "feeling the bottom." In a pencil-note to the Hon. Mrs. C——, Jan. 19, she says: "I really am too ill just now to write or read or think; but I must make the effort to undeceive you about my state of mind—it never was so low, so unable to enter at all 'into the sanctuary above.' No; I have had the full persuasion that God was unchangeable in all His feelings to me, though all mine to Him seem at an end. You little know how sorely unbelief tries me; but I suppose it is through these very depths of anguish that we learn most—and, therefore, while we cry, 'O wretched man that I am!' we may still be saying, 'I thank God through Jesus Christ.'"

And again: "I quite believe that this spiritual trial arises from bodily health. I feel you do right to direct me to the temptations of Jesus; for, after all, satisfying comfort can be found nowhere else. If there be one subject more than any other which I long to be helped to prize more, it is the love of Jesus. And perhaps the study of that love, as you have so kindly put it before me, may be God's way of setting me free."

And to another, Jan. 26: "Don't sorrow, dearest friend. When faith is lively, there is nothing I so long for as to be with Jesus—I do so want face to face communion; but pray for me just now as much as you can, for I seem to be ascending the mountain through mists which hide everything. Don't you know what I mean?"

Light once more arose in the darkness; and, as often before, it came through the Word. "I am happier now," she writes, Feb. 2. "I must first tell you, however, that, for some time past, it has been rather trying to me not to find anything in the Bible which quite suited my case. Isa. l. 10 did not; for I could not say I had 'no light.' Mic. vii. 9 did not; for, in this particular instance, I had no particular sin with which to charge myself. And so on with other similar texts; whilst I never could, for one moment, believe that God was hiding *His* face. I felt I was myself crushed, and I could not look up. You will believe therefore, how exactly I found myself described in Exod. vi. 9—'Moses spake so unto the children of Israel; but they hearkened not unto Moses for anguish (*marg.*, shortness, or *straitness*) of spirit and for cruel bondage.' And then I felt that redemption was only 'promised' to them; but for us it is 'obtained'—actually, for the soul, and, in Christ, for the body. And it seemed as if, for the first time, God had in this trial spoken through His Word and brought it home. I never am happy till I have verified my experience by the Word. "She brightened," says her sister, "from that moment."

Another consolation gladdened her. "This has sometimes tried and exercised my faith lately," she writes, on Feb. 10, "why such extremity of suffering must be; but, after all, it brings us into very, very little fellowship with what Jesus endured. His sufferings have been quite too much for me at times lately—I could not read them. I suppose you never felt that?" And again: "I have been thinking of those words of His to Zebedee's sons, 'Can ye drink of the cup which I drink of?' Oh! dearest ——, if I have learned but one lesson through this season of humiliation, it is that I stand from first to last in what Jesus has done for me. 'Thou wilt keep him in peace—peace, whose mind is stayed on thee!'"

About the end of February she speaks of being "wonderfully better," and of "certainly gaining strength." And she hastened to "occupy" the brief season of respite. "Whenever she was able to do so," says her sister, "her book on the Hebrews was generally her subject; she reserved all her strength for that—writing, or correcting what she had previously written, or searching works, especially *the* Book. She even gave up almost all correspondence with friends, that her little remaining power to hold a pen might be devoted to Him of whom she felt that that epistle especially testified." And, on March 14, she herself writes to the Hon. Mrs. C——, thus: "I thought you would like one line to know that, in spite of increasing weakness, Heb. ix. is done and chapter x. begun. I feel it is an effort to do it, but I am anxious to do what I can, while I can."

One of her earliest labours of love had been the aiding of the Irish Missions. With that steadfastness of purpose which characterised all her efforts, she had sustained this agency, year by year, with a zeal which time only deepened. "Thank you, a thousand times," are her closing words regarding it, "for all your love and thoughts of me. I have been, to my own feelings, at the very point of death, but just now have rallied again a little, and seize on the opportunity for sending my money. Dear G—— has kindly undertaken the care of my Scripture-reader (D. V.) for the future. I feel a little, sending it for the last time—the flesh is so very weak. But, thank God, I am not so spiritually crushed and kept down, now that the body is freer from pain. I knew it was physical depression. Exod. vi. 9 seemed exactly to suit me. Dr. —— has plainly told me, that with disease so 'active' as it was when he last tried my chest, it was impossible to tell how soon it might do its work. I can testify to GOD's faithfulness throughout, and have only been crushed through intense weakness and bodily suffering in myself."

And one or two other messages likewise engaged her pen. "I cannot refrain," she writes to Miss G——, March 9, "from trying to send you this evening a text which has seemed very full of beauty to me lately, Heb. ix. 24, Christ 'appearing' in the presence of God for us. The Greek is to 'appear, or shew one's-self.' Don't you think there is something very touching in the idea, that it is enough that Jesus should show Himself to God for us? That is the idea the words give me; and I have found it very sweet—as if the sight of Jesus quite satisfied the Father. And then to feel it is on our behalf He is there! But I am getting too tired to write any more, and will only add very fondest love. Pray for me, that I may not 'faint.'"

And to another, who had been bereaved: "The expression—be it ever so hasty—of the love and sympathy which I feel to you and each of you just now as fellow-members in Christ's body, must not be withheld, though it be given with all the infirmity of poor frail humanity! Jesus is your real Fountain of comfort; and friends at best can only be channels, and rills, and little streams, to convey to you some of His overflowing consolation. God Himself bless, and keep, and comfort, and shine upon you!"

And again to another: "I am anxious to scribble a few words to you as best I can. When I have been able, I have been thinking of the New Covenant—its marvellous perfection, and the very wonderful state it places us in. If we only believed it, I can hardly conceive how we could be happier. But it strikes me now, in getting nearer views of eternity, how little we know of true simple faith. I can't express it; but I do so feel it. However, I must stop: my writing will show how weak I am!"

About the middle of March she was once more prostrated. "I am again," she writes, "as weak as I can be. I think I decidedly decline; and my hopes lessen of any reviving—which I had fancied I should have liked, if I might have had it, just for a little while." And, a few days later, to the Hon. Mrs. C——: "The frequent shortness of breath, which has been more trying me lately, is what chiefly makes me feel the uncertainty I do about life." And, again, to another: "My throat has lately become extremely painful at times; and I have, in consequence, entirely lost my voice."

"I wish," said a friend who was visiting her one day, "I could take that pain and suffer it for you."

"But you know," replied dear Adelaide, with a smile of patient meekness which her friend says she never will forget, "you know that if I am to reign with Jesus, I must be conformed to His image in His sufferings also and in His death."

She used to lie upon the sofa, with her eyes fixed upward and her lips moving. Only occasionally she would whisper some brief word. "All is bright yonder!" she said one evening. The "glory to be revealed," seemed chiefly to absorb her thoughts. "Perhaps," was her remark, on another occasion, "as believers in a coming Redeemer, we ought hardly to let death dwell on our minds."

"I do not find the same comfort," she said one morning, "from isolated texts as I once did." "The last large portion of Scripture which I read to her," writes one of her sisters, "was the Book of Deuteronomy, in which she particularly delighted. As I was reading it this last time, she seemed to 'revel' (as she used to express it) in the view of God's character which she always gained from it. If I paused at any particular verse, she would inquire why that single sentence arrested me, and would add—'You should look at the grand whole.'"

At intervals she revived a little, and was able to enter into a whispering conversation. "His dealings with me are so mysterious," she said on one of those occasions, "so unlike anything I ever anticipated! He keeps me in such perfect peace! I can only think of the words, 'He shall carry the lambs in His bosom'—lift them up, and take them quite out of reach of the wolf, so that they shall not even hear his roaring."

And, another time, she said; "It is wonderful how little I have been tempted by Satan. But the Lord 'stayeth His rough wind in the day of His east wind:' when there is great bodily suffering, He does not let Satan harass me."

In one of her last brief notes, she wrote to the Hon. Mrs. C—— thus: "I hope you have got your Hebrew Bible, or, at all events, your German, and will enrich me with some of the exquisite things you get out of it. I should like to send you those words to think of—'Making melody in your heart to the Lord.' How sweet the occupation of singing to Him! (Ps. cv. 2)—and it just occurs to me how nice an opportunity you and —— have got for it, whilst shut out from more active service. It is the greatest comfort to me often to feel sure it is fragrant to Jesus. Will you give Eph. i. 12 to —— from me? It is such a precious verse for a sick-room; for, when we can absolutely neither write, nor speak, nor work at anything, we are 'to the praise of His glory' still, whilst lying 'trusting in Christ.'"

And in another note she bids a touching farewell to a humble saint, thus:—

"MY DEAREST M——,

"I must say good-bye in writing, as it is so impossible for us now to meet in the flesh. What a wonderful thing our union is in the True Vine! Oh, that we may get daily closer together in Jesus! Does He not seem to you every day to be more and more your 'All and in all?'—the Beloved on whom we lean every step of our way in coming up from the wilderness.

"'I travel through a desert drear and wild,
Yet is my heart with such sweet thoughts beguiled
Of Him on whom I lean—my strength, my stay,
I can forget the sorrows of the way.'

It really does put sad and gloomy thoughts quite away, to realize tke presence of Him whom our soul loveth.

"I was thinking to-day of Cant. viii. 14, and especially of 'the mountains of spices.' It appears to me as if that verse implied, that it is when we are highest and farthest up the mountains, earthly things look so small (as they gradually recede from our sight) that at length the only object we seem to care about is seeing Jesus again! They are mountains of spices, full of sweetness; but still we are not satisfied until we awake after His likeness, and see Him face to face! Will you constantly pray that I may be ever ready to meet my precious Saviour when the appointed time comes, and 'be found of Him in peace, without spot and blameless?' The verse I will specially ask you to plead for me is 1 Thess. v. 23, that I may be 'preserved blameless'—kept from falling, or from growing cold or languid.

"Oh! may the Spirit of our God take some live coals from off the altar, and set our hearts on fire with love to Jesus!

"Ever, my dearest M——, your own affectionate sister in Him,

"A. L. NEWTON."

About four, one morning, three weeks or so before her death, she was talking with one of her sisters about the ways of the Lord towards her. "Do you think you must go?" she said, as her sister was leaving, afraid of her exhausting herself. "I have been so little able to talk lately, that it is quite a pleasure. But the pain has been so intense. Oh! there is something so inconceivably precious in the firm conviction, that, as to one's safety, it is all done! When you draw near, or feel drawing near, to the end, it is nothing but the great foundation-realities of the Gospel which will do—one seems to care about nothing else; it is just Christ's finished work, nothing else, which will satisfy you then."

"I got up again to go," says her sister, "for she coughed so sadly; and though it was hard to tear one's-self away, I thought it cruel to stay. But she almost kept me, saying, 'There is something so unspeakably precious in speaking of HIM we love, remembering Him in the night-watches.'"

It is recorded of Legh Richmond, that, the last

fortnight of his life, he "was very silent, and appeared constantly in prayer and meditation, waiting his dismissal and the end of his earthly pilgrimage. Nothing seemed to disturb him, and he seemed to realize that blessed word, 'Thou wilt keep him in perfect peace, whose mind is stayed on thee.'" Very similar was the closing fortnight of dear Adelaide's course. "It looked like heaven," says one of her sisters. "She seemed already there in spirit though treading our vale of tears. There was nothing of triumph: but such solid, rock-like peace I scarcely hope ever to see again. As I used to close her room-door and sit silently beside her, she little able to speak, or even to listen to speaking or reading, yet 'looking heaven'—I could not but feel that we were three, and Jesus in our midst. 'Him! Him!' she once said, alluding to Rev. i. 5, 6, which I had begun to quote, 'I cannot get any further—that is enough—HIM!'"

One of those mornings, very early, she lay, with a happy smile on her worn countenance, meditating on the chapter (Tit. iii.) which had been read to her the previous evening. "'According to His mercy He saved us,'" she slowly repeated twice, alluding to v. 5; "'According to His mercy He saved us.' If I can say no more, angels and devils too shall hear me say, 'Mercy! mercy! According to His mercy He saved us!'"

A few days before he died, Payson—himself also enduring extreme bodily suffering—said: "My God is in this room. I see Him! Oh! how lovely is the sight! how glorious does He appear! worthy of ten thousand hearts, if I had so many to give!" Dear Adelaide "seemed now quite willing," says her sister, "to relinquish seeing ministers and Christian friends, or getting letters, though formerly all the three had been helps she felt solitary without. The Lord's Person seemed wholly to absorb her, as if she saw Him, heard Him, lived with Him. Certainly He was not only far dearer, but appeared to be nearer, to her than were any of us."

On a Saturday night (April 15), about ten days previous to her departure, one of her sisters, who was sitting up in the adjoining room (for Adelaide always preferred being alone), went in to mend her fire.

"What thought have you had," whispered Adelaide, observing her, "which makes you look so happy?"

"That word in the 65th Psalm, 'Praise waiteth for thee, O Lord, in Sion.'"

"Oh! I remember your thoughts about Sunday always. I hope you will have a very happy one to-morrow."

The next evening, on her sister's return from church, the thought seemed fresh in her mind. "I have been meditating so much all day," she said, "on that precious Psalm!"

"Don't you think," asked the other, "that its full meaning, especially verses 1 and 4, never can be realized here? Glimpses we may have; but 'praise waits,' does it not?"

"Yes," said Adelaide, turning her bright eye upwards; "we must go higher up to know what it is to be 'satisfied' with the goodness of His house."

"How glorious it will be to have Jesus 'declaring' His Father's 'name' to us! Man spoils it so."

"Yes," was her reply; "and the Hebrew is very striking; it is, 'He reckons up—enters into the minutest details;' and He will 'praise in the midst of the congregation.' It will not be long, G——, before He comes again, and with our bodies, knowing each other, we shall stand there."

The same evening, her mother "enjoyed a most delightful conversation with her." Few words she was able to utter; and these few only in a whisper. "Dear mamma," she said at its close, "here is my parting gift to you—'For one look to self, take ten of Jesus.'"

A day or two afterwards, one of her sisters was reading to her the 90th Psalm. "Alluding," says her sister, "to v. 8, which we had talked over seven years before, she asked if I had made up my mind about it. Then, passing to v. 17, and slowly repeating the words—'And let the beauty of the Lord our God be upon us,' she said, 'What a sublime prayer! how unlike it ours are!'"

Another morning, the sister who used always to take up her breakfast, found her deeply affected. "It is only the parting from all you dear creatures," she said, wiping the tear from her eye. "But never mind," she added, a few moments afterwards, with a brightening smile, "this corruption must put on incorruption."

The following Friday (April 21), the Rev. Mr. Dallas (of Wonston) came from Hull to see her. Naming some features of death, he inquired if the near prospect of it troubled her. "Oh!" she replied, turning her eye towards him and sweetly smiling, "there are many things about it which I shrink from; but, you know, I need not look at them." "He told me," says her sister, "that nothing would ever efface from his memory the impression of that brief visit—scarcely ever had he witnessed such maturity of faith and of love." And her mother adds: "He was much affected, and said how much he rejoiced that he had come."

The last Sabbath of her life was one of great agony. In the morning, she had been jotting down in pencil some thoughts on Heb. xi. 1, 2—intending it for her book then passing through the press; and, on her sister's return from morning-service, she had put a "small piece of paper" into her hand, saying eagerly, "I want you to tell me what you think of it." In the afternoon, she was seized with a violent cramp. "She was in great suffering," says her sister; "but not a word or look of impatience then or at any other time escaped her." And another sister says: "Three times that afternoon and evening, she told me of her thankfulness in being kept from any spiritual clouds."

"Affliction is ours," says Herbert, speaking of the family-discipline—

"We are the trees whom shaking fastens more,
While blust'ring winds destroy the wanton bowers,

And ruffle all their curious knots and store.
My God, so temper joy and woe,
That thy bright beams may tame thy bow."

Dear Adelaide's "woe," arising from extreme bodily suffering, was indeed "tempered" with a heavenly "joy." "As I watched her from day to day," says her sister, "I felt quite overcome, to see how she literally rejoiced in the tribulation of body which Jesus had appointed for her. A silent tear was the only expression of pain which ever came from her. I was really astonished at the long-continued grace she manifested in this particular, and could only glorify God in her, being often reminded of the remarks she used to make about Phil. i. 29, how it is 'given' to the believer 'in the behalf of Christ' to suffer for His sake. 'A gift' she would say, 'a gift!' and she did indeed accept it with a loving, acquiescing heart—a will which delighted in His will—so that the common term of 'resignation' had really in her case no meaning."

Her patience appeared also in another trial. "All through her illness," her sister says, "she had been so independent of help that she would let nothing of any kind be done for her, however costly the struggle which enabled her to do it for herself. But when at last she could struggle no more and she was obliged to be helped as you would help an infant, she never uttered anything like complaint, but most humbly, and gratefully, and lovingly accepted our services." "Ah!" she would say, with a kindly smile, to the faithful old family-nurse, as she was washing her or doing any other act of service, "a cup of cold water shall in no wise lose its reward."

On the Monday afternoon, she asked her sister to read the second chapter of Malachi. "I rather wondered," says the latter; "but, not liking to make her speak, I began to read, when she half looked up and said, 'I meant the third.' And that was the last portion," her sister adds, "of her precious companion which I ever enjoyed with her. For three weeks she had scarcely ever been able to read it for herself; but often I was struck by the eager way in which her bright eye followed it, if, when trying to place her food or medicine conveniently near to her, I ever moved it even a very little further off than where she had put it."

The next forenoon, after a few minutes' sleep, she said, "I *will* get up; I think I can write some more of 'Hebrews;' my mind is so full; give me my Bible." And for a little she sat with her pencil in her hand, but unable from exhaustion to put it to paper.

A faintness, however, came on; and, after another short sleep, she awoke with an excruciating pain in her head. At four P.M. this gave way to a distressing convulsion, which "gave us all (says her sister), as we gathered round her, the feeling that death had seized her." For about twenty minutes her distress was agonizing; yet "even with the grasp of that iron hand upon her (her sister adds), her expression of countenance never altered in the least, nor did her consciousness leave her for a moment."

The physician came in, and administered some

medicine; and the violence of the spasms subsided. As he retired, she said to one of her sisters, "I have just been asking Dr. —— how long he thinks I may continue in this state; and he told me it could not be long." "For your sake," said the other, "I cannot wish it should be." "I," Adelaide replied, "have no wish about it."

A little before eight she was lifted into bed, thanking those around her for their tender care. About nine, it seemed as if the painful struggle were again coming on; and she begged that the physician might be called, saying, "Surely the bitterness of death is past!" But she was spared any further conflict. Till four in the morning she was still and calm—not uttering a word, though apparently quite conscious. At length her happy spirit was evidently departing. "As she leaned against the pillows which supported her," says her sister, "I fancied she would have spoken to us, had she been spoken to; but no one broke the solemn silence." A smile of heavenly peace rested on her pale face—when, about five, her breathing ceased so insensibly, that not till the physician who supported her had said, "She is here no longer," did those around her know that she had gone to be with the Lord.

It was on April 26, 1854, and as she had just completed her thirtieth year.

"I bless thee," said Polycarp, as he stood at the stake, "that thou hast counted me worthy of this day and of this hour, to receive my portion in the number of the martyrs, in the cup of Christ." Dear Adelaide Newton had now finished her "living martyrdom," and finished right worthily.

Lord Bacon has remarked that, "when a man has obtained worthy ends and expectations, the sweetest canticle is, 'Nunc dimittis.'" Beloved Adelaide is gone upward, solaced by this canticle. "Yet a little while," and she shall receive her crown, which the Lord, the righteous Judge, shall give to her "at that day."

Our sister's fight is over,
 Her arduous race is run;
'Twas by THY grace and power
 The prize of life she won.

Soon wilt THOU come in glory,
 With all thy Church to shine,
Our bodies raised in honour
 And beauty, Lord, like thine

Then, then, we'll shout still louder
 The song which now we sing—
O grave, where is thy victory?
 O death, where is thy sting?

THE END.

BONAR'S (Rev. Andrew) Commentary on Leviticus. 8vo... 1 50
BONNET'S Family of Bethany. 18mo........................ 40
——— Meditations on the Lord's Prayer. 18mo............... 40
BOOTH'S Reign of Grace. 12mo............................ 75
BORROW'S Bible and Gypsies of Spain. 8vo, cloth.......... 1 00
BOSTON'S (Thomas) Select Works. Royal 8vo............... 2 00
——— Four-fold State. 18mo................................ 50
——— Crook in the Lot. 18mo............................... 30
BRETT'S (Rev. W. H.) Indian Tribes of Guiana. 18mo....... 50
BREWSTER'S More Worlds than One........................ 60
BRIDGEMAN'S Daughter of China. 18mo.................... 50
BRIDGES on the Christian Ministry. 8vo.................. 1 50
——— on the Proverbs. 8vo................................ 2 00
——— on the CXIXth Psalm. 8vo............................ 1 00
——— Memoir of Mary Jane Graham. 8vo...................... 1 00
BROKEN Bud; or, the Reminiscences of a Bereaved Mother. 75
BROTHER and Sister; or, the Way of Peace................. 50
BROWN'S (Rev. John, D.D.) Exposition of First Peter. 8vo.. 2 50
——— on the Sayings and Discourses of Christ. 2 vols. 8vo.. 4 00
——— on the Sufferings and Glories of the Messiah. 8vo...... 1 50
——— The Dead in Christ. 16mo............................ 50
BROWN'S Explication of the Assembly's Catechism. 12mo.. 60
BROWN (Rev. David) on the Second Advent. 12mo.......... 1 25
BROWN'S Concordance. 32mo, gilt, 30 cents. Plain......... 20
BUCHANAN'S Comfort in Affliction. 18mo.................. 40
——— on the Holy Spirit. 18mo............................. 50
BUNBURY'S Glory, Glory, Glory, and other Narratives...... 25
BUNYAN'S Pilgrim's Progress. Fine ed. Large type. 12mo. 1 00
——— 18mo. Close type..................................... 50
——— Jerusalem Sinner Saved. 18mo........................ 50
——— Greatness of the Soul. 18mo.......................... 50
BURNS' (John) Christian Fragments. 18mo.................. 40
BUTLER'S (Bishop) Complete Works. 8vo.................... 1 50
——— Sermons, alone. 8vo.................................. 1 00
——— Analogy, alone. 8vo.................................. 75
——— and Wilson's Analogy. 8vo........................... 1 25
CALVIN, The Life and Times of John Calvin. By Henry.... 2 00
CAMERON'S (Mrs.) Farmer's Daughter. Illustrated.......... 30
CATECHISMS—The Assembly's Catechism. Per hundred.... 1 25
——— Do. with proofs........................ " " 3 00
——— Brown's Short Catechism........ ...... " " 1 25
——— Brown on the Assembly's Catechism. Each............ 10
——— Willison's Communicant's Catechism. Per dozen....... 75
CECIL'S Works. 3 vols. 12mo, with portrait................ 3 00
——— Sermons, separate.................................... 1 00

CECIL'S Miscellanies and Remains, separate.................. 1 00
——— Original Thoughts, separate.......................... 1 00
——— (Catharine) Memoir of Mrs. Hawkes, with portrait...... 1 00
CHALMERS' Sermons. 2 vols. 8vo, with fine portrait....... 3 00
——— Lectures on Romans " " " 1 50
——— Miscellanies " " " 1 50
——— Select Works; comprising the above. 4 vols. 8vo..... 6 00
——— Evidences of Christian Revelation. 2 vols. 12mo...... 1 25
——— Natural Theology. 2 vols. 12mo...................... 1 25
——— Moral Philosophy.................................... 60
——— Commercial Discourses............................... 60
——— Astronomical Discourses.............................. 60
CHARLES ROUSSEL; or, Honesty and Industry............. 40
CHARNOCK on the Attributes. 2 vols. 8vo................ 3 00
——— Choice Works.. 50
CHEEVER'S Lectures on the Pilgrim's Progress. Illus. 12mo. 1 00
——— Powers of the World to Come. 12mo................... 1 00
——— Right of the Bible in our Common Schools............ 75
CHILDS' Own Story Book. Square.......................... 50
CHRISTIAN Retirement. 12mo.............................. 75
——— Experience. By the same author. 12mo............... 75
CLARA STANLEY; or, A Summer Among the Hills......... 50
CLAREMONT Tales (The). Illustrated. 18mo.............. 50
CLARK'S (Rev. John A.) Walk about Zion. 12mo........... 75
——— Pastor's Testimony.................................. 75
——— Awake, Thou Sleeper................................. 75
——— Young Disciple...................................... 88
——— Gathered Fragments.................................. 1 00
CLARKE'S Daily Scripture Promises. 32mo, gilt........... 30
COLLIER'S Tale (The).................................... 25
COLQUHOUN'S (Lady) World's Religion. New edition. 16mo 50
COMMANDMENT, with Promise. 18mo....................... 40
COWPER'S Poetical Works. Complete. 2 vols. 16mo. Illus. 1 50
——— Task. Illustrated by Birket Foster.................. 4 50
CUMMING'S (Rev. John, D.D.) Message from God. 18mo.... 30
——— Christ Receiving Sinners. 18mo....................... 30
CUNNINGHAM'S World without Souls. 18mo.............. 30
CUYLER'S (Rev. T. L.) Stray Arrows. New edition.......... 40
DAILY Commentary. For Family Reading. 8vo............ 3 00
D'AUBIGNE'S History of the Reformation. 5 vols. 12mo.... 2 50
Do. do. 8vo. Complete in 1 vol.... 1 50
——— Life of Cromwell the Protector. 12mo................ 50
——— Germany, England and Scotland. 12mo................ 75
——— Luther and Calvin. 18mo............................ 25
——— Authority of God. 16mo............................. 75

DAVIDSON'S Connection of Sacred and Profane History...... 1 00
DAVID'S Psalms, in meter. Large type. 12mo. Embossed.. 75
Do. do. do. gilt edges........... 1 00
Do. do. do. Turkey morocco..... 2 00
Do. 18mo. Good type. Plain sheep............... 38
Do. 48mo. Very neat pocket edition. Sheep...... 20
Do. " " " morocco.... 25
Do. " " " gilt edges.. 31
Do. " " " tucks...... 50
Do. with Brown's Notes. 18mo................... 50
Do. " " " morocco, gilt 1 25
DAVIES' Sermons. 3 vols. 12mo............................ 2 00
DICK'S (John, D.D.) Lectures on Theology. 2 vols. in 1. Cloth 2 50
Do. do. do. Sheep, $3. 2 vols. Cloth... 3 00
——— Lectures on Acts. 8vo................................ 1 50
DICKINSON'S (Rev. R. W.) Scenes from Sacred History...... 1 00
——— Responses from Sacred Oracles......................... 1 00
DILL'S Ireland's Miseries, their Cause and Cure............... 75
DODDRIDGE'S Rise and Progress. 18mo.................... 40
——— Life of Colonel Gardiner. 18mo....................... 30
DRUMMOND'S (Mrs.) Emily Vernon. A Tale. 16mo......... 75
——— (Rev. D. T. K.) on the Parables. 8vo..................
DUNCAN'S (Rev. Dr.) Sacred Philosophy of the Seasons. 2 vols. 2 50
——— Life, by his Son. With portrait. 12mo................ 75
——— Tales of the Scottish Peasantry. 18mo. Illustrated.... 50
——— Cottage Fireside. 18mo. Illustrated................. 40
——— (Mrs.) Life of Mary Lundie Duncan. 16mo............. 75
——— ——— Life of George A. Lundie. 18mo................ 50
——— ——— Memoir of George B. Phillips. 18mo............ 25
——— ——— Children of the Manse.......................... 50
——— ——— America as I Found It... .... 1 00
——— (Mary Lundie) Rhymes for my Children. Illustrated.... 25
EDWARD'S (Jonathan, D.D.) Charity and its Fruits. 18mo... 50
ENGLISH Pulpit (The). 8vo...... .... 1 50
ERSKINE'S Gospel Sonnets. 18mo. Portrait................ 50
EVENING Hours with my Children. Colored, $1 75. Plain.. 1 25
EVIDENCES of Christianity—University of Virginia. 8vo.... 2 50
FAMILY Worship. 8vo. Morocco, $5. Half calf, $4. Cloth 3 00
FANNY and her Mamma. Square........................... 50
FISK'S Memorial of the Holy Land, with steel plates.......... 1 00
——— Orphan Tale... 25
FLEETWOOD'S History of the Bible. Illustrated............. 2 00
FLORENCE Egerton; or, Sunshine and Shadow. Illustrated. 75
FOLLOW Jesus. By the author of "Come to Jesus".......... 25
FORD'S Decapolis. 18mo.................................. 25

FOSTER'S Essays on Decision of Character, &c. 12mo........ 75
FOSTER'S Essays on the Evils of Popular Ignorance. 12mo.. 75
FOX'S Acts and Monuments. Complete. Illustrated........ 4 00
FRANK Harrison.. 30
FRANK Netherton; or, the Talisman. 18mo................. 40
FRITZ Harold; or, the Temptation. 16mo.................. 60
FRY (Caroline) The Listener. Illustrated edition. 16mo...... 1 00
——— Christ our Law. 16mo.............................. 60
——— Christ our Example and Autobiography. 16mo......... 75
——— Sabbath Musings. 18mo............................. 40
——— Scripture Reader's Guide. 18mo..................... 30
GELDART'S May Dundas. A Tale. 18mo.................... 50
GILFILLAN'S Martyrs, Heroes and Bards of Covenant. 16mo. 60
GOODE'S Better Covenant.................................. 60
GOODRICH'S Geography of the Bible.......................
GRAY'S Poems. Illust. Mor. $2 50. Gilt extra $1 50. Plain 1 00
HALDANE'S (Robert) Exposition of Romans. 8vo........... 2 50
——— (Robert and James A.) Lives. 8vo.................... 2 00
HAMILTON'S (Rev. James, D.D.) Life in Earnest. 18mo...... 30
——— Mount of Olives. 18mo.............................. 30
——— Harp on Willows. 18mo.............................. 30
——— Thankfulness, and other Essays. 18mo................ 30
——— Life of Hall. 32mo, gilt............................. 30
——— Lamp and Lantern. 18mo............................ 40
——— Happy Home. 18mo.................................. 50
——— Life of Lady Colquhoun. 16mo....................... 75
——— Life of Richard Williams. 16mo...................... 75
——— Royal Preacher. 16mo............................... 85
HAWKER'S Poor Man's Morning Portion. 12mo............. 60
Do do. Evening Portion. 12mo............. 60
——— Zion's Pilgrim. 18mo................................ 30
HENRY'S Commentary. 5 vols. Quarto. Fine edition......
——— Miscellaneous Works. 2 vols. Royal 8vo.............. 4 00
——— Method for Prayer. 18mo............................ 40
——— Communicant's Companion. 18mo..................... 40
——— Daily Communion with God. 18mo.................... 30
——— Pleasantness of a Religious Life. 24mo, gilt........... 30
HENRY (Philip) Life of. 18mo............................. 50
HERVEY'S Meditations. 18mo.............................. 40
HETHERINGTON'S History of the Church of Scotland. 8vo.. 1 50
——— History of Westminster Assembly. 12mo............. 75
——— Minister's Family. A Tale........................... 75
HEWITSON, Memoir of the Rev. W. H. Hewitson. 12mo.... 85
HILL'S (George) Lectures on Divinity. 8vo.................. 2 00
HISTORIC Doubts.. 50

HISTORY of the Puritans and Pilgrim Fathers. 12mo........ 1 00
HISTORY of the Reformation in Europe. 18mo.............. 40
HOOKER (Rev. H.), The Uses of Adversity. 18mo............ 30
——— Philosophy of Unbelief. 12mo......................... 75
HORNE'S Introduction. 2 vols. Royal 8vo. Half cloth...... 3 50
Do. 1 vol., sheep, $4. 2 vols., sheep, $5. 2 vols., cloth. 4 00
HORNE'S (Bishop) Commentary on the Book of Psalms. 8vo. 1 50
HOWARD (John); or, the Prison World of Europe. 16mo.... 75
HOWELL'S Life—Perfect Peace. 18mo...................... 30
HOWE'S Redeemer's Tears. 18mo........................... 50
HOWIE'S Scots Worthies. 8vo............................. 1 50
HUSS (John) Life of. Translated from the German... 25
INFANT'S Progress. 18mo. Illustrated...................... 50
JACOBUS on Matthew. With a Harmony. Illustrated....... 75
——— on Mark and Luke.................................. 75
——— on John and Acts (preparing)........................ 75
——— Catechetical Questions on each vol. Per dozen.......... 1 50
JAMES' Anxious Inquirer. 18mo............................ 30
——— Christian Progress. 18mo............................ 30
——— True Christian. 18mo................................ 30
——— Widow Directed. 18mo................................ 30
——— Young Man from Home. 18mo........................ 30
——— Christian Professor. 16mo............................ 75
——— Christian Duty. 16mo................................ 75
——— Christian Father's Present. 16mo..................... 75
——— Course of Faith. 16mo................................ 75
——— Young Woman's Friend. 16mo........................ 75
——— Young Man's Friend. 16mo.......................... 75
JAMIE Gordon; or, the Orphan. Illustrated. 18mo.......... 50
JANEWAY'S Heaven upon Earth. 18mo..................... 50
——— Token for Children. 18mo............................ 50
JAY'S Morning and Evening Exercises. Large type. 4 vols.. 4 00
Do. do. Cheap edition. 2 vols........ 1 50
——— Autobiography and Reminiscences. 2 vols. 12mo..... 2 50
——— Female Scripture Characters. 12mo.................. 1 00
——— Christian Contemplated. 18mo........................ 40
JEANIE Morrison; or, the Discipline of Life. 16mo.......... 75

By the same Author.

A New Volume, uniform with the above............... 75
THE Pastor's Family. 18mo.......................... 25
JOHNSON'S Rasselas. Elegant edition. 16mo................ 50
KENNEDY'S (Grace) Profession is not Principle. 18mo...... 30
——— Father Clement. 18mo............................... 30
——— Anna Ross. 18mo. Illustrated........................ 30
——— Philip Colville. A Covenanter's Story.................. 30

KENNEDY'S Decision. 18mo................................ 25
——— Jessy Allan, the Lame Girl. 18mo..................... 25
KEY to the Shorter Catechism. 18mo........................ 20
KING'S (Rev. David, L.L.D.) Geology and Religion. 16mo.... 75
——— on the Eldership...................................... 50
KITTO'S Daily Bible Illustrations. 8 vols. 12mo........... 8 00
——— Lost Senses.. 1 00
KRUMMACHER'S Martyr Lamb. 18mo..................... 40
——— Elijah the Tishbite. 18mo............................ 40
——— Last Days of Elisha. 18mo............................ 50
LAW and Testimony. By Miss Warner. 8vo................ 3 00
LEYBURN'S Soldier of the Cross. 12mo..................... 1 00
LIFE in New York. 18mo.................................. 40
LIFE of a Vagrant. Written by himself. 18mo............. 30
LIGHTED Valley; or, the Memoir of Miss Bolton............ 75
LITTLE Annie's First Book. Square........................ 35
——— Annie's Second do. Square........................ 40
LITTLE Lessons for Little Learners. Square................ 50
LIVING to Christ.. 40
LUTHER'S Commentary on the Galatians. 8vo............... 1 50
MACKAY, The Wycliffites.................................. 75
——— Family at Heatherdale. 18mo........................ 50
MAMMA'S Bible Stories..................................... 50
Do. do. Sequel.............................. 50
MARSHALL on Sanctification. 18mo......................... 50
MARTYRS and Covenanters of Scotland. 18mo.............. 40
McCHEYNE'S (Rev. Robert Murray) Works. 2 vols. 8vo.... 3 00
——— Life, Lectures and Letters. Separate.................. 1 50
——— Sermons. Separate.................................. 2 00
McCLELLAND (Prof. Alex.) on the Canon and Interpretation. 75
McCOSH on the Divine Government, Physical and Moral...... 2 00
McCRINDELL, The Convent. A Narrative. 18mo............ 50
——— The School Girl in France. 16mo..................... 50
McFARLANE, The Mountains of the Bible. Illustrated....... 75
McGHEE'S (Rev. R. J.) Lectures on the Ephesians. 8vo...... 2 00
McILVAINE'S Truth and Life. A Series of Discourses........ 2 00
MEIKLE'S Solitude Sweetened. 12mo....................... 60
MENTEATH, Lays of the Kirk and Covenant. Illust. 16mo.. 75
MICHAEL Kemp, The Happy Farmer's Lad. 18mo.......... 40
MILLER (Hugh), The Geology of the Bass Rock. Illustrated.. 75
MISSIONARY of Kilmany.................................. 40
MISSIONS, The Origin and History of. 25 steel plates. 4to.... 3 50
MOFFAT'S Southern Africa. 12mo.......................... 75
MONOD'S Lucilla; or, the Reading of the Bible. 18mo........ 40
MOORE (Rev. T. V.) Com. on Haggai, Zechariah and Malachi.

MORE'S (Hannah) Private Devotion. 18mo.................. 30
Do. do. do. 32mo. 20 cents. Gilt... 30
MORELL'S History of Modern Philosophy. 8vo............. 3 00
MORNING of Life. 18mo.................................. 40
MORNING and Night Watches.............................. 60

By the same Author:—

FOOTSTEPS of St. Paul. 12mo. Illustrated.......... 1 00
FAMILY Prayers. 12mo........................... 75
WOOD-CUTTER of Lebanon, and Exiles of Lucerna.... 50
THE Great Journey. Illustrated..................... 50
THE Words of Jesus................................. 40
THE Mind of Jesus.................................. 40

MY School-Boy Days. 18mo. Illustrated.................. 30
MY Youthful Companions. 18mo Illustrated............... 30
The above two in one volume......................... 50
NEW Cobwebs to Catch Little Flies...................... 50
NEWTON'S (Rev. John) Works. 2 vols. in 1. Portrait....... 2 00
NOEL'S Infant Piety. 18mo.............................. 25
OBERLIN (John Frederick) Memoirs of.................... 40
OLD White Meeting-House. 18mo.......................... 40
OLD Humphrey's Observations—Addresses—Thoughts for Thoughtful—Walks in London—Homely Hints—Country Strolls—Old Sea Captain—Grand parents—Isle of Wight—Pithy Papers—Pleasant Tales—North American Indians. 12 vols. 18mo. Each.................................. 40
OPIE on Lying. New edition. 18mo. Illustrated............ 40
OSBORNE (Mrs.) The World of Waters. Illustrated. 18mo... 50
OWEN on Spiritual Mindedness. 12mo...................... 60
PALEY'S Evidences. Edited by Prof. Nairne................. 1 25
——— Horæ Paulinæ. 8vo................................. 75
PASCAL (Jaqueline); or, Convent Life in Port Royal. 12mo.. 1 00
——— Provincial Letters.................................. 1 00
PASTOR'S Daughter. By Louisa Payson Hopkins............ 40
PATTERSON on the Assembly's Shorter Catechism........... 50
PEARSON on Infidelity. Fine edition. 8vo. $2. Cheap ed... 60
PEEP of Day... 30

By the same Author:—

LINE upon Line...................................... 30
PRECEPT on Precept.................................. 30
NEAR Home... 50
FAR Off... 50
SCRIPTURE Facts..................................... 50

PHILIP'S Devotional Guides. 2 vols........................ 1 50
——— Young Man's Closet Library........................... 75

PHILIP'S Mary's, Martha's, Lydia's and Hannah's Love of the Spirit. Each........ 40
PIKE'S True Happiness. 18mo........ 30
——— Divine Origin of Christianity........ 30
POLLOK'S Course of Time. Elegant edition. 16mo. Portrait 1 00
——— Do. 18mo. Small copy. Close type........ 40
——— Life, Letters and Remains. By the Rev. J. Scott, D.D... 1 00
——— Tales of the Scottish Covenanters. Illustrated........ 50
——— Helen of the Glen. 18mo. Illustrated........ 25
——— Persecuted Family " " 25
——— Ralph Germnell " " 25
POOL'S Annotations. 3 vols. 8vo. Half calf, $12. Cloth.... 10 00
PRAYERS of St. Paul. 16mo........ 75
QUARLE'S Emblems. Illustrated........ 1 00
RETROSPECT (The). By Aliquis. 18mo........ 40
RICHMOND'S Domestic Portraiture. Illustrated. 16mo...... 75
——— Annals of the Poor. 18mo........ 40
RIDGELY'S Body of Divinity. 2 vols. Royal 8vo........ 4 00
ROGER Miller; or, Heroism in Humble Life. 18mo........ 30
ROGER'S Jacob's Well. 18mo........ 40
——— Folded Lamb. 18mo........ 40
ROMAINE on Faith. 12mo........ 60
——— Letters. 12mo........ 60
RUTHERFORD'S Letters. With Life by Bonar........ 1 50
RYLE'S Living or Dead. A Series of Home Truths........ 75
——— Wheat or Chaff........ 75
——— Startling Questions........ 75
——— Rich and Poor........ 75
——— Priest, Puritan and Preacher........ 75
SAPHIR (Philip) Life of........ 30
SCHMID'S Hundred Short Tales........ 50
SCOTIA'S Bards. A Collection of the Scottish Poets........ 2 00
SCOTT'S Daniel. A Model for Young Men........ 1 50
——— (Thos.) Force of Truth. 18mo........ 25
SELECT Works of James Venn, Wilson, Philip and Jay....... 1 50
——— Christian Authors. 2 vols. 8vo........ 2 00
SELF Explanatory Bible. Half calf, $4 50. Morocco........ 6 00
SERLE'S Christian Remembrancer........ 50
SHERWOOD'S Clever Stories. Square........ 50
——— Jack the Sailor Boy........ 25
——— Duty is Safety........ 25
——— Think before you Act........ 25
SINNER'S Friend. 18mo........ 25
SIGOURNEY'S (Mrs. L. H.) Water Drops. Illust. 16mo...... 75
——— Letters to my Pupils. With portrait. 16mo........ 75

SIGOURNEY'S Memoir of Mrs. L. H. Cook.................... 75
—— Olive Leaves.. 50
—— Faded Hope.. 50
—— Boy's Book. 18mo...................................... 40
—— Girl's Book. 18mo..................................... 40
—— Child's Book. Square.................................. 35
SINCLAIR'S Modern Accomplishments......................... 75
—— Modern Society... 75
—— Hill and Valley.. 75
—— Holyday House.. 50
—— Charlie Seymour.. 30
SMITH'S (Rev. James) Green Pastures for the Lord's Flock.... 1 00
SMYTH'S Bereaved Parents Consoled. 12mo................... 75
SONGS in the House of my Pilgrimage. 16mo. 75
SORROWING yet Rejoicing................................... 30
STEVENSON'S Christ on the Cross. 12mo..................... 75
—— Lord our Shepherd. 12mo................................ 60
—— Gratitude. 12mo.. 75
STORIES on the Lord's Prayer.............................. 30
STUCKLEY'S Gospel Glass................................... 75
SUMNER'S Exposition of Matthew and Mark. 12mo............. 75
SYMINGTON on Atonement. 12mo.............................. 75
TALES from English History. Illustrated................... 75
TAYLOR'S (Jane) Hymns for Infant Minds. Square. Illust... 40
—— Rhymes for the Nursery. Square. Illustrated........... 50
—— Limed Twigs to Catch Young Birds. Square. Illust... 50
—— Life and Correspondence. 18mo.......................... 40
—— Display. A Tale. 18mo.................................. 30
—— Original Poems and Poetical Remains. Illustrated..... 40
—— (Isaac) Loyola; or, Jesuitism in its Rudiments.......... 1 00
—— —— Natural History of Enthusiasm....................... 75
—— (Jeremy) Sermons. Complete in 1 vol. 8vo............ 1 50
TENNENT'S Life.. 25
THEOLOGICAL Sketch Book. 2 vols........................... 3 00
THREE Months under the Snow. 18mo......................... 30
THORNWELL'S Discourses on Truth........................... 1 00
TUCKER, The Rainbow in the North. 18mo.................... 50
—— Abbeokuta or, Sunrise in the Tropics. 18mo............ 50
—— The Southern Cross and the Southern Crown.............. 75
TURNBULLS Genius of Scotland. Illustrated. 16mo.......... 1 00
—— Pulpit Orators of France and Switzerland............... 1 00
TYNG'S Lectures on the Law and Gospel. With portrait..... 1 50
—— Christ is All. 8vo. With portrait...................... 1 50
—— Israel of God. 8vo. Enlarged edition.................. 1 50
—— Rich Kinsman... 1 00

TYNG'S Recollections of England. 12mo.................... 1 00
—— Christian Titles.................................... 75
—— A Lamb from the Flock. 18mo......................... 25
VARA; or, the Child of Adoption.......................... 1 00
VERY Little Tales, First and Second Series. 2 vols........... 75
WARDLAW on Miracles.................................... 75
WATERBURY'S Book of the Sabbath. 18mo................ 40
WATSON'S Body of Divinity. 8vo.......................... 2 00
WATTS' Divine Songs. Illustrated. Square................. 40
WEEK (The). Illustrated. 16mo........................... 50
WHATELY'S Kingdom of Christ and Errors of Romanism.... 75
WHITECROSS' Anecdotes on Assembly's Catechism.......... 30
WHITE'S (Hugh) Meditations on Prayer. 18mo.............. 40
—— Believer. A Series of Discourses. 18mo............... 40
—— Practical Reflections on the Second Advent. 18mo..... 40
—— (Henry Kirke) Complete Works. Life by Southey...... 1 00
WILBERFORCE'S (Wm.) Practical View. Large type. 12mo. 1 00
—— Life. By Mary A. Collier............................. 75
WILLISON'S Sacramental Meditations and Advices. 18mo.... 50
WILSON'S Lights and Shadows of Scottish Life. 16mo. Illust. 75
WINSLOW on Personal Declension and Revival.............. 60
—— Midnight Harmonies................................... 60
WOODROOFFE'S Shades of Character........................ 1 50
WYLIE'S Journey over the Region of Fulfilled Prophecy..... 30
YOUNG'S Night Thoughts. 16mo. Large type, with portrait 1 00
Do " " Extra gilt, $1 50. Mor. $2. 18mo. 40

BOOKS NOT STEREOTYPED.

BICKERSTETH'S Works. 16 vols. 16mo..................... 10 00
—— On John and Jude.................................... 60
BINNEY'S Make the Best of Both Worlds.................... 60
BRIDGES' Manual for the Young........................... 50
BUXTON (Sir T. F.), A Study for Young Men................. 50
CHART of Sacred History. Folio.......................... 1 50
DA COSTA'S Israel and the Gentiles. 12mo................. 1 25
—— Four Witnesses...................................... 2 00
EADIE on Colossians.......................................
—— on Ephesians.. 3 00
FLETCHER'S Addresses to the Young....................... 60
HALL'S Forum and the Vatican............................. 1 00
HEWITSON'S Remains. 2 vols.............................. 2 00

HOWELL'S Remains	75
LONDON Lectures to Young Men, 1853-4	1 00
" " " 1854-5	1 00
MALAN'S Pictures from Switzerland	60
OWEN'S Works. 16 vols. 8vo	20 00
PRATT (Josiah) Memoirs of	1 50
SMITH'S (Jno. Pye) Scripture Testimony to Messiah	5 00
SELF-EXPLANATORY Bible, half calf, $4,50 mor	6 00
SWETE'S Family Prayers	60
THOLUCK'S Hours of Devotion	60
VILLAGE Churchyard. 18mo	40
—— Pastor. 18mo	40
—— Observer. 18mo	30
WILSON (Prof.), The Forester, a Tale	75
WORDS to Win Souls. 12mo	75

THE FIRESIDE SERIES.

A Series of beautiful volumes of the Narrative kind, uniform in binding, and prettily Illustrated. 18mo. Price 50 cents each.

The following are now ready:

MABEL GRANT. A Highland Story.
THE WOODCUTTER OF LEBANON.
LOUIS AND FRANK.
CLARA STANLEY. A Story for Girls.
THE CLAREMONT TALES.
THE CONVENT. By Miss M'Crindell.
FAR OFF. By the author of the "Peep of Day."
NEAR HOME. By the same author.
HAPPY HOME. By Dr. Hamilton.
JAMIE GORDON; or, the Orphan.
THE CHILDREN OF THE MANSE. By Mrs. Duncan.
TALES OF THE SCOTTISH PEASANTRY.
SCHOOL DAYS AND COMPANIONS.
THE INDIAN TRIBES OF GUIANA.
HOLIDAY HOUSE. By Miss Sinclair.
OLIVE LEAVES. By Mrs. Sigourney.
BROTHER AND SISTER.
POLLOK'S TALES OF THE COVENANTERS.
THE RAINBOW IN THE NORTH.
THE INFANT'S PROGRESS. By Mrs. Sherwood.
THE WORLD OF WATERS.
BLOSSOMS OF CHILDHOOD.
MAY DUNDAS. A Tale.
ABBEOKUTA; or, Sunrise in the Tropics.
THE FAMILY AT HEATHERDALE.

www.ingramcontent.com/pod-product-compliance
Lightning Source LLC
LaVergne TN
LVHW010130110826
845151LV00002B/318

* 9 7 8 1 4 2 5 5 4 0 3 9 5 *